The Smithsonian Guides to Natural America

THE SOUTHEAST

WA

The Pacific Northwest

OR

MT

The Northern Rockies

ID

WY

ND

The Norther Plains

SD

NE

NV

The Far West

CA

UT

The Southern Rockies

CO

K

AZ

The Southwest

NM

O

T

HI

The Pacific

AK

THE SOUTHEAST
SOUTH CAROLINA – GEORGIA
ALABAMA – FLORIDA

THE SMITHSONIAN GUIDES TO NATURAL AMERICA

THE SOUTHEAST

SOUTH CAROLINA, GEORGIA, ALABAMA, AND FLORIDA

TEXT
Michele Strutin

TEXT FOR SOUTH CAROLINA
Harry Middleton

PHOTOGRAPHY
Tony Arruza

PREFACE
Thomas E. Lovejoy

SMITHSONIAN BOOKS • WASHINGTON, D.C.
RANDOM HOUSE • NEW YORK, N.Y.

Front cover: Wood stork rookery, Everglades National Park, Florida
Half-title page: Sand dollar, Bull Island, South Carolina
Frontispiece: Spanish moss, Lake Talquin, Apalachicola National Forest, Florida
Back cover: Great egret; water lily; Palamedes swallowtail butterfly

THE SMITHSONIAN INSTITUTION
SECRETARY I. Michael Heyman
COUNSELOR TO THE SECRETARY FOR
BIODIVERSITY AND ENVIRONMENTAL AFFAIRS Thomas E. Lovejoy
DIRECTOR, SMITHSONIAN PRESS/SMITHSONIAN PRODUCTIONS Daniel H. Goodwin
EDITOR, SMITHSONIAN BOOKS Alexis Doster III

THE SMITHSONIAN GUIDES TO NATURAL AMERICA
SERIES EDITOR Sandra Wilmot
MANAGING EDITOR Ellen Scordato
SERIES PHOTO EDITOR Mary Jenkins
PHOTO EDITOR Sarah Longacre
ART DIRECTOR Mervyn Clay
ASSISTANT PHOTO EDITOR Ferris Cook
ASSISTANT PHOTO EDITOR Rebecca Williams
ASSISTANT EDITOR Seth Ginsberg
COPY EDITORS Helen Dunn, Karen Hammonds
FACT CHECKER Jean Cotterell
PRODUCTION DIRECTOR Katherine Rosenbloom

Library of Congress Cataloging-in-Publication Data
Strutin, Michele.
 The Smithsonian guides to natural America. The Southeast—South
 Carolina, Georgia, Alabama, Florida/text by Michele Strutin;
 photography by Tony Arruza; preface by Thomas E. Lovejoy.
   p.   cm.
 Includes bibliographical references (p. 256) and index.
 ISBN 0-679-76480-1 (pbk.)
  1. Natural history—Southern States—Guidebooks. 2. Southern
 States—Guidebooks. I. Arruza, Tony. II. Title.
 QH104.5.S59S765 1996
 508.75—dc20   95-48072
                                                  CIP
Manufactured in the United States of America
98765432

How to Use This Book

The Smithsonian Guides to Natural America explore and celebrate the preserved and protected natural areas of this country that are open for the public to use and enjoy. From world-famous national parks to tiny local preserves, the places featured in these guides offer a splendid panoply of this nation's natural wonders.

Divided by state and region, this book offers suggested itineraries for travelers, briefly describing the high points of each preserve, refuge, park, or wilderness area along the way. Each site was chosen for a specific reason: Some are noted for their botanical, zoological, or geological significance, others simply for their exceptional scenic beauty.

Information pertaining to the area as a whole can be found in the introductory sections to the book and to each chapter. In addition, specialized maps at the beginning of each book and chapter highlight an area's geography and geological features as well as pinpoint the specific locales that the author describes.

For quick reference, places of interest are set in **boldface** type; those set in **boldface** followed by the symbol ❖ are listed in the Site Guide at the back of the book. (This feature begins on page 263, just before the index.) Here noteworthy sites are listed alphabetically by state, and each entry provides practical information that visitors need: telephone numbers, mailing addresses, and specific services available.

Addresses and telephone numbers of national, state, and local agencies and organizations are also listed. Also in appendices are a glossary of pertinent scientific terms and designations used to describe natural areas; the author's recommendations for further reading (both nonfiction and fiction); and a list of sources that can aid travelers planning a guided visit.

The words and images of these guides are meant to help both the active naturalist and the armchair traveler to appreciate more fully the environmental diversity and natural splendor of this country. To ensure a successful visit, always contact a site in advance to obtain detailed maps, updated information on hours and fees, and current weather conditions. Many areas maintain a fragile ecological balance. Remember that their continued vitality depends in part on responsible visitors who tread the land lightly.

C O N T E N T S

PREFACE

In the Southeast, natural America suffers from pervasive stereotypes—a surfeit of bald cypress swamps, live oaks, magnolias, and palmettos. Yet for me there is nothing quite so glorious as a Southeast spring day when gentle breezes caress the Spanish moss fluttering from live oaks, buds pop into bloom, and a kaleidoscope of birds pursue their vernal urge to propagate.

With so many remarkable places in South Carolina, Georgia, Alabama, and Florida, it is tough for me to decide what the region first brings to mind. In the end, though, Georgia's magnificent Okefenokee Swamp stands out. One of the most splendid wetlands in all of North America, the Cherokees' "Land of the Trembling Earth" first transfixed me as a college undergraduate, and it always springs to mind as a metaphor whenever I want to refer to a shaky proposition.

Encompassing far more than wetlands, South Carolina, so tidily divided into Up-country and Low Country, ranges from the Blue Ridge Mountains, shared with Georgia and Alabama, to the coastal plain, which is home to fully one quarter of the East Coast's salt marshes. Within the state's borders are nesting beaches for threatened loggerhead turtles as well as the curious peat-filled bays called pocosins. Natural highlights include Sassafras Mountain, at 3,554 feet the highest point in the state; the Chattooga River (which has national wild and scenic status); the biologically fascinating sand hills region; and the Congaree, the best remnant of the once extensive Great Swamp, which now shelters the last major stand of virgin hardwood bottomland swamp.

Scattered throughout the state, South Carolina's excellent heritage preserves offer a bounty of native flora and fauna. Grass-of-Parnassus and carnivorous sundews and bladderworts grow at Ashmore; swamp pinks and bog rose orchids thrive in the rare mountain bog at Watson; the largest known population of endangered mountain sweet pitcher plants is found at Chandler. The undisturbed valley of Eastatoe Creek supports quasitropical plants and a trio of uncommon ferns—bristle, dwarf, and Tunbridge. On the jagged granite cliffs of Glassy Mountain and the marble outcrops of Buzzard Roost rare plant populations find purchase. Steven Creek protects endangered Webster's salamanders.

Beyond the Blue Ridge and piedmont, South Carolina's Low Country is festooned with great wetlands such as Four Holes Swamp—home to one of the continent's single largest stands of bald cypress and tupelo gum—as well as extensive coastal wetlands. Among the finest of the latter is the ACE Basin, named for the Ashpoo, Combahee, and Edisto rivers, which flow together there. I was

---

PRECEDING PAGES: *The sun sets at Alabama's Lake Guntersville, an impounded lake formed where the Tennessee River bends north toward the Ohio.*

introduced to this place of spectacular beauty by former Smithsonian National Board member Tony Merck. Its exquisite landscapes (photographed so brilliantly by Tom Blagden in *South Carolina's Wetland Wilderness*) harbor least terns, rare beach pigweed, sea oats, Wilson's plover, painted buntings, and black skimmers.

Georgia boasts the second largest river basin in the East, that of the Altamaha. It was here in the mid-eighteenth century that Philadelphia naturalist William Bartram, the second generation of the famous botanical founding family of America, discovered the white-flowered Franklinia. Named for Benjamin Franklin, this beautiful small tree is most likely America's first recognized endangered species (although the concept as such did not exist until many years later). The trees now grown in domestic gardens are descendants of plants originally cultivated by the Bartrams; the Franklinia has been extinct in the wild since 1803.

ABOVE: *A sleek but damp American anhinga spreads its gray patterned wings to dry in the Florida sun.*

In the mountains of northern Georgia the Chattooga River appears again, its sprays of white water marking the state's boundary with South Carolina. Distinctive granite domes, or balds, top a number of peaks here: Brasstown Bald, at 4,784 feet the highest in the state, supports a pygmy oak forest below its bald, and the summit of Panola Mountain displays a fascinating succession of flora—beginning with a tiny red-stemmed diamorpha bearing white flowers and proceeding to summer-blooming white mountain sandwort, yellow Confederate daisies, yuccas, and persimmons of bonsai dimensions.

Georgia's portion of the Blue Ridge is well represented by the lush growth and fertile soils of the Rich Mountain and Cohutta wildernesses. Some old-growth forests of the Cumberland Plateau can still be visited at the Marshall Forest Preserve and at Pigeon Mountain, named for the huge flocks of now-extinct passenger pigeons that once roosted there. At Pigeon's base, Ellison's Cave is the deepest cavern in the East; on the mountain's western side, a moist woodland cove called the Pocket presents a nonpareil wildflower spectacle.

And there is still more to see in Georgia: sun-drenched barrier islands and Cumberland Island National Seashore, where dolphins play nearby; Tallulah Falls in the eastern Blue Ridge, with its mixture of pine species and persistent trillium; Franklin D. Roosevelt State Park near Warm Springs where the polio-stricken 32nd president repaired for a cure; Dowdell's Knob, where Roosevelt liked to sit and think; and finally, of course, Okefenokee itself, with its water moccasins, anhingas, alligators, and sandhill cranes.

Alabama, a state of modest mountains and rivers, may be a bit short on superlatives, but it has a considerable variety of natural America to offer. De Soto
State Park harbors 650 wildflower species and features great sweeps of pink
lady's slippers. Russell Cave National Monument reveals thousands of years of
human habitation, while the caves at Wheeler National Wildlife Refuge shelter
two endangered bat species, which provide quite a summer spectacle during
their twilight flights. In the central part of the state lies its wildest area, the 26,000-
acre Sipsey Wilderness, and in the south the 84,000-acre Conecuh National
Forest protects longleaf pines essential to endangered red-cockaded woodpeckers, as well as woodland ponds and endangered dusky gopher frogs. Mobile
Bay, site of the Dauphin Island Bird Sanctuary and capital of the Louisiana
Territory before the U.S. purchase, is second only to Chesapeake Bay in size.

Far and away the richest part of the Southeast, naturally speaking, lies within the state of Florida, which is invariably associated in my mind with the voice
of its greatest naturalist, Archie Carr (see his *A Naturalist in Florida: A Celebration of Eden*, 1994). Highlights here surely include Wakulla Springs, which
gushes 400,000 gallons per minute; the 3,000 sinkhole lakes; and Paynes Prairie
near Gainesville (and the Carr home). The extensive longleaf pines within the
500,000 acres of the Apalachicola National Forest and Gulf Islands National
Seashore are also not to be ignored. And that's all just in northern Florida.

South Florida, characterized by author Marjorie Stoneman Douglas as the
"river of grass," is a single gigantic ecosystem, which extends from the Kissimmee
River through the Everglades, Florida Bay, the Keys, and adjacent coral reefs. It is
one of the great natural systems of the world, but many of its essential ele-
ments—coral reefs, American crocodiles, roseate spoonbills—are in serious trouble. Half a century of seemingly reasonable decisions have, in aggregate, drastically changed South Florida hydrology. Today a highly important experiment in
restoration and ecosystem management is underway. Despite the project's ex-
pense and lack of precedent, its prospects look good. If that is the case, what we
may learn in South Florida may prove useful in other parts of the world.

So my advice to you is to savor the evocative words of Harry Middleton
and Michele Strutin, glory in the spectacular photographs of Tony Arruza, and
then head to the Southeast, where there is so much to enjoy and so much to
discover. You may never want to come back.

—Thomas E. Lovejoy
Counselor to the Secretary for
Biodiversity and Environmental Affairs,
SMITHSONIAN INSTITUTION

LEFT: *Twisting channels wind through a bald cypress swamp on Okefenokee's western side. Thousands of alligators thrive in this watery world.*

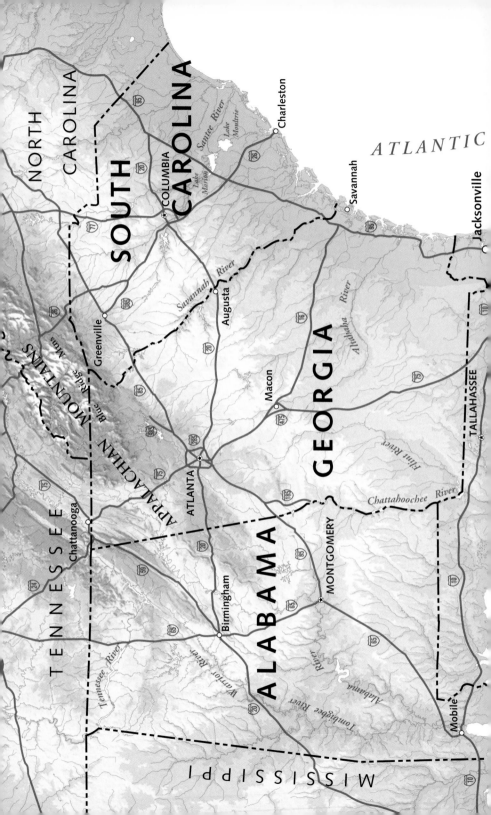

INTRODUCTION

INTRODUCTION: THE SOUTHEAST

The first images that the states of the Southeast bring to mind are of plantations, new sun-bright cities, languid grace, Disney World, shiny highrises pressed against the beach. All these pictures are of human additions, yet the Southeast is far older than our cultural memories.

The natural Southeast presents timeless images of sea and sky, of sultry forests and rounded mountains, of places that have existed much longer than humankind and will exist far into the future if we protect them. Streams gurgle among worn peaks, and warblers sing amid the damp, lush foliage of shadowed coves. In primordial swamps, shafts of sunlight probe between huge tumid cypress trees to illuminate dark waters inhabited by lilies and alligators. In coastal forests, ponderous live oaks mingle with waxy magnolias whose fat white blooms perfume the air. Along the ocean, panicles of sea oats shiver atop sand dunes in the soft coral light of sunrise.

Although the political boundaries of the four southeastern states—South Carolina, Georgia, Alabama, and Florida—were drawn by people, their natural divisions were formed by larger forces over unimaginably long periods. Northwestern South Carolina, northern Georgia, and northern Alabama are joined in the rocky grip of the southern Appalachian Mountains. About 400 million years ago, continents slammed together to raise these mountains, among the oldest in the Western Hemisphere, for the first time. The legacy of that event is a glorious confusion of peaks and balds, of cove valleys and gorges that shelter profuse life.

Over millennia, the Appalachians have created countless fascinating habitats. Each ridge, cove, and dell in this jumble of ancient mountains harbors its own blend of soil, moisture, and temperature. Millions of years of specialization have produced profound biological diversity—wildflowers and ferns

---

PRECEDING PAGES: *In South Carolina's coastal ACE Basin, loblolly pines and live oaks edge Mosquito Creek; the branches are hung with Spanish moss, actually an epiphyte that absorbs moisture and nutrients from the air.*

found nowhere else, salamanders exquisitely adapted to a particular damp gorge, mountaintop plants able to withstand drastic temperature fluctuations.

A ridge with gravelly soil sports a fringe of scented silver bells. The golds and blues of celandine poppies and bluebells spill over the sides of one low-walled cove in Alabama while carnivorous plants thrive in bogs on the plateau above. A gorge in South Carolina resembles steamy South American jungles. Looking like tonsured monks, mountain balds in Georgia are ringed by pygmy forests of northern birches and oaks. Some waterfalls slip silkily down smooth, water-polished stone as others nearby crash over jagged rock lips in noisy, careless tumult. The great Chattooga River, which forms part of the border between Georgia and South Carolina, growls past snarls of boulders in a pinched gorge and then—released—leaps over rocks as if it cannot contain the silvery joy of running.

Rolling east and south from the mountains is the piedmont, a broad band of foothills that arc from South Carolina through Georgia and Alabama. The mountains look more natural than the piedmont because they support scant agriculture, and although most of the big trees have been logged, second- and third-growth forests cover the slopes. By contrast, large areas of the more accessible piedmont and coastal plain are devoted to agriculture and other human development—but not all.

The rivers that begin in the mountains gather force in the piedmont. The Savannah, Chattahoochee, Flint, Black Warrior, and others carry seeds of mountain plants and deposit them among piedmont habitats in anomalous and surprising variety. Also within the forests and river valleys of the piedmont are relict communities of more northerly plants that migrated south during the ice ages, found a comfortable niche, and stayed. The resulting strange blend of plants attracts equally strange groupings of animals. Along waterways and sloughs, national wildlife refuges become winter headquarters for myriad birds. Dabbling ducks and diving ducks, sandhill cranes, geese, bald eagles and other raptors—birds by the hundreds of thousands find winter succor in the piedmont.

Studded through the foothills are giant granite domes, hulking gray heights composed of magma that cooled beneath the surface and were exposed as wind and water eroded more friable ground above and around them. South Carolina's Glassy Mountain and Georgia's Panola Mountain, two of the best, support small colonies of rare plants that eke out tenuous livings on the sunbaked domes.

Splayed beyond the piedmont is the coastal plain—a broad, flat lowland that stretches to the Atlantic and Gulf coasts and deep into northern Florida. As continental ice caps ebbed and flowed during great glacial periods, sometimes much of the present landscape was covered with water. Sometimes land's end extended farther into the sea. Always the littoral has been lavish with life.

Between piedmont and shore, the Southeast's coastal plain is a vast sandy beach lightly overlain by vegetation. Because the region's copious precipitation drains right through the sandy soil, some have likened this sweeping coastal area to a desert with rain. Such tough conditions have produced a forest unique in the world: the longleaf pine and wire-grass community. When they first encountered the upland longleaf forests that covered much of the Southeast's coastal plain, European settlers dubbed them parklands because longleaf pines space themselves widely, allowing sun to pour onto the forest floor. Low gauzy blankets of tan-and-green wire grass and sun-loving wildflowers give longleaf forests the look of prairies punctuated by pine trees. In their midst lives an interwoven community of endangered birds, snakes, tortoises, and others.

ABOVE: *Once near extinction, alligators are now protected and flourish in moist areas such as the Shark Valley in Everglades National Park.*

LEFT: *From South Carolina's Cherokee Foothills Scenic Highway, Table Rock Mountain dominates scenic Lake Oolenoy, a jewel set amid the folds of the Blue Ridge.*

The wetlands that dot the lower areas of the coastal plain are a luxuriant weave of swamps, bottomland hardwoods, and bayheads. (Less wet than swamps, bayheads support a variety of bay trees.) In central South Carolina, Congaree Swamp's bottomland forest—teaming with sycamores, tupelos, and a host of smaller hardwoods—has no equal in the region. Straddling the Georgia-Florida border, renowned Okefenokee Swamp is the largest in the land, its brooding cypresses draped with Spanish moss and its sunny channels dotted with basking alligators.

Loaded with silt, the Altamaha, Apalachicola, and other big, languid rivers etch sinuous paths across the plain. At their deltas, salt marshes mix the silt

5

ABOVE LEFT: *Although water lilies, such as these growing in Georgia's Okefenokee Swamp, look delicate, below the surface their rhizomes are thick enough to provide food for muskrat and other aquatic animals.*

with organic material flushed in from the sea, producing unparalleled fecundity. Southeastern shores are braided by the world's largest and most fertile salt marshes, where oysters, crabs, clams, shrimp, hundreds of species of fish, manatees, and wading birds all crowd mile upon mile of softly swaying grasses.

Beyond the marshes, just off the mainland, lie necklaces of barrier islands. Coastal forests of live oak anchor the middle sections of the fragile isles, and the edges are mounded with scrub oak, undulating dunes, and dazzling beaches busy with clubby groups of shorebirds and armadas of brown pelicans. Barrier islands are ephemeral places. The product of powerful winds and insistent waves, they are at the mercy of these forces, which can in turn easily destroy them.

Weather is a prime sculptor of the southeastern landscape. This hurricane country is often lashed by sea and winds that can reduce the creations of human industry to a pile of rubble. Fire plays a leading role in the Southeast because scrub and longleaf pine forests depend on fires to keep them healthy; each summer, lightning-sparked blazes frequently oblige.

South of the coastal plain stretches South Florida, a long thumb of land that recently emerged from the sea, forming the bridge between the temperate and tropical zones. Here salt marshes give way to coastlines dense with the arched and twisted roots of mangroves. Azure springs bubble up from Florida's porous limestone base, and south of the state's central ridge, lowlands ease slowly into the sea. The watery saw-grass prairies of the Ever-

ABOVE: *At Florida's Myakka River State Park, rare roseate spoonbills (left) wade and hunt in the shallows. Yellow trilliums (right) signal spring along Rocky Bottom Creek in South Carolina's Eastatoe Valley.*

glades—presenting horizon-to-horizon views of spare beauty—slope a scant two inches per mile toward the Gulf of Mexico.

The Everglades ecosystem, which once spread across the entire tip of southern Florida, is unique in the world. The arching tops of six-foot-tall saw grass undulate like the sea and conceal a realm like no other. From painted snails to seabirds, crocodiles to cougars, the Everglades preserves an Eden of subtropical wildlife. At the edges of the Everglades, along the coast, the heart of the world's most extensive mangrove swamps create an emerald maze where myriad birds and marine life make their homes. The health of the Everglades and Florida Bay has been severely impaired, however, by major changes in water delivery to satisfy urban and agricultural needs. Although habitat restoration is beginning, much has already been lost.

Below South Florida, coral island Keys arc toward the Caribbean Basin. At this southernmost edge of America, plants and animals are reminiscent of the West Indies. Mahoganies, gumbo-limbos, and other tropical hardwoods populate the woodlands; pink roseate spoonbills forage for shrimp in brackish lagoons; pelagic frigate birds wing overhead; and rare American crocodiles bask alongside balmy waters. The sea teems with uncommon life: Reefs pulse with fish and corals in colors more varied and brilliant than a painter's palette.

The Southeast is a land of startling diversity, of life forms tested over millions of years. As visitors to this realm, humans should enter thoughtfully into a world of such natural majesty, where each species, from red-cockaded woodpecker to Florida panther, has its place.

SOUTH CAROLINA

PART ONE

SOUTH CAROLINA

A t certain times of day—in the blush of dawn or in the last hour of sunset, when the day's light bleeds from the sky— South Carolina seems a contiguous and undiluted expression of its natural history. In these moments of deep solitude, human history seems far removed. From horizon to horizon, from mountains to seashore, the land glows in great ranges of wild and abiding light. This light eventually permeates the countryside, etching every detail in shadow and color, defining every mountain ridge, every rolling sand hill, every radiant expanse of marsh; it finds every sweaty dark-water swamp, every bay and bright river, every dune. And as it takes hold, the light embraces the state's remaining natural areas—large and small, mysterious and common—and illuminates South Carolina's natural heritage, a vital legacy of wildness that still enriches the state.

Beauty prospers within this light: the harsh beauty of the rugged Ellicott Rock Wilderness in the Blue Ridge Mountains, which crowd the northwestern region of the state; the hypnotic beauty of sea oats swaying in a cool ocean wind along the coast; the violent beauty of pounding cataracts in the Chattooga River; the fragile beauty of a tiny carpet of stonecrop shuddering in small pools among the eroded outcrops at Flatcreek; the primordial beauty of an alligator hauling itself out of the black water of Four Holes Swamp; and the surreal beauty of a cloud of brown pelicans settling into the waters off Capers Island.

Despite its size (it ranks 40th out of 50), South Carolina embraces a startling variety of natural areas in its mountains, piedmont, and coastal plain. Small isolated pockets guarantee the survival of varied flora and fauna and sustain at least some of the land's legacy of wildness. From the hulking mass of Glassy Mountain, rich with unexpected life, to Congaree Swamp, one of the last great stands of virgin hardwood bottom-land swamp, South Carolina's biological diversity is important—not only to this small southern state but to the planet as a whole.

In the Up-country, the abraded hogback ridges of the Blue Ridge Mountains wrinkle across the sky like an arthritic stone finger. Ridgelines trace their images in the low clouds, especially near Sassafras Mountain, the highest peak in the state at 3,554 feet. Despite the Palmetto State's extensive development—especially along the coast—the mountain country retains a genuine wildness sustained by a wide array of state parks, sanctuaries, and the sprawling Sumter National Forest. Many of these protected lands lie so close together that they form one huge swath of untamed high country. They are South Carolina's glorious contribution to the wilderness corridor that links natural sites from the vast sweeps of Georgia's Chattahoochee National Forest to the rough and difficult reaches of North Carolina's Nantahala National Forest.

If the mind glories in the majesty of mountains, it finds renewal in the sea, the indomitable spirit of life rising and falling with every gray-beard wave. Even far inland, the evening wind is drenched with the smell of salt water, a smell that raises atavistic hairs on the back of the neck. One of the state's clearest successes in habitat conservation is the ACE Basin, a vast coastal acreage preserved by coalitions of private and public interests. From Salkehatchie Swamp to Jehossee Island in the Edisto River to the waters of Saint Helena Sound, this protected area exudes a sense of the wild earth: intact, dynamic, vital. Here an immense ecosystem trembles with life in a world of sunlight and water, sand and wind, where textures and forms change from moment to moment.

Every region of the state conveys its own moods and character, its own beauty. To those visitors willing to take the time to connect, each landscape imparts an ancient sense of place that soothes and nourishes the human spirit. Every step in the wilderness brings visitors to new destinations and to the assurance that life endures here, among the stones and the marshes, in the swamps and the deep bays. The natural areas of South Carolina speak in wild tongues, the language of the natural world, which human beings once spoke. Part of us still—in blood and bone, muscle and nerve—this language is life's common ground. It is a silent but undeniable reminder that we are yet another mysterious expression of life and an integral part of the continuum of history and time.

SOUTH CAROLINA:
MOUNTAIN RIVERS TO BARRIER ISLANDS

O
n an early morning in May—a good month to be traveling the mountain highways, even the interstate, in South Carolina's high country—the rugged peaks of the southern Appalachians crowd the horizon, and the dome of pale blue sky widens overhead. The wind from the mountains smells sweetly of wild onion, and in the distance the sound of an unseen river conjures images of bright water tumbling over the smooth backs of dark stones.

These rushing waters are central to South Carolina's natural and human history. Seekers of wilderness beauty can find cold mountain streams, dense forests, fecund salt marshes, and unusual floral communities in South Carolina's three distinct physical provinces: the mountains, the piedmont, and the coastal plain, which includes the intriguing sand hills region. The rivers' headwaters rise in the mountainous Blue Ridge, pour across the piedmont plateau to the fall line, and snake lazily through the flat coastal plain. Three important rivers—the Savannah, the Santee, and the Pee Dee—traverse South Carolina's coastal plain and are navigable up to the fall line, which separates Up-country from Low Country—long an important social and political division in South Carolina.

The Up-country has historically been home to isolated communi-

LEFT: *Bald cypresses thrive in Congaree Swamp, a fecund bottomland dotted with rare old-growth hardwoods. The flanged bases of these towering trees help support them in the shallow, waterlogged soils.*

ties—first hardy bands of Cherokee and later fiercely independent small farmers. The Revolutionary War battles of Kings Mountain and Cowpens were fought here. Charleston, the state's oldest and best-known city, is the center of Low Country influence. Settled by the English in the late 1600s, Charleston commanded an area that both the Spanish and French unsuccessfully attempted to claim in the 1500s. Overwhelmingly agricultural, South Carolina's Low Country produced rice, cotton, and indigo in the eighteenth and nineteenth centuries. A large population of African slaves was imported to work the extensive plantations, usually sited along the myriad rivers that provided ready access to far-flung markets. Its wealth firmly rooted in the slave-based plantation system, the state was the first to secede from the Union, and the shots fired at Fort Sumter in Charleston Harbor marked the beginning of the Civil War. Today, many of the historic plantations, once dependent on wetlands diked to create fields, have been returned to wildlife.

The dominance of wetlands arises partly from the state's geology and geography. Two thirds of South Carolina is coastal plain, the low, mostly flat sedimentary legacy of ancient oceans that traces the Atlantic and Gulf states from southern New Jersey to southeastern Texas. In South Carolina, the unconsolidated sediments of the coastal plain stretch westward through the sand hills to the fall line, a lip of hard metamorphic rock that marks the edge of the piedmont. At the far western tip of the state lie the Blue Ridge Mountains, last uplifted along with the rest of the southern Appalachians at the end of the Paleozoic era, approximately 245 million years ago.

Encompassing plunging waterfalls, rapids-studded streams, and craggy peaks, the Blue Ridge Mountains of South Carolina's Up-country are its surprisingly rugged contribution to the Appalachian chain. Here warm, moist winds from the coast and points south hit cooler air above the magnificent Blue Ridge Escarpment, the towering eastern edge of the southern Appalachians. The result is some of the heaviest rainfall in the Southeast, which sustains tumultuous mountain rivers (including the roaring Chattooga, where the movie *Deliverance* was filmed), cuts deep gorges in the eroded escarpment (one small valley is home to quasitropical plants otherwise found only in South America), and feeds the spectacular waterfalls that plummet over remote cliffs and sheer ravines.

ABOVE: *Landscape artist Esteban Chartrand (1825–89), who attained great success in his native Cuba, visited the Charleston area around*

Below the escarpment the piedmont plateau stretches from foothills to the fall line. Heavily influenced by human use, the piedmont was once mostly flat, rolling farmland, though its red clay soils are ill-suited for agriculture and have been extensively overworked. Today manufacturing—especially the textile industry—is the hallmark of the area, dotted with orchards in the north and recreation areas created by impoundments of the upper Savannah River to the south.

The coastal plain begins at the fall line, which slants diagonally from Cheraw in the northeast to Aiken in the southwest. (Route 1 runs approximately along this natural division.) Also at the plain's western edge are the sand hills, evidence of an ancient ocean. When prehistoric seas lapped at the fall line, rivers deposited sand and silt here, debris that remained after the waters retreated. Subsequently the dunelike

***1870. His* Sunset at the Savannas, South Carolina, *reveals his consider-*
able skill at rendering the natural mystery of the tropical landscape.

hills were blanketed with vast pine forests, which European settlers logged almost to extinction. In the 1930s the federal government reforested this region, and the modern sand hills delight botanists and other naturalists with their surprising biotic diversity.

Fanning eastward from the fall line and sand hills to South Carolina's 198 miles of shoreline (3,000 miles when sounds, bays, and estuaries are included), the coastal plain encompasses more swamps than any other state except Louisiana. Salt marshes anchor the productive coastal food chain, supporting myriad life-forms, as well as commercial fishing and tourism. Still, these bounteous wetlands can only hint at the erstwhile magnificence of the Great Swamp, which once covered much of northeast South Carolina in the Pee Dee River area. Drained by settlers, farmers, and slaves, the Great Swamp now exists

17

only in small pockets; the best-known remnant is the biologically rich Congaree, south of Columbia.

Through the centuries, floods washing over these flat lands created great oxbow lakes, sloughs, and channels; now the waters, controlled by dams and dikes, form large impoundments and lakes. Just beyond the coast, 16 barrier islands are home to scrub vegetation and dwarf deer. The battering of hurricanes and the relentless force of the ocean constantly sculpt the islands' outlines as their fragile sandbars protect the mainland shores.

Powerful storms can wrack the coast in fall and winter, while baking heat and unimaginable clouds of mosquitoes, the bane of hikers everywhere, descend in summer. Along the coast, winters are mild (temperatures fall only to about 50 degrees Fahrenheit); in the mountains winter can be bitter, but a pleasant coolness prevails the other three-quarters of the year. Up-country hikers are wise to beware of spring's torrential rains, which nourish the lacy veils of waterfalls and thundering river rapids. In the Low Country, summer humidity can send even avid naturalists and birders to a shady piazza for an icy sip of tea.

Because these varied regions harbor more than 60 different habitats, the state is home to an astounding diversity of plants and wildlife, protected by a variety of public and private groups. Two national forests—Sumter in the piedmont and Francis Marion in the Low Country near Charleston—are complemented by South Carolina heritage preserves, Nature Conservancy sites, National Audubon Society refuges, and local conservation areas.

Since the mid-1970s, dedicated individuals have worked to save the Blue Ridge Mountain wilderness, and the multifaceted efforts of private landowners, nonprofit organizations, and state and federal agencies have preserved the vital wetlands complex of the ACE Basin. In a 1996 victory for environmentalists, the state acquired part of Sandy Island and blocked plans to construct a bridge. The state and Nature Conservancy plan to maintain intact the offshore island's largely undisturbed wetland habitat.

Modern travelers in a hurry to sample the various delights of South Carolina can follow approximately the line of the ancient Cherokee Path by zooming down Interstate 26. Bisecting the state from northwest to southeast, I-26 rushes efficiently from the Up-country near Landrum through the piedmont—Spartanburg and the capital at Columbia—to the lush coastal sunlight of Charleston. Interstate highways such as I-26, however, are for making time, not for exploring a land's natural history or experiencing a region's unique sense of place. For such journeys, the best choices are state roads, secondary roads, forest roads, and back roads; narrow waterways and coastal channels for canoeing and kayaking; and country lanes in the flatlands that grant bicyclists the freedom of open sky. These smaller byways—often nameless and meandering—seem part of the landscape they traverse, and following them adds immeasurably to a visitor's appreciation of the state.

This chapter begins in northwest South Carolina on such a road, the Cherokee Foothills Scenic Highway (Route 11), which winds among the low-lying clouds, dense forests, and cold mountain rivers of the Blue Ridge Escarpment and Sumter National Forest. Next the itinerary angles southeast along the high bluffs of the Savannah River on the Georgia–South Carolina border and zigzags northeast through sites in the piedmont to the sand hills, mysterious remnants of an ancient seacoast. After visiting the Little Pee Dee River basin, unusual Carolina bays, Lakes Marion and Moultrie, and the Frances Marion National Forest, the route moves to the coast. There it travels south through the fabulous ACE Basin wetland complex, pausing at the estuaries, marshes, and constantly shifting Sea Islands on the way to Georgia.

THE UP-COUNTRY: FROM JONES GAP TO TABLE ROCK

Entering South Carolina from the north is a selfish pleasure. Just a few miles from the state line, travelers exiting Interstate 26 at Campobello can find themselves on the **Cherokee Foothills Scenic Highway** (Route 11), which serpentines westward through the high country, tracing a broad crescent along the North Carolina and Georgia state lines. Easing gently into the soothing, demulcent rhythms of the mountains, the Foothills Highway leads directly into the wide embrace of the state's six Up-country counties, where some of the most gorgeous mountain scenery in the entire Southeast awaits at every point of the compass.

Wisps of mountain fog rise from the two-lane highway like tendrils of smoke as a light the color of bruised apricots slouches down the ridges. Gowensville, where the single traffic light seems always to be green, marks the edge of this vast corridor of rugged mountain country, which is studded with a magnificent array of state parks; public and private preserves; natural, scenic, and wilderness areas; and one unit of a tripartite national forest.

Much of South Carolina's Blue Ridge Escarpment is encompassed by the immense **Mountain Bridge Wilderness and Recreation Area❖,** which now stretches over ten miles from Route 276 to Route 25. Established gradually since the mid-1970s, by 1996 the wilderness area protected more than 10,000 acres of rugged, undeveloped mountain terrain, once largely privately owned. It provides a "bridge" of state-protected land between two vast watersheds—the Poinsett on the east and Table Rock on the west—owned by the city of Greenville. Including the 30,000-acre watersheds currently under conservation easement, Mountain Bridge includes three state parks and three heritage preserves that constitute an additional 20,000 acres.

Like all the Up-country, this region is rich in natural and human history. The Cherokee lived in these mountains, their villages and influence reaching from Tennessee to Georgia. Allied with the British during the Revolutionary War, they were harshly treated by the victorious United States and pushed deep into the mountains. By the early 1800s the Cherokee were displaced altogether—except for a few hardy bands that continued to survive in the most inaccessible high country. The rest were herded together and marched over what became known as the Trail of Tears to new Indian Territory in Oklahoma, land promised to them forever. Forever lasted fewer than 70 years.

Between 1840 and 1848, according to local history, an early pioneer in the harsh mountain uplands, one Solomon Jones, single-handedly built a mountain road from River Falls to Cedar Mountain, North Carolina, a distance of more than five miles. In virtually continuous use as a toll road until the early 1900s, Old Jones Gap Road was, even by today's standards, an engineering marvel. Beyond the road, however, Jones Gap, as this break in the mountains came to be called, was never settled and remains a premier natural area, its thick understory home to black bears and ruffed grouse, white-tailed deer, foxes, and bobcat.

These days backpackers, not wagons heavy with commerce, travel the Old Jones Gap Road. Stretching along the banks of the Middle

Much of South Carolina's mountainous northwest section is protected by watershed easements, parks, and a huge wilderness area. Here the distinctive profile of Table Rock Mountain rises in the distance.

Fork of the Saluda (the state's first wild and scenic river), **Jones Gap State Park✦** is most easily reached from the Cherokee Foothills Scenic Highway on River Falls Road. The nearly pristine wildness of Jones Gap continues to harbor a thriving diversity of biological communities, including more than 300 species of wildflowers, many of them rare. By late spring, the hardwood forests resonate with the confusing calls and chips, whistles and trills of warblers. In a blur of wing and color, furtive vireos flit among the trees, their territorial calls edged with raspy temper and aggressiveness.

Several trails wend through the craggy, unspoiled Jones Gap country, a number connecting it with nearby **Caesars Head State Park✦.** (By road the park is about ten miles farther northwest off Route 276.) The park's namesake scarp is a weather-blasted chunk of exposed granite that rises 3,226 feet above the surrounding hogback mountains, sluicing waterfalls, and trilling mountain rivers. Climbing Caesars Head means negotiating Devils Kitchen, a perpetually cool natural fissure linking the flank of the mountain with the pinnacle.

The massive slab of stone takes its name either from history or from

ABOVE: *At Jones Gap park in the Mountain Bridge Wilderness Area, the Middle Fork of the Saluda River plunges past basswood, beech, and an understory of rhododendron—all classic southern Appalachian flora.*

a moment of nostalgia. One local legend maintains that the outcrop's essentially chinless profile reminded an early settler (blessed with a smidgen of classical education) of Julius Caesar. Another story claims the rock face was named for a local hunting dog named Caesar, who died bravely here. Whatever the source of its name, this platform of stone presents a sweeping view of the Up-country. The misty Blue Ridge Mountains fall away into northern Georgia and southwestern North Carolina, and in the near distance, the imposing outline of Table Rock and the summit of **Sassafras Mountain,** the state's highest peak, rise to the west; encased in a fold of clouds, they resemble blue islands anchored in a surreal white sea. Trails ranging from easy to strenuous crisscross the area. Taking the Jones Gap Trail through the magnificent gorge that embraces the tumbling waters of the Middle Fork of the Saluda River is an unforgettable experience. The far more difficult Rim of the Gap Trail should be approached with caution; even experienced hikers need at least six hours to negotiate it one way.

Another favorite is the Raven Cliff Falls Trail, which covers more than two miles (one-way) of spectacular mountain country from Caesars Head into the Mountain Bridge Wilderness Area. Although difficult at times, the trail yields a reward heard before it is seen. From a dis-

ABOVE: *Hoary with slow-growing lichen, the granite profile of Caesars Head—named either for an ancient Roman or for a prized hunting dog—surveys the vast reaches of the Mountain Bridge Wilderness Area.*

tance the sound of cascading water heralds a mountain waterfall, which materializes in the drifting clouds of cold mist rising from its plunge pool. Spilling over a rocky ledge on Matthews Creek, **Raven Cliff Falls** is a dramatic 420-foot veil of icy water tumbling down a dark wall of glistening stone.

The patchwork of trails through the Mountain Bridge Wilderness Area offers a grand assault on the senses: woods redolent with the heady smell of magnolia and the sweet scent of rhododendron and mountain laurel. Basswood, ash, red maple, and birch crowd the gorge, and along the higher ridges oaks and hickory, pine, wild dogwood, tulip poplar, and black locust dominate woods thick with blueblack shadows and cool breezes.

Two tracts of the Mountain Bridge area owned by the state's Heritage Trust as Heritage Preserves—the Ashmore and Watson—are as unspoiled as Jones Gap and far less visited. Both areas support unique populations of mountain plants. The well-marked Foothills Trail goes through the Watson Heritage Preserve, and an old logging road serves as the trail on the Ashmore Heritage Preserve. Their uncommon botanical diversity makes both preserves well worth the compass and topographic map needed to find and enjoy them. Once at these sites,

23

visitors should linger a bit in their undiluted solace.

Extending along the edge of the Blue Ridge Escarpment, the remote **Ashmore Heritage Preserve❖** is an uncommon mountain cataract area. Small rivulets continually flowing down exposed outcrops of eroded stone create "water slicks." Because the surrounding soil is too thin to support a canopy of large trees, the cataract is an open area, frequently flooded in sunlight. Where they occur, mountain cataracts often provide the perfect habitat for an unmatched diversity of unusual Up-country plants. At Ashmore insectivorous sundews and bladderworts sway gently in the warming sunlight. Nearby, scarlet Indian paintbrush casts a delicate red glow on the edges of the cataract. Rare grass-of-Parnassus flashes in the pale sunlight near snarls of southeastern tickseed and stands of the endangered and beautiful mountain sweet pitcher plant, one of only five such insectivorous species found in South Carolina.

Covering 496 acres, the Ashmore tract also protects lovely stands of Appalachian hardwood forest thick with oaks (white and scarlet and chestnut), big hickories, sourwood, and handsome yellow poplar. A careful climb to the apex of the cataract reveals a view of uncluttered grandeur, mountains rising and falling across the distance, defining the land and its history. In the distance, dominating this seemingly endless gallery of rolling stone spines and worn summits, are the burly rock shoulders of Paris Mountain.

Close by, along the headwaters of Matthews Creek and the North Carolina border, is the 1,660-acre **Watson Heritage Preserve❖,** which protects a rare, undisturbed mountain, or depression, bog; once common, these are now unusual in the Appalachians. At an elevation of 3,000 feet, the Watson bog is one of very few mountain bogs known to exist in South Carolina. Thickets of wine-red chokeberry and alder sink their roots deep into layers of cold mud and rich sphagnum moss. Climbing ferns lace pockets of this wetland like gossamer green spiderwebs as shadows reflect the blush of swamp pinks and twayblade and bog rose orchids. The preserve is especially renowned for its population

RIGHT: *Framed by hemlocks, hickories, tulip poplars, and magnolias, the tiered cascades of Raven Cliff Falls mist the air; this moisture helps small hanging gardens to thrive in the cracks on the rock faces.*

ABOVE: *Clumps of reindeer moss (left), a lichen that prefers tundra or sandy soils, carpet the Eva Russell Chandler preserve. A fragrant dwarf iris (right) lights up Rocky Bottom Creek in the Eastatoe Valley.*

of swamp pinks, a nationally threatened species that survives here among tangles of huckleberry, greenbrier, and mountain laurel. Along Matthews and Julian creeks, huge hemlocks stand like ancient sentries, their shade imparting a deep blue patina to the rushing streams where brook trout cloaked in brilliant colors rise to feed on insects.

Between the Ashmore and Watson tracts is the 25-acre **Eva Russell Chandler Heritage Preserve❖,** also owned by the Heritage Trust (north of the hamlet of Little Bald Rock on Route 276, turn right on Persimmon Ridge Road and follow it to the Heritage Trust signs). Two well-marked trails loop through this backcountry mountain sanctuary, which supports the largest known population of endangered mountain sweet pitcher plants (*Sarracenia jonesii*) in the Carolina uplands. The Upper Trail parallels Slickum Creek, home to another mountain cataract ecosystem. Cloaked in slippery algae, the stream's stones glisten among legions of mountain sweet pitcher plants.

The banks of smaller nearby creeks are festooned with glades of Christmas, New York, and Southern lady ferns. In spring, the clearings are vivid with blooming wild violets and native azalea. The Upper Trail wanders through scrubs of mountain laurel and stands of chestnut oak, among spongy carpets of reindeer moss and even pods of prickly-pear cactus. At trail's end is a memorable view of Table Rock Mountain in the distance.

Tucked quietly between Jones Gap and Caesars Head is **Wildcat Wayside❖.** Like many of the Southeast's older natural areas, Wildcat Wayside is the handiwork of the WPA (Works Progress Administration). Just off the Cherokee Foothills Scenic Highway west of the small community of Cleveland, these 63 acres rarely draw the crowds that throng better-known parks nearby. However, those familiar with Wildcat Wayside, like pilgrims at a holy shrine, return to it again and again. The park's initial allure is a diminutive waterfall that empties into the cold waters of a plunge pool. A little exploration, however, deposits the adventurous on trails choked with rafts of rhododendron, stands of hardwoods, and an understory strewn with wildflowers.

A 15-minute walk along a stream trilling softly in its channel of stones brings a hiker to the base of a wondrous slickrock water slide more than a hundred feet long. Layers of cold, slippery water sluice down the 45-degree angle of the slickrock, which is edged with knots of mountain witch alder, patchworks of divided-leaved groundsel, and Carey saxifrage.

Despite its popularity and often considerable crowds, **Table Rock State Park❖,** about 10 miles farther west along the Foothills Highway and 16 miles north of Pickens, enfolds another great pocket of wild country. Laid out by the Civilian Conservation Corps during the Great Depression, Table Rock has seen its share of development, but it maintains a solid reputation for sternly protecting its natural areas and the region's rich Cherokee legacy. Along with another "rock" (actually an adjacent mountain) known locally as the Stool, 3,200-foot Table Rock dominates the surrounding high country, which is rich in both plant and animal life. According to Cherokee legend, chiefs and holy men sat on the Stool and dined at the Table, awaiting visions and contemplating the wonder of the great mountain world around them.

One of the park's highlights is the portion of the **Foothills Trail**—perhaps the most ambitious in the Carolina Up-country—that passes through Table Rock State Park. Switchbacking up and down, the Foothills Trail covers more than 100 miles of spectacular mountain country and provides a hikeable link among Jones Gap, Caesars Head, Table Rock, and Oconee state parks. The trail curls over a broad sampling of mountain and valley topography and visits sublime river

---

OVERLEAF: *As though they had just risen, bare and new, above hills clothed in trees, the stark granite walls of Table Rock Mountain shimmer in the rosy glow of sunrise above the blue Table Rock Reservoir.*

canyons, Sassafras Mountain (South Carolina's highest peak), Raven Cliff Falls, Drawbar Cliffs, and the hushed beauty of the Middle Fork of the Saluda River at Jones Gap. It snakes from Pinnacle Mountain at Table Rock across the North Carolina state line to Whitewater Falls, the largest river falls east of the Mississippi in the south, and eventually loops south to Oconee State Park in the Andrew Pickens Ranger District of the Sumter National Forest.

NORTHWEST MOUNTAINS: PRESERVES, FORESTS, AND WHITE WATER

Straddling the North Carolina border just east of the Sumter's Pickens Ranger District is a jewel of the Up-country, the Eastatoe Valley. (Follow Route 178 north approximately 8 miles from its junction with the Foothills Highway; beyond the hamlet of Rocky Bottom, just over the Eastatoe Creek Bridge, is a trailhead for the Foothills Trail; access to the preserve is about an eighth of a mile up the trail.) The heart of the 373-acre **Eastatoe Creek Heritage Preserve❖** is the narrow seven-mile-long valley of the Eastatoe Creek. Closely associated with the Cherokee, this undisturbed valley is tucked deep into the shadow of the Blue Ridge, which surrounds the Eastatoe on three sides. Three small creeks—Laurel Branch, Rocky Bottom, and Side of Mountain—join to form the larger Eastatoe, which then tumbles 600 feet into a hauntingly beautiful ravine. Compressed by this gorge—often called the Narrows—the waters can turn turbulent, and after a sudden rain, even dangerous.

Because it is bathed in extremely high humidity, the gorge has an eerie tropical feel and supports an unusual ecosystem. Indeed, several species of quasitropical plants grow here, including uncommon ferns such as bristle, dwarf, and Tunbridge, which naturalists have been unable to find anywhere else in North America. Mosses normally seen only in the jungles of South America have been discovered in the **Eastatoe Gorge Natural Area,** which is part of the preserve, and at least one of the mosses in the gorge has been found nowhere else in the world. Some naturalists believe the Eastatoe Valley may be the only genuine tropical habitat in the Southeast outside of southernmost Florida.

Peeling off the Foothills Trail at the parking area off Horsepasture Road, the Eastatoe Creek Trail continues lazily through forests of chestnut oaks, red maples, and black locusts and penetrates some re-

ABOVE: *Ferns, violets, and trilliums create natural gardens beside the rushing waters of Rocky Bottom, a tributary of Eastatoe Creek; the gorge here harbors rare vegetation, otherwise found only in South America.*

markable scrubland. An alert walker might well see the blur of indigo buntings on the wing or hear the unmistakable call of prairie warblers deep in the brambles. Soon the gnarled scrub forest gives way to mature forest habitat marked by a healthy canopy and a sun-dappled understory. Winds high among the trees rattle with the songs of red-eyed vireos and shy wood thrushes. Red-spotted newts scurry among the plethora of fallen trees rotting on the forest floor, and small trout rise in the nearby stream. Near its end, the trail crosses a stream near a wide wet basin laced with wild geraniums, foamflowers, delicate wake-robins, stands of majestic old-growth hemlocks, and more than ten species of wild violets.

From Table Rock, the Cherokee Foothills Scenic Highway heads due south, paralleling the Andrew Pickens Ranger District of the **Sumter National Forest❖.** Covering 360,000 acres, Sumter is divided into three noncontiguous areas: the Andrew Pickens Ranger District, which includes a significant chunk of the mountainous northwest; the Long Cane Ranger District, along the Savannah River and Georgia border north of Augusta; and the more central Enoree Ranger District,

ABOVE: *Near Eastatoe Creek, red-spotted newts (left) scurry in damp forests where indigo buntings (top right) return each spring. Catesby's trillium (bottom right) puts on a show in the Ellicott Rock Wilderness.*

about halfway between Columbia and Spartanburg.

As the Cherokee Foothills Scenic Highway twists and turns southwest toward the entrance to Sumter's Andrew Pickens Ranger District, Glassy Mountain gradually begins to command attention. The centerpiece of the **Glassy Mountain Heritage Preserve❖** is well worth a short detour; take Route 183 east 1.5 miles from Route 8. Go north (left) on South Glassy Mountain Road, which continues about 200 feet to the mountain trailhead on the east side of the road.

A natural siren, Glassy Mountain signals the gradual transformation of the landscape from rugged mountain Up-country to rolling piedmont. Glassy Mountain is a natural area of considerable interest. Its 65 acres are characterized by jagged cliffs—some dropping more than 400 feet—and granite outcrops supporting rare plant populations, including talinum, yucca, and regionally threatened thousand-leaf groundsel. A trail strays pleasantly through a stately forest dominated by Virginia pine and, on the north side, more traditional upland hardwoods, including chestnut oaks. The summit affords a spectacular

ABOVE: *In the Ellicott Rock Wilderness of the Sumter National Forest, the East Fork of the Chattooga River flows through a river cove forest thick with rhododendron, mountain laurel, buffalo nut, and hemlock.*

panoramic view of the hulking Blue Ridge Escarpment and in the distance the rolling sprawl of the piedmont plateau.

Taking Route 28 north from Walhalla to enter the **Andrew Pickens Ranger District❖** of the **Sumter National Forest** is like being engulfed by an endless expanse of Up-country—deep cool shadows, blue-black woods, the dizzying splash of mountain cascades. Covering more than 78,000 acres, the Andrew Pickens Ranger District includes part of the imposing 8,274-acre **Ellicott Rock Wilderness❖,** named for the surveyor who determined in the early 1800s where Georgia, North Carolina, and South Carolina met; a long stretch of the **Foothills Trail❖,** which roams 25 miles north through the forest from Oconee State Park to Table Rock State Park and a rendezvous with the North Carolina line; and the Chattooga River, a natural white-water roller coaster, which plummets 2,500 feet over a stretch of about 50 miles.

The only truly mountainous section of national forest in the state, the Andrew Pickens Ranger District is a labyrinth of peaks and rocky gorges, valleys and trilling waterfalls. Here 13 trails covering nearly 50

ABOVE: *The heart-stopping rapids at roiling Big Bend Falls are one of the wildest sections along the legendary Chattooga River, which forms part of South Carolina's northwestern border with neighboring Georgia.*

miles crisscross wild uplands and culminate in the rugged ridges that crowd a narrow apex where the high fastnesses of Georgia, North Carolina, and South Carolina seem to collide. From a distance, this dramatic chaos of uplifted mountains resembles a great earthen bowl of gigantic crushed stones.

Each year thousands explore the mighty **Chattooga National Wild and Scenic River❖,** drawn to the surging rapids as though the waters hold the answers to unfathomable mysteries. Once seen and experienced, the Chattooga buzzes down the spine like ragged charges of electricity. It gets under the skin and stays there, flashing in and out of memory, soothing and frightening, dangerous and forever unknowable.

The river is a deafening cacophony of truncated waterfalls and rapids, beginning with the thumping, hissing waters of Bull Sluice Falls, whose low groaning is easily heard from the Route 76 bridge. Here the river falls with the suddenness of a failed elevator, cascading 14 feet over three falls in a matter of seconds to create one of the most challenging, thrilling, and deadly white-water runs in the country. And the ride has just begun. Plummeting downstream, the river plunges past steep bluffs and drops 120 feet at Rock Gorge Falls near Moody Springs. Reaching this section on foot can be as risky as negotiating it by white-water raft: During high water Rock Gorge Falls becomes a Dante's Inferno of thwacking, grinding water and violent beauty better enjoyed from a distance.

Probably the most famous series of rapids along the river occurs at Big Bend Falls. (Take the Big Bend trail from Cherry Hill Campground and allow at least six hours for the round-trip hike.) On high ground well above the river, the din of Big Bend echoes like the distant roar of a steam train hurtling through a mountain tunnel. Here the Chattooga takes its single largest drop as the channel slopes 30 degrees. Water roils madly over tilted slabs of stone. In a heartbeat, the river seems to shrug off gravity, free-falling at least 15 feet to leave rafters giddy, scared, thrilled, their hearts lodged trembling in either stomach or throat.

At evening a cool wind rises off the river, and high in the hard-woods above the shadows, woodpeckers drum incessantly. The trail up Buzzard Roost Mountain is flanked by Virginia pine and mockernut hickory; among older stands scarlet and black oaks prevail. The pines are probably no more than 50 years old, an indication that the mountain and surrounding region were once heavily logged. The thickening woods are reclaiming long-abandoned forest roads, which now serve hikers instead of logging trucks. Just before sundown, the view from the summit is like a glimpse of creation, as the day's last illumination bleeds from the sky, wrapping Poor Mountain and Hurricane Mountain in sheets of fiery light.

Buzzard Roost Heritage Preserve❖ is adjacent to the national forest about 12 miles northwest of Walhalla and accessible via Routes 193 and 290 (near the Stumphouse Ranger Station) and then Forest Roads F-744 and F-7441 (the barricade is on Forest Road F-7441). Green and green-and-white blazes mark the boundaries of the preserve; red blazes mark the national forest boundary. Buzzard Roost boasts South Carolina's largest marble outcrops. Its marble makes the mountain home to several rare plant communities, including purple cliffbrake,

OVERLEAF: *In early fall, reflections of hardwoods (oak, sourwood, red maple, black gum) and pines tint a placid mountain lake in Oconee State Park, which is surrounded by the vast Sumter National Forest.*

ABOVE: *A rare Florida gooseberry, a prickly cousin of the currant, thrives at the botanically diverse Stevens Creek preserve.*
BELOW: *Carpeting forest floors, spring beauties grow from tubers. Cherokees and colonists once dined on these roots.*

woolly lipfern, stoneroot, blackstem spleenwort, and a variety of ferns. The woods reverberate with the confusing songs of warblers and the unmistakable call of rose-breasted grosbeaks. High above the ridge, black and turkey vultures cut lazy arcs in the sky. At nightfall, the stone surfaces shimmer with the dim light of distant stars and the yellow blush of a rising moon.

At day's end most visitors to the Pickens Ranger District of Sumter National Forest make their way to **Oconee State Park❖.** Situated on a Blue Ridge plateau, the park embraces more than 1,600 acres. More important, at least to exhausted rafters, hikers, and backpackers, the park contains amenities—cabins, a store. Although such conveniences are unnatural fixtures in the protected wilderness areas of the national forest, after a week of scurrying up and down mountain trails, eating cold chili, and drinking tepid water laced with purification tablets, even the hardiest adventurer would rank a hot shower at least as high as a kaleidoscopic sunset.

THE PIEDMONT PLATEAU: ALONG THE SAVANNAH RIVER

Passing from one scenic drive to another, about 17 miles south of Oconee a traveler on Route 11 reaches Route 24, which along with Routes 187 and 81 forms the Savannah River Scenic Highway. Paralleling the impounded lakes of the Savannah River on the Georgia state line, Route 81 leads to the **Long Cane Ranger District❖** of **Sumter National Forest,** which sprawls over more than 60,000 acres in parts of Edgefield, McCormick, Saluda, and Greenwood counties. Here remnants of the rich and sophisticated culture and history of the Cherokee have been preserved, along with relics of the region's antebellum era.

South of Sumter's Long Cane Ranger District, along the Savannah River off County Route 88, the **Stevens Creek Heritage Preserve❖** shelters more than 200 acres of complex piedmont habitat that supports a fine diversity of plant and animal species. The ecological value of Stevens Creek was discovered early; the tract was purchased by the Nature Conservancy in 1976 and turned over to the state. So uncommon and important are the plant species at Stevens Creek that the preserve is considered one of the two most important extant lower piedmont ecosystems.

In mood and character, Stevens Creek often seems more typical of the Up-country, perhaps because many plant species now found in this patchwork of isolated habitats retreated here ahead of the glaciers during the last ice age. Many of the preserve's most interesting plant varieties appear between the floodplain and the upper ridgeline, along the northern bluffs. Hunkered among the stones are plants whose ancestors thrived in the state's ancient forests. Mountain varieties grow alongside coastal and piedmont plants, including such rare and threatened species as the spiny perennial shrub Florida gooseberry, which has been found only here and near Lake Miccosukee, Florida. Underfoot, endangered Webster's salamanders coil quietly among the damp stones, the muted strips on their backs glowing orange in the soft light of dawn and dusk.

The Stevens Creek Trail explores most of the preserve's sensitive habitats. Hikers should respect the fragile character of the plant communities and keep to the trail, leaving the creek to the vagaries of time. Smaller streams are lined with shooting stars, saxifrage, and butterweed. At the base of the bluffs and on the floodplain, spring initiates one of the state's most dramatic wildflower displays—white clusters of false rue anemones and arching stalks of creamy Dutchman's-breeches; pink-striped spring beauties and large-leaved trilliums; spicebush, with its dense clusters of pale yellow flowers that appear before the leaves, and blue spiderwort; wild ginger and delicate foamflowers; sweet chervil and green violets. Stop often to listen to the dissonant chorus of pileated woodpeckers. Observe this thriving legacy of an ancient habitat, a living fossil growing among transition hardwoods, shagbark and butternut hickory and oaks. Enjoy it all—the bluffs, the creek, the flowers—and walk on.

Because it shelters both piedmont and coastal-plains habitats, the 70-acre **Savannah River Bluffs Heritage Preserve❖** is one of the state's important natural areas. Located just beyond North Augusta, off I-20 and Old Plantation Road, the preserve's granite bluffs and abundant hardwood forest crowd along a thousand feet of the Savannah River, flanking one of its last intact shoals. The bluffs provide a wild corridor between the coastal and piedmont ecosystems, but development to the north and south has been isolating this area. Such natural bridges are vital to the survival of species that live in marginal regions.

The plant communities on these bluffs are often as rare as they are diverse. Indeed, eighteenth-century American naturalist William Bartram reported locating the first specimen of the extremely rare Rocky Shoals spider lily here. These delicate wildflowers still bloom briefly—their appearance as fleeting as passing clouds—along the river shoal in May and June. Tendrils of Spanish moss hang like gray beards from bald cypress trees, and the shade of the understory sustains glades of yellow-green dwarf palmetto. Mingled with these coastal species are such piedmont plants as upland swamp privet, endangered relict trillium, and bottlebrush buckeye. Volunteers built and maintain the trail that traverses the bluffs, allowing visitors to experience the amazing diversity of plant life without disturbing the rare quiet or disrupting the rare union of Carolina Low Country and piedmont.

The natural world perseveres wherever it can—not always in places removed from the human touch or the malaise of the modern world. **Hitchcock Woods❖,** a splendid natural area, is not far from downtown Aiken (take Route 1 east 15 miles from North Augusta and the Georgia state line). Visitors entering Hitchcock Woods off South Boundary Avenue are stepping into a portion of the swath of pine uplands and wiregrass lowlands that once extended across the middle southeastern states.

In 1939 Thomas Hitchcock and his daughter established a foundation to preserve almost 1,200 acres of nearly virgin longleaf pine forest as a gift for the city to enjoy in perpetuity. Over the years, additional tracts have been acquired, and now the preserve protects almost 2,000 acres. Variety is the hallmark of Hitchcock Woods, from sweet bay and red bay trees to bloodroot and hepatica, from lupine and wood sorrel to

ABOVE: *On the border between piedmont and coastal ecosytems, the Savannah River Bluffs preserve includes a variety of vegetation, including trees draped with Spanish moss—a sure sign of the lowlands.*

resurrection fern, ebony spleenwort, and thickets of mountain laurel. This botanical diversity is also attractive to many birds, which dart among the trees and shrubs in a whirl of song, motion, and color: indigo buntings and eastern bluebirds, ruby-crowned kinglets, screech owls, warblers, redheaded woodpeckers, summer tanagers, and eastern pewees. A complex latticework of more than 60 miles of trails explores the beauty of Hitchcock Woods and reveals its rich biodiversity—including more than 100 species of birds and 350 species of plants.

THE NORTHEAST: MIDLANDS AND SAND HILLS

In the rural country north of Columbia, about 50 miles northeast of the Long Cane Ranger District, lies the third section of the **Sumter National Forest,** the **Enoree Ranger District❖** (including the former Tyger District), covering more than 80,000 acres. Just before the Great Depression, this region was largely in ruins. Most of the trees had been cut, and the majority of the land was farmed out and often abandoned, its soil exhausted or eroded. The federal government acquired thousands of

41

LEFT: *Cross vine's trumpet flowers are dazzling. Missionaries accompanying early explorers named the plant for the cross that appears on the cross-section of a cut stem.* **RIGHT:** *Seen here at the Savannah River Bluffs preserve, cross vine is native to the lowlands of the Southeast, rambling 50 feet and more up trees and across shrubs.*

acres, planted trees, and transformed seemingly dead and useless country into a national forest. Today the land is again rich with nature's endless possibilities.

Many trails wander along the rivers and through the woodlands of the national forest, including one to **Mollys Rock❖,** a small picnic area accessible from Route 176 and Forest Road 367. A perpetual cowl of chilly shade enshrouds Mollys Rock. The glassy surface of a nearby pond reflects the sky and every detail of branches shimmering in a wind soaked with the smell of sassafras trees. Settling nervously on the water's surface, dragonflies flash neon greens and reds and blues as rafts of painted turtles bask in the sun. Around the pond are knots of mulberry trees, which grow consistently along the edge of the piedmont. White-tailed deer are easily spotted and a fortunate few may see red and gray foxes dashing about. Rabbits and fox squirrels make many a fine meal for reclusive bobcat, and the ever-present raccoon feed omnivorously on whatever they find.

In the northeast corner of the state between Interstates 77 and 95, the **Flat Creek Heritage Preserve and Forty Acre Rock❖,** off Route 601 near Taxahaw, occupies a significant transition zone where the habitats of South Carolina's piedmont plateau and coastal plain overlap. The preserve's 1,550 acres are an ecologist's dream. This ensemble of unusual granite outcrops, floodplain, tiny seasonal creeks, beaver ponds, patches of resplendent piedmont cove forest, and upland pines makes the preserve one of the richest natural areas in northeastern South Carolina.

Physically, the preserve is dominated by the corpulent bulk of Forty

Acre Rock (actually only 14 acres), an eroded stone outcrop that shelters the most magnificent example of flat-rock habitat in the eastern United States. Geologists report that the 200-million-year-old diabase dike underlying the preserve is the most extensive formation of its kind east of the Mississippi. Constant weathering and erosion of this bedrock has produced a calcium-rich soil, which supports a wide variety of plant communities, many exceptionally rare.

Numerous plants at Forty Acre Rock are endemic species. One such native flora is the pool sprite, which survives the harsh environment on exposed outcrops by blooming twice a year. Each time it blossoms, it produces a completely different set of leaves and flowers, thus doubling its chances of survival. Plants use every resource in the Forty Acre Rock ecosystem. Some depend on water that pools in eroded depressions pocking the rock surfaces. After a rain, the seemingly dead stone suddenly wrinkles to life: Fuzzy mosses and lichens, as well as Puck's orpine and thick wine-red mats of diamorpha (both members of the stonecrop family) appear and then spin out their life cycles elegantly, efficiently, quickly. Plants such as yucca survive in rock fissures and cracks, and riparian species—nodding trillium, creeping phlox, yellow buckeye, and papooseroot—abound along the creek and pond. Even before winter has loosened its grip on the land, bloodroot brings the hope of spring.

Like a buckled backbone, South Carolina's sand hills, the western edge of the coastal plain, form a thin boundary

ABOVE: *A denizen of the coastal plain, woolly ragwort with its narrow fleecy leaves emerges from the forest floor of the Flat Creek preserve.*

LEFT: *At Forty Acre Rock, solution pits begin when lichens colonize cracks created by erosion. The weak acids formed as organic matter decomposes then dissolve more rock, eventually producing the large depressions.*

OVERLEAF: *Gauzy in the moist spring air, flowering dogwoods complement moss- and lichen-covered rocks within the Flat Creek preserve.*

between the piedmont and the Low Country. East of Forty Acre Rock, just north of the junction of Routes 1 and 151, lies the heart of the state's sand hills country. Here the 46,000-acre **Carolina Sandhills National Wildlife Refuge❖** sprawls along the fall line that separates the higher plateau from the lower coastal plain. Visible from Route 1, which bisects the adjacent **Sand Hills State Forest❖,** the sandy ridges are probably remnants of ancient sand dunes. According to geologists, the layers of sand that underlie this region are debris left by rivers pouring into an ocean that probably last covered the region 50 to 60 million years ago. (A Nature Conservancy site, **Peachtree Rock Preserve❖,** off Route 6 just west of Columbia, provides more evidence of this prehistoric sea; Peachtree's 20-foot-high chunk of stone is laced with fossils and fossilized burrows of ancient marine creatures.)

The Carolina Sandhills refuge is vital, living evidence that exhausted land can be reclaimed over time. Its 30 lakes and ponds, open meadows, and pine forests make the refuge an important wintering ground for migrating waterfowl—Canada geese and many species of ducks, including mallard, American wigeon, hooded mergansers, wood ducks, and black ducks. Bobcat and deer, beavers and otters, wild turkeys and eastern fox squirrels roam the woodlands and rolling terrain.

The refuge also shelters a number of rare and unusual species, including the eastern cougar, the bright green Pine Barrens tree frog, a tiny pyxie moss *(Pyxidanthera barbulata),* and clumps of three different species of pitcher plants. Biologists now estimate that the refuge's century-old longleaf pine forest is home to more than a hundred red-cockaded woodpecker clans (each clan usually numbers from three to five birds), more than at any other national wildlife refuge. These endangered woodpeckers make their homes in mature longleaf pines—an increasingly rare habitat as development and logging spread.

About 60 miles east of the sand hills via Route 9 is the 3,771-acre **Little Pee Dee Heritage Preserve❖,** protecting nine miles of blackwater river frontage. The Little Pee Dee welcomes canoe campers with ten river access points, and paddlers who pause in their exertions can drift through mysterious cypress-gum swamps, bottomland forests that nourish stands of hardwoods, and fascinating sand ridges. Among the floral and vegetative denizens sheltered by the preserve are three rare species: sarvis holly *(Ilex amelanchier),* pyxie moss (actually a shrublet rather than a true moss), and dayflower *(Stylisma pickeringii).*

Southwest of the Little Pee Dee, about 20 miles southwest of Florence and east of I-95 near Olanta, **Woods Bay State Park**❖ harbors an unusual regional habitat known as a Carolina bay. Usually elliptical, this rare natural wetland depression takes its name from the evergreen bay trees that characteristically colonize its waters. Today undisturbed bay ecosystems thrive only in isolated remnants along the Carolina coastal plain. Unfortunately, few bay habitats survive because most have been drained, logged, and abandoned. Woods Bay is an exception: It remains heavily wooded, wet, and intact—part bog, part hard-bottom wetland, part swamp.

A strange characteristic of Carolina bays is their natural alignment from northwest to southeast, as true as a compass needle. The exact origin of the bay habitat is a matter of some dispute. An early theory contended that the egg-shaped depressions were the result of past meteorite activity. More recently scientists have speculated that they developed from shallow lakes that have been modified by the dominant southwest wind. Another belief holds that they, like the sand ridges of the sand hills, are beached remnants of an ancient sea. However they were created, unspoiled bays can support an impressive diversity of life, especially in tree species—from the unusual bays to wild dogwood and sweet gum, tupelo and water oak. At Woods Bay, a 500-foot boardwalk leaves visitors poised over the dark waters, just inches above marsh grasses and bladderworts, sunning alligators and wading birds.

CENTRAL COASTAL PLAIN: SWAMPS, LAKES, AND BIG TREES

On the Low Country side of the sand hills' snaking backbone is the **Congaree Swamp National Monument**❖, about 20 miles southeast of Columbia. (Access is from Gadsden via Route 48.) One of the most significant natural areas in the Southeast, Congaree Swamp is an untouched remnant of the region's once sprawling hardwood bottomland forest, an ecosystem reminiscent of Louisiana's Atchafalaya Swamp. Preserved and protected by the National Park Service since 1976, Congaree Swamp was designated a United Nations Man and the Biosphere Reserve in 1983 because of its great biological diversity.

Routinely flooded with sediment-rich waters, the low-lying swamp

ABOVE: *In Congaree Swamp, the fertile black waters of Cedar Creek reflect a pedestrian bridge and an arching ironwood, a dense understory tree, also known as musclewood because of its smooth sinewy bark.*

is a mesmerizing maze of black-water creeks and floodplain forest, an incredibly fertile habitat that supports magnificent hardwood trees, some of them national record holders for their species. Denizens include 160-foot loblolly pines, enormous bald cypresses, water oaks, ghostly sycamores, and tupelo trees embroidered with wild grape vines and draped with green shawls of poison ivy. The spreading crowns of massive sweet gums, sugarberries, oaks, elms, ashes, and black gums veil the swamp in a perpetual humid shade, perfect conditions for Spanish moss and ferns.

The 22,000-acre swamp trembles with life. Time spent on any of the monument's six trails—including a canoe trail on Cedar Creek—only deepens an appreciation of Congaree's wild beauty and incredible diversity. This hard-bottom floodplain nourishes more than 300 plant species, some 90 of them trees; among its many birds are the endangered red-cockaded woodpecker and the threatened bald eagle. Raccoon, squirrels, and an occasional bobcat are a few of the 40 or so species of mammals coexisting with 24 species of reptiles. Travelers expecting a few venomous swamp residents are not disappointed. Cottonmouth, canebrake rattler, and copperhead snakes dwell here.

ABOVE: *Wildlife at Congaree includes large, noisy pileated woodpeckers (top left), water-loving mink that nest in hollow logs (top right), and a young alligator (bottom) whose creamy stripes will fade with age.*

Like the Okefenokee Swamp in southern Georgia, the Congaree presents a haunting landscape. Its moods and turns of character are distinctive: surreal, primeval, always wild. One feels that at any moment almost anything might haul itself out of the marvelous muck, a leftover creature seeking the Cretaceous dawn, or even evolution's newest mutation, eager to begin life on earth.

The Congaree River winds southeast from the swamp and 60 miles later joins the Wateree to form the Santee River. In between lie two of the state's largest artificial lakes, Marion and Moultrie, formed when dams were constructed for hydroelectric power and to control flooding before World War II. Created as a sanctuary for birds displaced by the impoundments, the **Santee National Wildlife Refuge❖,** just off I-95, hugs the northern shore of Lake Marion.

Today the refuge's constant winds from fall through spring rattle with the racket of birds on the wing, especially populations of wintering waterfowl. So thick are the migratory flocks that at times they shade the bold setting sun. As many as 30,000 ducks have been known to spend the winter within refuge boundaries; hundreds of other avian species—from warblers to woodpeckers, bluebirds to eagles—visit as well. A tapestry of trails explores the refuge's varied habitats of ponds, small lakes, open meadows, and extensive wetlands. Although reclamation work here began barely half a century ago, the land has already regained its wild edge.

South of the Santee refuge, below the junction of I-95 and I-26 near the town of Harleyville, **Four Holes Swamp** encompasses the incomparable **Francis Beidler Forest❖,** administered as a wildlife sanctuary by the National Audubon Society. Like the Congaree Swamp or Great Smoky Mountains National Park, Beidler Forest ranks among North America's most important natural areas because it shelters a crucial pocket of biological diversity—one of the largest stands of virgin swamp forest of bald cypress and tupelo gum left on the planet.

Francis Beidler, a successful lumberman who understood the significance of undisturbed old-growth trees, preserved the site, and the family kept it until the 1960s. Before logging rights could be sold, the National Audubon Society and the Nature Conservancy managed to buy more than 3,000 acres of Beidler Forest, guaranteeing its preservation. Later, additional tracts of swamp and forest were added.

Today the Audubon Society interferes as little as possible with this rare ecosystem. The only permanent evidence of human presence is a boardwalk that probes the forest for more than a mile, ending at Goodson Lake. After a few steps into the forest, visitors are wrapped in a cocoon of smells and colors, in a deep solitude interrupted only by the wind. An alligator slips into the dark water, and birds call from the damp woodlands and open wetlands. Hundreds of avian species reside here: herons and egrets, kites and swallows, warblers and thrushes in the damp shadows. Giant cypress trees, some thought to be at least a thousand years old, glow in the dappled light, which burnishes the assemblage of trees lining Goodson Lake—swamp cottonwoods, overcup oaks, winged elms, bays, water locusts, black cherries, tupelo gums, hickories, and sweet leaf, or horse sugar, trees.

To go beyond the boardwalk and pierce the heart of the sanctuary, visitors must take to the water. Just six canoes are permitted on guided trips where participants are routinely awed, startled, and humbled. Canoeists are reluctant to paddle too often because the noise seems out of place among the swamp's ongoing symphony of sounds: the sigh of water trickling over an outcrop of cypress knees, the whir of a bright yellow prothonotary warbler suddenly taking wing, the diminutive splash of sunning turtles sliding off rotting logs into the cool black water, the rattle of crickets, the peeping of tree frogs. Great mats of resurrection ferns grow along the massive limbs of bald cypress, and in midsummer fragile greenfly orchids, the state's only epiphytic orchids, produce delicate blooms in the dense understory. Among the fallen trees and scrub grow great varieties of herbaceous plants, including dwarf trillium, Atamasco lily, lavender lobelia, creeping coral honeysuckle, supplejack, greenbrier, climbing hydrangea, muscadine, and yellow jasmine (also called jessamine).

COASTAL CAROLINA: NORTH OF CHARLESTON

Despite ever greater concentrations of people and a startling amount of development, the South Carolina coast still shelters numerous dynamic natural areas, from lush maritime forests and great swaths of fecund marsh and wetlands to bays and estuaries teeming with marine life, dune-lined beaches, and secluded barrier islands.

Where Route 6 from Lakes Marion and Moultrie gives way to Route 52 near Moncks Corner, the highway slips quietly through a back door into **Francis Marion National Forest❖.** Established in 1936 to reclaim depleted farm fields, the Francis Marion National Forest now covers 250,000 acres. More than 14,000 acres occupy four beautiful coastal wilderness areas—Wambaw Creek, Hellhole Bay, Wambaw Swamp, and Little Wambaw Swamp. Several excellent trails crisscross the forest, including the 50-mile Swamp Fox Passage of the statewide Palmetto Trail that meanders from Awendaw to the rim of Lake Moultrie. Due to damage from Hurricane Hugo in 1989, red-cockaded woodpeckers lost more than half their nests in the forest, but biologists drilled into the mature trees, making new homes for the birds.

A tributary of the Santee River, **Wambaw Creek** encompasses the endlessly haunting Wambaw Creek Wilderness Canoe Trail. Slithering seductively into the forest's interior, this water route coils nine miles through a thousand acres of tangled swamp and wetlands, the dark water seemingly motionless, the air heavy and humid and often abuzz with clouds of mosquitoes. In the shadows birds call from islands of cypress and tupelo. Alligators haul out of channels to warm their cold blood in the dark muck of the swamp. Nearby, anhingas hunt patiently,

awaiting just the right moment to plunge for a fish and then swallow it whole. Because their feathers do not shed moisture, anhingas must perch in the sun to dry their dark iridescent plumage after each watery meal. Often two or three birds, wings outstretched to catch the warming sunlight, pose in a craggy half-dead tree. Motionless and primeval, they seem caricatures of themselves, as though carved from tupelo and left in the branches as primitive totems.

Exiting the national forest on the coast near McClellanville and Bulls Bay, Route 45 gives way to Route 17, the Ocean Highway, which seems to mimic each twist and turn of the Carolina coast. To the south near Charleston lies Capers Island (accessible by boat from Capers Beach) and to the north is Cape Island, part of the surrounding Cape Romain National Wildlife Refuge. All are uncommon remnants of South Carolina's once-pristine coastal plain. One of the best ways to see these islands is by sea kayak; guided tours from the Charleston area allow kayakers to absorb the beauty of this watery world at sea level, to breathe the odors of the estuaries, to watch bottle-nosed dolphins frol-

ic, and to hear mullet plop and flop in and out of the water as they elude hungry predators.

Although completely devoted to cotton and vegetables in the 1800s, **Capers Island❖** became a state preserve in the mid-1970s and has now reverted to its barrier-island roots. A narrow trail winds from the island's south beach through a fine stand of maritime forest to a large impoundment created in 1952. Since the impoundment's original dike eroded, the tidal mixing of freshwater and salt water has made the island a major refuge for bird species favoring both environments.

On the south end of the island, dune ridges rise and fall like white waves. In the back dunes harsh coastal storms have twisted live oaks into bizarre poses; the oaks survive amid the largest stand of mature coastal magnolia forest left in South Carolina. On the backside of the island facing Capers Inlet, forest gives way to meadows of panic grass intertwined with mats of pink and purple morning glory and dune heads thatched with tenacious, ever-swaying sea oats. Here grass blades are encased in a film of sea salt, and intense coastal sunlight washes over the landscape like the swollen tides of spring.

Like the sea and sand, barrier islands are always on the move. As the Atlantic continues its slow, steady rise, Capers Island creeps ever closer to the mainland. Few movements are more seductive than the imperceptible drift of wild islands like Capers, where the wind is constant, the seclusion genuine, and sea bass flash silver in the rolling surf.

Ocean dreams spun on Capers Island only deepen nearby in the shallow bays, creeks,

In Francis Marion National Forest, an endangered red-cockaded woodpecker (above) pecks at its hole high in an old-growth pine. Nearby tall pond cypresses grow in a mysterious depression called a Carolina bay (left). Carnivorous yellow trumpets (below) dot the sandy, infertile soil of the forest's wet pinelands.

marshes, and wetlands of the 60,000-acre **Cape Romain National Wildlife Refuge❖.** Some 22 miles north of Charleston, Route 17 begins its 20-mile sweep along the shore-side boundary of the island-dotted refuge. Still recovering from extensive damage caused by Hurricane Hugo in 1989, Cape Romain, accessible only by boat (Charleston-area outfitters run tours), remains one of the most popular birding spots on the Atlantic coast. Ponds on Bull Island attract crowds of waterfowl each winter, including most of the Atlantic coast's population of American oystercatchers. Its wetlands and coastal forest (on Bull Island) of magnolia, oak, and palmetto lure more than 250 species of birds, from the common and occasional to the rare and accidental—loons and herons and grebes, falcons and gallinules, cuckoos, goatsuckers, storks, shrikes, and skimmers.

On Bull Island alligators slide from land to water, perhaps seeking a young, unwary shorebird. Farther inland, deer browse on post-hurricane growth as marsh rabbits bound underfoot. And nearly every day at dusk Marsh Island, in the shallow waters of Bulls Bay, is cloaked with brown pelicans, endangered throughout the United States except on the Atlantic coast and in Florida and Alabama.

As tides rise and fall here, the worlds of land and water quietly collide, join, separate. What was land a moment before succumbs to water, and what was sunk in a tidal pool glistens in the sunlight, suddenly a hammock of dry land. At the edges of the marsh, where spartina grass seems impenetrable, shallow water teems with immature shrimp, crabs, and small fish.

At the northern end of the refuge on Cape Island, thousands of least terns nest, and female loggerhead turtles still crawl ponderously onto the sand to lay their thousands of eggs. Indeed, the island is one of the more important natural sea-turtle rookeries remaining on the southeastern coast. So many birds nest within the boundaries of the refuge that portions of it are officially closed from mid-February until September 15 to protect the birds and their young.

North of Cape Romain near Georgetown, the Ocean Highway parallels the **Santee Coastal Reserve❖,** a state-managed area comprising swamp, abandoned rice fields, a private sportsmen's club, and a Nature Conservancy property. Healthy, beautiful vestiges of all the state's coastal ecosystems thrive here—maritime forest, marsh, and more than a thou-

ABOVE: *Backed by a strand populated with sabal palms, the "boneyard" beach at Cape Romain's Bull Island is strewn with the dead silvery hulks of massive live oaks. The trees' roots were undercut by changing tides.*

sand acres of bald cypress, pine flatwoods, and tupelo gum swamp in the **Washo Reserve.** Rich in coastal fauna and flora, the reserve is a favorite among birders, especially in winter, when the waterfowl arrive, and during the spring migrations of shorebirds and wading birds.

Just ten miles north on Route 17 is the **Tom Yawkey Wildlife Center❖,** land willed to the state in 1976 at the death of Tom Yawkey, the longtime owner of the Boston Red Sox baseball team. The center includes three relatively untainted coastal islands at the mouth of Winyah Bay—the majority of Cat Island and all of North and South islands. (Access is limited to prearranged field trips and boats run by public vendors in Georgetown to the outer beaches.) Prime waterfowl habitat, the Yawkey Wildlife Center protects 20,000 acres of wetlands—marshes, bays, estuaries, marsh creeks, and ponds. Archaeological evidence suggests that ancient coastal Indians lived on Cat Island as long ago as 1500 B.C. Today, in addition to its active role as an environmental research

ABOVE: *At the Santee Coastal Reserve fish-eating ospreys nest above the water (left); red-bellied woodpeckers (right top) inhabit the canopy of the forest; and a barn owl (right bottom) roosts in a loblolly pine.*

station, the center enjoys a richly deserved reputation as a birder's paradise. In summer the islands are home to hundreds of increasingly rare wood storks, which, come winter, relinquish their lease to more than a thousand arriving American avocets—one of the largest gatherings of avocets anywhere on the Atlantic coast.

Wildlife center biologists lead half-day field trips into the preserve periodically; groups are limited to the capacity of the van—about 14 eager souls—and reservations are a must. The outings begin with a ferry ride to Cat Island and proceed first to the hardwood bottomlands and piney ridges and then to Goose Pasture, where Canada geese and thousands of ducks feed in the winter. Next comes South Island's maritime forest and its complex of brackish marshes, where rafts of spikerush, widgeongrass, salt-marsh bulrush, and sea purslane attract an immense chaos of ducks—pintail, scaup, wigeon, and blue- and green-winged teal.

Farther north, nestled next to busy Myrtle Beach and the Intra-coastal Waterway, is the surprising **Lewis Ocean Bay Heritage Pre-serve❖.** Near the intersection of Routes 9 and 17 just outside North Myrtle Beach, the preserve protects more than 20 Carolina bays within its 9,343 acres. Unlike the depressions at Woods Bay, these bays are filled with peat, which leaches tannic acid into the groundwater and soaks up surface water like a blanket. Here the bays support pocosins, nearly impenetrable tangles of blueberries, huckleberries, zenobia, and fetterbush intertwined with catbrier, titi, and gallberry. Topped with scattered loblolly bay trees, some of the bays are surrounded by desic-cated sandrims where prickly-pear cactus, dwarf live oak, and dwarf azalea dominate. White-tailed deer bound between pocosins, red-cockaded woodpeckers excavate mature pines, and a few black bears search for berries and grubs. Between the pocosins and sandrims, damp, sandy ground is home to seemingly sinister sundews and Venus's-flytraps, both of which invert the common natural order with their insectivorous ways. This unusual adaptation to acidic, nutrient-poor soils also appears in yellow and purple pitcher plants, which pre-fer the interior of wildfire-cleared bays.

THE SEA ISLANDS: ACE BASIN TO SAVANNAH RIVER

Stretching south from Charleston to Savannah, a chain of windswept, sunlit islands, which early Spanish explorers called the Golden Isles, form a vital barrier protecting the mainland from the vicissitudes of the sea. In their fertile, sheltered bays lie some of the most fecund wetlands on the East Coast, home to oysters, shrimp, and hundreds of thousands of birds. Blessed with warm temperatures, arresting natural beauty, and abundant wildlife, the region drew native peoples thousands of years ago, and today Edisto, Ashepoo, Kiawah, and Combahee are familiar place names. European settlement brought rice plantations to the fresh and saltwater marshes and development to the long idyllic beaches. At

OVERLEAF: *The most fertile saltwater marshes in the world—including this marshland mosaic at the Santee Coastal Reserve—stretch from the coast of the Carolinas through Georgia and into northern Florida.*

present, despite the resorts and shopping malls, the Sea Islands still protect critically important ecosystems.

About 45 minutes south of Charleston, a group of parks and preserves form a loose semicircle around Saint Helena Sound. All are part of a 350,000-acre Low Country ecosystem known as the **ACE Basin,** which encompasses the lower watersheds of the Ashepoo, Combahee, and Edisto rivers, all emptying into Saint Helena Sound. The basin shelters some of the most outstanding coastal habitat in the nation. A regional task force—comprising the state's Department of Natural Resources, the U.S. Fish and Wildlife Service, the Nature Conservancy, Ducks Unlimited, and many private landowners—has worked for years to ensure that this critically important coastal ecosystem is protected from encroaching commercial development.

Here an intact estuarine ecosystem still functions—from black-water rivers and upland pine ridges to bottomland hardwood forests and more than 90,000 acres of protean freshwater and saltwater marshland. Hundreds of species of native flora and fauna, a number rare or threatened, thrive here largely undisturbed—from wood storks and bald eagles to loggerhead turtles and alligators. Endangered short-nosed sturgeon cruise the rivers; white-tailed deer, bobcat, and wild turkeys frequent bottomland forests dominated by sweet gums, water oaks, cabbage palmettos, and tupelo gum trees. Trilliums, mayapples, and anemones bloom on low ridges between the rivers, among lovely stands of mixed hardwoods and loblolly and longleaf pine.

Bustling rookeries of wading birds—herons, ibis, egrets—thrive in the fertile wetlands, as do large numbers of reptiles and amphibians. The impressive array of shrubs and plants surviving here includes water lilies, native orchids, and meadows of cane, sedge, and soft rush. Where the water is brackish, wet prairies sustain bulrushes and panic grasses, redroot and wild millet. Nearly 15 percent of the dabbling ducks on the Atlantic Flyway and other varieties of ducks visit and winter throughout the basin, and more bald eagles nest here than anywhere else in the Southeast except parts of Florida.

LEFT: *In the recently protected ACE Basin, 350,000 acres of wildlife-rich coastland south of Charleston, a Bear Island tidal marsh is thick with smooth cordgrass, black needle rush, and yellow groundsel bush.*

Although private individuals own most of the land within the basin, a number of natural sites are open to the public. At the **ACE Basin National Wildlife Refuge❖** (26 miles from Charleston via Route 17, then south off Route 174), wood storks and ospreys feed and dabbling ducks reside each winter. Nearby (13 miles off Route 17 on Bennett Point Road), the **Bear Island Wildlife Management Area❖** encompasses 12,000 acres of marshland and bottomland forest. Also used for hunting and fishing, Bear Island supports game animals as well as tundra swans, red-winged blackbirds, ducks, and wading birds. At **Edisto Beach State Park❖,** off Route 174 on the south shore of Edisto Island, white sands and sunbathers share space with a four-mile nature trail and marsh boardwalk; threatened small terns and loggerhead turtles nest on the beach. The basin complex also includes several barrier islands such as **Devaux Bank,** which all but disappeared after Hurricane David in 1980, only to reappear in 1991 a mile and a half from its former location. The island is an important nesting site for brown pelicans and sandwich and royal terns.

ABOVE: *A brown pelican spreads its wings as it glides over a shallow lake. The wingspan of these large fish-eaters can reach seven and a half feet.*

Beaufort makes a convenient base for exploring the area north of Hilton Head Island, particularly Saint Helena Island. Level and laced with quiet dead-end lanes, Saint Helena is a fine place for a leisurely bicycle tour, allowing peddlers to savor the subtleties of the surrounding marshes and inlets. Just beyond Saint Helena, some 16 miles east of Beaufort, **Hunting Island State Park❖** on Route 21 embraces 5,000 acres of coastal dune ridges, maritime scrub forest, tidal pools and lagoons, saltwater marsh, and one of the least disturbed stands of slash pine and palmetto forest left along the Carolina coast. More than 900 acres at the southern end of the park have been designated a Heritage Site, protecting an intact dune-beach-estuary ecosystem that hosts two endangered species, one a bird (the least tern), the other a plant (the rare beach pigweed). The least terns that visit the wilder reaches of the park each summer form one of the largest nesting concentrations anywhere. Patience soon garners other rare delights at Hunting, especially along the Sea Oats Nature Trail—perhaps a glimpse of a Wilson's plover, increasingly rare along the South Carolina coast; or the call of an incomparably beautiful painted bunting hidden among wax myrtle growing beyond the back dunes; or the spectacle of black skimmers flashing iridescent as they glide inches above the blue-green sea.

South of the ACE Basin are Port Royal Sound, the resort island of Hilton Head, and the Savannah River, on the Georgia state line. Off Route 278 East, which branches off I-95 near Ridgeland, the **Pinckney Island National Wildlife Refuge❖** occupies a small island in Port Royal Sound, just one bridge away from the often crowded environs of Hilton Head Island. Here populations of seabirds

Above: *Tricolored herons, which prefer salt marshes and mangrove swamps, find bountiful hunting grounds along the South Carolina coast.*

and wading birds—along with swelling numbers of people seeking surcease from Hilton Head's throngs—find sanctuary within the refuge's 4,000 acres.

More birds than people still inhabit the natural splendor of these parts (the refuge includes a number of small islands such as Buzzard, Corn, Little, and Big Harry). Despite its proximity to Hilton Head, the preserve has yet to embrace paved roads. Miles of hiking trails and bike paths, often circling the refuge's major impoundments, explore Pinckney's extensive saltwater marshes, wooded hammocks, and freshwater ponds. At Ibis Pond, white ibis often fill nearby trees while tricolored and little blue herons silently stalk their prey along the cattail-lined shore. The refuge is popular with the coast's rare wood storks, and its enormous offshore oyster beds attract great swarms of oystercatchers and other shorebirds.

As they head south toward Savannah, both I-95 and Route 170 tra-

verse the Savannah Wildlife Refuge. Like deep-sea divers who let the
bodies readjust slowly to the pressures of the surface, some travele
would do well to savor the solace of a wildlife refuge or a small pa
winding through cool woods before confronting the neon temptatio
of Savannah, just across the river.

The **Savannah National Wildlife Refuge❖** is an older preserv
founded in 1927 on former rice plantations interspersed with tid
creeks, marshland, bottomland swamp, and freshwater impoundmen
This mix of coastal and marshland habitat quickly attracted migratir
ducks, especially after another 13,000 acres were added in 1978; pinta
wigeon, gadwall, ring-necked ducks, and occasionally some sno
geese and tundra swans stop in during winter months. South Carolir
and Georgia share the Savannah refuge, which, along with the Pincl
ney and Tybee Island preserves, are administered from Savannah a
parts of the **Savannah Coastal Refuges.** The 20 miles of dikes arour
the major impoundments double as excellent bike paths and hikir
trails, providing access to the interior of the refuge.

Warm summers bring nesting Mississippi and swallow-tailed kit
to the refuge. Clogged with carpets of water lilies and lotuses, por
surfaces become almost motionless, their deep greens broken only l
the sudden rush of a feeding purple gallinule. The refuge is known f
sightings of rare wood storks, surges of uncommon warblers (blu
winged, bay-breasted, and chestnut-sided warblers among them), ar
accounts of not-so-rare mammoth alligators. In the 1980s the large
gator ever captured in South Carolina—a female more than 11 feet
length—was released at the Savannah refuge. Still bigger gators ma
lurk in the dark waters; reported sightings include one alligator th
edgy witnesses insist is at least 14 feet long.

Boats, canoes, and kayaks provide the best access to the wate
refuge. However, car-bound visitors on Laurel Hill Wildlife Driv
(Route 170 as it passes through the refuge), are also surrounded I
natural wonders beyond the windows—the wild coast that does n
end here but only changes its name from South Carolina to Georgia.

RIGHT: *In the Bear Island Wildlife Management Area, a dark green*
loblolly pine is crowned by the elegant white silhouette of a great egr
once hunted nearly to extinction for its exquisite breeding plumage.

GEORGIA

PART TWO

G E O R G I A

From its mountain ridges and moist woodland coves to its massive live-oak forests and some of the greatest cypress swamps in the nation, Georgia's landscape is the quintessence of the South. The state is the largest east of the Mississippi River, and its natural diversity matches its size.

In north Georgia, banjo-taut rivers sing over boulders in the rhododendron haunts of the southern Appalachians. Clay hills stain the lower piedmont a distinctive terra-cotta red. Beaded across the coastal plain are remnants of the endless pine forests that once covered much of the Southeast. Broad, lazy rivers meander across the plain to the continent's edge, traversing vast salt marshes whose thick grasses and tangled channels blur the distinction between land and sea. In the south, where Georgia melds into northern Florida, the nation's largest swamp, Okefenokee, mesmerizes with its dark moss-hung cypress trees, cranes crying overhead, and sly-eyed gators hovering just beneath the water's surface.

Mountains, piedmont, and coastal plain are Georgia's three great geographic divisions. Another distinct region, the Cumberland Plateau in the northwest corner of the state, is a distant cousin of the jumbled peaks and coves—sheltered mountain hollows—that crowd the eastern Blue Ridge. Composed of sandstone, limestone, and shale, the Cumberland Plateau was deposited, layer upon layer, when shallow inland seas washed the American midlands millions of years ago. Since then, rivers have incised this layer cake of stone, creating ridges and valleys and a canyon called Cloudland, which catches rainbows and bits of sky alike.

The Blue Ridge rocks are old so-called "basement" material faulted and smashed onto North America. When Africa slammed into North

---

PRECEDING PAGES: *Slipping languidly past a moss-hung white tupelo, the Altamaha River winds through swamp forest and salt marsh to the sea.*

America about 400 million years ago, the ancient layers were transformed—metamorphosed—by extreme heat and pressure. Squeezed between the mighty continents, the Blue Ridge bulged and buckled like soft asphalt under a blazing sun. After the nascent Atlantic Ocean separated the continents again, the Blue Ridge remained an eastern bulwark of North America. Today the reverberations of those cataclysmic eras are evident in western Georgia, where rippled ridge-and-valley lands lie between the Blue Ridge and the Cumberland Plateau.

The ponderous continental collisions wrought a magnificent muddle of ridges, coves, and gorges in today's Chattahoochee National Forest. The southern Appalachians' wealth of microhabitats have nurtured floral opulence unmatched in North America. Dark hemlocks, relics of the ice ages, shade cool, narrow stream valleys. Oaks, maples, and magnolias are the most common of dozens of types of trees, many found only in the southern Appalachians. Dainty silver bells, fringe trees with their perfumed flowers, and brassy orange flame azaleas occupy their own niches here. On every slope hundreds of wildflower species turn springtime into a kaleidoscope of white, pink, purple, gold, and blue.

Below the fortress of north Georgia's mountains, the piedmont cants down to the coastal plain. In this rolling transition, hardwoods give way to pines as the climate becomes hotter and drier. Strewn through the piedmont like raisins in a pudding are granite domes, such as Panola Mountain near Atlanta, that eons ago pushed their way toward the surface from molten depths.

Dividing piedmont and coastal plain, a fall line of sand hills and Georgia's famous red clay hills cuts a diagonal from Augusta southwest to Columbus. Farther south lies the coastal plain, once a sweep of longleaf pine forests dotted with cooler, moister hammocks of magnolias, beeches, and other hardwoods. And where swamps such as Okefenokee intrude, cypress, tupelo, and thick, tangled bayheads push into the pinelands.

At the ocean's edge, rivers heavy with silt striate broad bands of salt marshes. These fecund expanses of spartina grass are estuarine nurseries for fish, oysters, shrimp, scallops, birds, alligators, and turtles that hide and feed in the rich black muck of the marshes—the richest soils of the South. And beyond, sheltering the coast from the worst of the Atlantic's storms, are the fabled Golden Isles: Wassaw, Cumberland, and the other bright semitropical barrier islands of the Georgia coast.

GEORGIA:
MOUNTAINS TO COASTAL MARSHES

O ver millennia, Georgia's natural wealth has provided a good living for diverse peoples and wildlife. The rich coastal marine life afforded fertile fishing grounds for Paleo-Indians thousands of years ago. Much later, the Creek fished and farmed along the coastal plain, and the Cherokee prospered farther north, in the mountains and piedmont.

During the 1540s, Spain's Hernando de Soto pushed north along the Georgia coast, establishing missions on Sapelo and Saint Simons islands. As it broadened its base in North America, Britain wanted to curb Spanish advancement, and in 1733 James Oglethorpe provided the buffer when he established a colony of debtors and indigents and built Savannah as its nucleus. This unprepossessing beginning led to rapid settlement after the Revolutionary War. Among the early visitors was William Bartram, son of America's first native-born naturalist, John Bartram. William traveled through the Southeast in search of botanical specimens, and his writings, published in 1791, still paint a vivid picture of a natural Georgia teeming with life.

Most who settled in Georgia, however, lived off the land in more conventional ways. Because they were the most arable, the forests of the piedmont and the grasses of the coastal plain fell before ax and plow. What remained were lands too hard to farm—the mountains—

LEFT: *All of Georgia's largest barrier island is included in the Cumberland Island National Seashore, which is rich in maritime forests, dunes, and beaches and crowded with shorebirds rather than sunbathers.*

or too wet to drain—the marshes. The Chattahoochee, Altamaha, and Georgia's other great rivers became the highways for the South's premier product: cotton, a kingdom built on slavery. During the nineteenth century, Georgia was central to two human tragedies: the infamous Trail of Tears—the forced relocation of Creek and Cherokee to Oklahoma during the 1830s—and the Civil War.

Today the engine of the new South is a far different place from the Georgia of the 1800s, but the lands of the piedmont and plain remain agricultural. Environmental organizations have been working to protect the granite outcrops, riverine sand dunes, and other precious anomalies, but the longleaf forests of the coastal plain are, for the most part, gone. The coastal salt marshes are now protected, although effluent from industry and urban areas, and barrier island development, are still concerns.

In the national forests of the mountainous north, timber harvesting remains economically important. Yet, as people realize that only fragments of the bountiful natural heritage described by William Bartram remain, forest wilderness areas, state "conservation parks," and other land preservation projects are proliferating.

A tour of Georgia's natural heritage starts where the coasts of Georgia and South Carolina meet, travels south through the marshes and islands of coastal Georgia, swings west across the coastal plain, and then turns north into the piedmont. From there, the itinerary explores the Blue Ridge in Georgia's northeast corner, culminating in the west, where the Cumberland Plateau spans the border of Georgia and Alabama.

BARRIER ISLANDS AND COASTAL PLAIN

Although it is fewer than 20 miles from Savannah, **Wassaw National Wildlife Refuge❖** is not within easy reach. Its inaccessibility has doubtless kept Wassaw Island the most pristine of Georgia's barrier islands—perhaps the most pristine along the entire southeastern coast. Wassaw lies at the seaward side of the lush, dense Romerly Marsh, an undulating maze of some of the world's finest salt marshes. Protected within the **Savannah Coastal Refuges❖** (which also manage preserves on Harris Neck, Blackbeard and Wolf islands) and not far from the mouth of the Savannah River, the Wassaw sanctuary includes two smaller islands: Pine and Little Wassaw.

TENN

DLAND
ON SP

Chickamauga Valley

LAKE
CONASAUGA
REC AREA

APPALACHIAN TRAIL

NORTH CAROLINA

59

COHUTTA
WILDERNESS

Cohutta Mtn

Blue Ridge Mtns

CHATTAHOOCHEE
NATIONAL FOREST

RICH MTN
WILDERNESS

PIGEON
MTN WMA

Eton

Blairsville

Clayton

Chatsworth

RAVEN CLIFF
FALLS

UNICOI SP

La
ette

Villanow

ED JENKINS
NRA

Helen

TALLULAH
FALLS SP

SOUTH

KEOWN
FALLS
SCENIC
AREA

AMICALOLA
FALLS SP

Dahlonega

ANNA RUBY
FALLS SCENIC
AREA

PANTHER
CREEK
REC AREA

Tugaloo R.

CAROLINA

CHATTAHOOCHEE
NATIONAL FOREST

Rome

411

Elowah R.

75

85

23

17

78

ATLANTA

Stone
Mtn

OCONEE
NATIONAL
FOREST

Appling

20

Augusta

20

PANOLA MTN
CONSERVATION PARK

HEGGIES'S
ROCK PRESERVE

Savannah River

27

SWEETWATER
CREEK STATE
CONSERVATION
PARK

OCONEE
NAT FOR

Eatonton

221

1

Chattahoochee R.

75

129

Pine
Mtn

SPREWELL
BLUFF SP

Thomaston

475

PIEDMONT
NATIONAL
WILDLIFE
REFUGE

441

Oconee River

16

185

F.D.
ROOSEVELT
SP

27

Macon

SAVANNAH
NATIONAL
WILDLIFE REFUGE

280

Columbus

27

Ohoopee River

Savannah

280

PROVIDENCE CANYON
STATE CONSERVATION PARK

Ocmulgee River

BROXTON ROCKS
PRESERVE

BIG HAMMOCK
NATURAL AREA

WASSAW
ISLAND NWR

27

Lake
Eufaula

Broxton

Altamaha River

17

95

GRAY'S REEF
NAT MARINE
SANCTUARY

27

LEWIS ISLAND
NATURAL AREA

Flint River

75

37

BANKS
LAKE NWR

Homerville

Darien

Brunswick

Chattahoochee R.

BANKS
LAKE
PRES

Lakeland

OKEFENOKEE
NATIONAL
WILDLIFE
REFUGE

121

CUMBERLAND
ISLAND NAT
SEASHORE

STEPHEN
FOSTER
STATE PARK

Okefenokee
Swamp

Folkston

St Marys

Lake
Seminole

Suwannee R.

St Marys
River

2

94

ATLANTIC
OCEAN

FLORIDA

GEORGIA

25   0   25 Miles

25   0   25 Kilometers

Accessible by private or rented boat from many marinas including Skidaway Island (once a barrier island now joined to the mainland), Wassaw is open to the public sunrise to sunset. Knowing the tides is critical to avoid becoming stuck in the muck of the salt marsh, where channels as twisted as a griffin's claws can shrivel to dead ends when the tides change.

ABOVE: *An exceedingly rare sight: Loggerhead turtles mate off the Atlantic coast. Because the open beaches where females lay their eggs are now increasingly scarce, these giant sea turtles are in jeopardy all over the world.*

Dolphins play in the open channels leading to Wassaw. From the edges of the marsh, a great blue heron looks up to watch boats approach before returning to its slow-motion stalking. At its feet, oysters encrust black soils cemented by a thick mat of spartina grass.

Crisscrossing the island are 20 miles of dirt roads, the legacy of former owners who sold most of Wassaw for conservation in 1969 (they retain a few hundred acres of private land). A series of parallel dune ridges run the length of the island. At about 30 feet, the tallest of the ridges is also among the highest spots in Chatham County, which includes Savannah. Swales between the ridges are wet during winter, but these long ponds dry up in summer, when gator holes are the only source of freshwater. Alligators excavate deep holes in the shallow wetlands, thus providing year-round ponds for themselves, as well as for turtles, fish, and wading birds. In return for this service, every week or two the liege of the pond takes its payment in the form of a fat duck, a fish, or even an occasional deer.

About 200 alligators live on Wassaw in wetlands surrounded by a forest of live oak, magnolia, red bay, sabal palm, and rambling wild grape, which provides the island's only fall color and a bounty of fruit for island wildlife. Here *Magnolia grandiflora* with grand shiny leaves as well as grand flowers makes its statement as a hallmark tree of the South. Noisy pileated woodpeckers feast on the berries of magnolias, beautifully patterned wood ducks nest in tree cavities above the ponds, and tiny parula warblers trill and buzz from the highest branches.

In a section of the refuge dominated by tall, thin slash pines, bald eagles have built a home high in a crotch of a pine. In a nearby nest, a pair of ospreys watch until both eagles are out hunting. Perhaps knowing that the eagles may try to rob them of fish, one of the ospreys lands on the eagles' nest and struts along its massive edge—a clear, if unseen, challenge.

The seven miles of sandy beach along the Atlantic side of Wassaw Island are strewn with ark shells, sea whips, skate cases, sponges, and crowds of shorebirds ranging from laughing gulls and royal terns to sanderlings and dowitchers. Along the north strand, the scene resembles an illustration from a child's book of fairy tales because everything is oversize. Here the Atlantic Ocean erodes the seaward side of the beach and topples whole trees at the edge of the forest. The boneyard beach is so called because the felled live oaks, their massive outspread arms bleached silver, look like a mile-long jungle of giants' bones or gargantuan elk antlers.

ABOVE: *Ponderous looking on land, endangered wood storks are graceful fliers that glide above wetlands with neck and legs extended. These gregarious wading birds nest together in swamp trees and mangroves.*

During the summer, loggerhead sea turtles lay their eggs on the open beach. As development devours the unspoiled coastlines of the world, sea turtles find fewer and fewer places to lay their eggs, and all species of the large ancient reptiles are now in danger. Because it is still wild, Wassaw Island has been the site of a sea turtle monitoring and protection program since 1973.

From Wassaw, Interstate 95 and Route 17 (the old Ocean Highway) offer access routes to **Ossabaw, Saint Catherines, Blackbeard, Sapelo,** and **Wolf islands**—all barrier islands under some form of protection. Sapelo, a national estuarine reserve, offers educational day trips that demonstrate the importance of estuaries, those fertile areas where salt and fresh waters meet. Seventeen miles east of Sapelo is **Gray's Reef National Marine Sanctuary❖,** one of only a handful off United

FRANKLINIA *alatamaha Bart. Journ.*

LEFT: *In 1765 botanist William Bartram, who painted this watercolor, discovered a rare Franklinia near the Altamaha River. The tree had disappeared from the wild by 1803.*

RIGHT: *Near the sea the Altamaha divides into channels that coil through some of the world's largest, most fecund salt marshes.*

States waters. Although most coastal seabeds are sandy "deserts" where little grows, Gray's Reef is called a live bottom because sandstone outcrops support an array of corals, sponges, crabs, squids, sea stars, octopuses, plants, and the fishes attracted to this outpost of life.

The town of Darien lies near the mouth of the **Altamaha River,** a strategic position that in the last century made the now-sleepy town one of the wealthiest in the country. Once a clearinghouse for timber, cotton, tobacco, and rice floated in from isolated plantations, Darien is still a gateway to a river system rich in natural resources. The Altamaha begins about 140 miles upriver, where the Oconee and Ocmulgee join to form Georgia's mightiest waterway. Boasting the second-largest river basin on the Atlantic seaboard, the Altamaha drains more than 25 percent of the state. Undammed from its confluence to the sea, this broad waterway flows past some of the rarest woodlands in the Southeast.

Approximately 50 rare or endangered species live along the Altamaha, including the red-cockaded woodpecker, wood stork, shortnose sturgeon, manatee, gopher tortoise, eastern indigo snake, and Georgia's only population of Florida corkwood. In 1765 naturalists John and William Bartram found the elusive Franklinia tree (*Franklinia alatamaha*) here. Although propagated from the Bartrams' collection and now grown in southeastern gardens, the lovely white-blossomed Franklinia, named after Benjamin Franklin, has never been seen in the wild since 1803.

A third of the way to the sea, **Big Hammock Natural Area**❖ protects hardwoods, pines, and a host of birds as well as one of only 50 naturally occurring populations of the threatened Georgia plume, a

shrub as magnificent in flower as it is rare. Along the tributary Ohoopee River lie parabolic sand dunes that harbor unusual habitats and plants.

Five miles upriver from Darien, accessible by boat (available for charter in Brunswick and Darien), **Lewis Island Natural Area❖** contains the largest groves of virgin tidewater cypress and tupelo in the state. A lightly marked trail leads from water's edge back into the swamp, but when the river is running hard and stained red by silt from the clay hills, Lewis Island's dark swamplands flood. At those times it is best seen from the river.

The oldest cypresses at Lewis Island rise from broadly flanged bases, huge red-brown columns with ponderous flat tops and feathery blue-green needles. Many of these ancients are misshapen, and in some, living tissue has grown around burnt-out lightning strikes. Like the gnarled bristlecone pines of high western forests, these are trees with character. Also, like bristlecones, they live for centuries. One grove of Lewis Island cypress is thought to be about a thousand years old.

Rare Ogeechee lime trees droop over the water, and behind them,

water tupelos stand on swollen bases, a design that works well for waterlogged trees with shallow roots. A swallow-tailed kite soars and
swoops overhead. The waters are home to river otters, redear and
bluegill (types of sunfish), catfish, and world-record largemouth bass.
In an unfortunate fish story, flatheads, a huge alien species of catfish
introduced to the river system for sport fishing, are now outcompeting
many native fish.

Not far from Lewis Island is a mudflat called **Alligator Congress,**
where dozens of alligators haul themselves out to sun alongside the
river. River managers note that the best time to count alligators is at
night, when the reptiles become active hunters. Then one can simply
shine a light and count the pairs of red eyes.

At its delta, the Altamaha drifts into salt marshes and divides into
five branches: the Darien, Altamaha, Butler, Champney, and Cathead
Creek. Because the Altamaha lies at the bend of a sweeping curve of
land that runs from South Carolina to Florida, seawater is funneled toward it, causing river tides to run seven to eight feet high and travel as
far as 20 miles inland. When the Altamaha is in flood stage, however,
the powerful waters reach a stalemate: Where roiling freshwater and
salt water meet, the river just keeps rising.

Continue south on I-95 almost to the Florida border, then swing
east on Route 40 to the historic town of Saint Marys and the ferry to
Cumberland Island National Seashore❖. Unlike most other National Park System areas, no visitor cars are allowed on the island. (Only
families that still own land on this largest of Georgia's barrier islands
may use their cars.) Seeing the island on foot, visitors can take time to
inspect a precisely "crafted" whelk egg case rather than motoring
quickly to the next point of interest. They can linger over shapely
mounds of scrub live oak, pruned low and tight by wind and salt
water, or observe the fishing techniques of brown pelicans as they
stall above the water, then plunge, stunning prey with their thick bills.

Although Cumberland Island offers fine wilderness camping, visi-

---

LEFT: *Access to some preserves is restricted so that birds, such as these
royal terns on a small island in Altamaha Sound, can nest undisturbed.*
OVERLEAF: *Feathery sea oats and a solitary cabbage palm help anchor
the ever-shifting sands of the Cumberland Island National Seashore.*

ABOVE: *Armadillos range from Texas to the South-east, where somehow they reached Cumberland Island.*
RIGHT: *Live oaks with saw palmetto growing around their feet reign in Cumber-land's maritime forests.*
BELOW: *Originally brought to Cumberland during the plantation period, feral horses now compete with white-tailed deer for forage.*

tors can easily see most of the major habitats on the island in one long, leisurely day. From the Dungeness ferry dock walk east to the beach, then north along the ocean to the trail leading back to the Cumberland Sound side and Sea Camp. Take the River Trail south to return to the Dungeness dock.

Early in the island's long history of habitation, Timucuan peoples, a coastal tribe found mainly in present-day Florida, wove clothing from Spanish moss and brewed painkillers from resurrection ferns, which cloak the tops of live oak branches. By 1610, Cumberland was the site of Spain's second-largest mission on the East Coast. During the South's plantation period, sea island cotton was an important crop here. In the late 1880s, a colony of mansions and a polo field appeared as the Carnegies made the island a retreat. Since 1972, Cumberland Island has been a national seashore including about 9,000 acres of wilderness. Unfortunately, humans introduced pigs and horses, some of which gave rise to feral populations that now compete with native wildlife for food. The National Park Service is working both to eliminate the pigs and to manage the horse population. Armadillos, recent interlopers, arrived mysteriously. Such problems, however, do not detract from the island's sea-swept beauty.

As cormorants and ring-billed gulls escort a ferry toward the island, a white cloud of ibis lift from an unseen spot in the marsh. In the distance, a huge paper mill is visible. Because the mill flushes warm water into the river and marsh, the area has become Georgia's only manatee preserve. The walk from

Dungeness dock to the beach passes gracefully crumbling mansions and scattered violets, pink and yellow oxalis, chokecherry and yaupon holly. Abruptly, the sandy footing becomes deeper as the dunes appear ahead. Lacy dog fennel and prickly-pear cactus punctuate the open sand between forest and the mounds of scrub oak and myrtle hugging the dunes.

The beach is broad, especially at low tide, and sea treasures litter the tide line. Skate cases resembling black taffeta change purses, leopard-spotted shells of calico crabs, knobbed whelk shells, a dying blue-domed man-of-war jellyfish, pearly clamshells, and sensuously round snails called moon shells transform the shore into an exquisite natural history lesson. Complacent as dowagers, a flock of royal terns stand together as ruddy turnstones busily probe the sand for tidbits: run, probe, run.

Because the island is subtropical, the year offers plenty of warm, dreamy days along the 18-mile beach, one of the longest undeveloped stretches on the East Coast. The shadowy live oak forest just beyond the dunes presents a night-and-day contrast to the bright sunbaked sand. Their huge limbs twisted in fantastic shapes above fan-leaf saw palmettos, these live oaks form a cool and stately refuge. Dimly seen, an osprey grasping a flailing silvery mullet flies overhead.

Dotting the interior of the island are freshwater ponds where deer and raccoon drink and alligators raise their young. Tall stands of long-leaf pine anchor the wild north end of the island, where the forest canopy is filled with the warbling voices of wrens, yellowthroats, and painted buntings.

OKEFENOKEE SWAMP

From Saint Marys, Route 40 runs west to Folkston, gateway to the great Okefenokee Swamp; Route 121 and its spur lead directly into the swamp. A visitor center offers a comprehensive overview of the area, which includes primeval cypress swamps, teeming freshwater marshes, and open pinelands. Clearly, the 650-square-mile **Okefenokee National Wildlife Refuge❖** has many faces. The refuge can be explored in cars, boats, or canoes or on foot by boardwalks and hiking trails.

The Swamp Island Wildlife Drive provides a good introduction to the drier parts of the refuge, where tall stands of old-growth longleaf pine provide homes for a few colonies of endangered red-cockaded woodpeckers. The airy understory of saw palmetto gives cover to a gabbling line of wild turkeys. Nearby, the surface of a black-water pond is dotted with water lily pads and dainty yellow spires of bladderwort, a carnivorous plant whose floating balloon-tipped roots contain traps for prey. The domed eyebrows and knobby snouts of alligators just break the surface of the water.

As the wildlife drive begins to circle back, a parking lot affords entry to a three-quarter-mile-long boardwalk winding past a strangle of bay trees with hummocks of peat at their feet. Red-flowered lyonia fights for space, and tall pond cypress rises above the snarl of shrubs. A water moccasin slithers among tall fiddleheads of cinnamon fern, and an aural mosaic breaks the morning quiet: trills of peepers, clicks of cricket frogs, and the deep grunting of pig frogs. At the end of the boardwalk the dense vegetation falls away, and the top of the observation tower reveals wet prairies stretching to the horizon.

The defining characteristic of Okefenokee's east side, wet prairies at-

---

RIGHT: *Chesser Prairie on Okefenokee's east side is more wet prairie than swamp; here saw grasses mingle with water lilies (center) and loblolly bay (foreground). Wood storks and cranes often drift above.*

tract myriad marsh and wading birds and are abloom with flowering plants in spring. Perched on a branch, an elegant anhinga spreads its wings to dry, preening like a fashion model showing off a silver-and-black cloak. A rotary cackle reveals the presence of rare Florida sandhill cranes, and soon a trio of the large redheaded birds flashes past. Below, herons and egrets hunt in the shallows, and green anole lizards with pink throat pouches scurry along the tower railings. Although ivory-billed woodpeckers have not been seen since the 1940s, some wildlife managers believe that the endangered birds may still exist here.

Tour boats or canoes, available at the east entrance of the **Suwannee Canal Recreation Area** within the refuge, are the best way to see the swamp close up. Marked trails guide canoeists down the canal and through Chesser Prairie. Along the way, large white wood storks swoop over the water and maiden-cane grass, scaring a green heron. Next a pair of wood ducks glides past. Clumps of brilliant blue iris emerge from the sun-speckled water while pitcher plants lie low—patient predators.

Seen from these prairies, Okefenokee does not seem like a swamp.

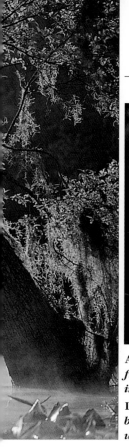

ABOVE: *In estimating an alligator's length, each inch from the eye to tip of the snout equals about one foot in length. Okefenokee's 15,000 gators come in all sizes.*
LEFT: *In the swamp forest on Okefenokee's west side, bald cypresses drip with Spanish moss; the trees were once heavily logged for their rot-resistant wood.*

It is actually a broad flowing wetland, one of the largest of its kind in the United States. The bed of Okefenokee was once sea bottom. About 7,000 years ago, as the seas retreated, a dune ridge rose along what was then the East Coast, creating a saucer-shaped depression that gradually filled with peat due to continental climatic changes. A five-to-ten-foot bed of peat still layers the bottom of this boggy bowl. Now fed primarily by rain, Okefenokee waters are not stagnant like a true swamp, but flow south and west so slowly that 80 percent of the water evaporates or is naturally transpired by vegetation before it leaves the wetlands. The dark tannin-stained waters gather in two areas to form the Saint Marys River, which flows eastward toward the Atlantic Ocean, and the Suwannee River, which crosses into Florida and empties into the Gulf of Mexico.

Stephen Foster State Park❖, at the west entrance of the refuge, exhibits a completely different personality. (Routes 121/23 south and 94 west, dipping briefly into Florida as Route 2, lead to Route 177 and the western entrance to Okefenokee.) On the west side of the park, water trails circumnavigate classic swamp, where tall, dark cypresses draped with Spanish moss and other epiphytes guard the gloomy forested depths. Although the cypresses look thick, more than half a billion board feet were hauled out of Okefenokee between 1899 and 1930, much from 1,500-to-2,000-year-old trees. Where lakes and channels open paths to the light, alligators sun themselves along the banks seeming to smile with contentment at their relaxed warmth. About 10,000–12,000 alligators—one of the world's largest populations—live in the swamp, along with bluegill, bream, catfish, chain pickerel, snakes, and turtles. The numbers and species of birds, amphibians, reptiles, fish, and mammals (including bobcat) are extraordinary. So are the numbers of butterflies, especially Georgia's state lepidopteron, the strikingly colored swallowtail. Okefenokee supports one of the largest concentrations of the black bear in the Deep South.

In narrow bayous that push into the swamp forest, spikes of the aquatic plant golden club light up the tea-colored waters like yellow flames atop long white tapers. Floating islands of peat called blowups occupy parts of the channels. Blowups are formed when methane from decaying swamp-bottom peat builds up and the gas blows rafts of dead peat to the surface, creating a quaking nascent island. Herbs, then shrubs and trees, colonize these islands, producing what are known as houses, where eventually black bears, deer, bobcat, barred owls, and other creatures live. Tree roots reaching deep into the sand base of the swamp stabilize the blowups, but the earth still quivers. Okefenokee is a Native American term meaning Land of the Trembling Earth.

WESTERN COASTAL PLAIN

Northwest on Route 441 toward Broxton, a trip west at Homerville toward Lakeland leads to **Banks Lake National Wildlife Refuge❖** and the adjoining **Banks Lake Preserve,** which is a black-water refuge second only to Okefenokee in Georgia's coastal plain. The lake and surrounding marshes support wading birds and shorebirds, wood ducks, sandhill cranes, and a thriving population of bass.

Proceed north again on Route 441 into Coffee County. Here **Broxton Rocks Preserve❖,** a Nature Conservancy property, is open to the public, but only for conservancy-scheduled tours because the area is so fragile. A rare extrusion of the sandstone layer that underlies much of the coastal plain, Broxton Rocks is a haven for equally rare plants. Carved by Rocky Creek, the preserve's rockbound ravines shade filmy ferns and shoestring ferns and provide purchase for greenfly orchids. Threatened Georgia plume grows here, as does the endangered silky creeping morning glory. Also in residence are owls, endangered indigo snakes, and gopher tortoises, the last two species indigenous to longleaf pine forests, which are Broxton Rocks's original habitat. The Conservancy is using prescribed burn techniques to restore the longleaf–wire grass community.

West on Route 280 and north on Routes 27 and 39 near the Alabama border about 30 miles south of Columbus lies **Providence Canyon State Conservation Park❖,** sometimes called the Little Grand Canyon (like so many other spectacular canyons across the United States). Surprisingly the fins and sculpted pinnacles of Providence Canyon did not exist in the early 1800s. As they cleared the land, nineteenth-century settlers uncovered the underlying sedimentary rock, delicately colored pink, peach, ocher, and chalky white. With little vegetation left to hold the soil, rainwater ripped through the exposed terrain, gouging gullies and eventually carving the 150-foot canyon. Only one day of heavy rain can wash away as much as six feet of canyon floor. To contain erosion, land managers planted kudzu before they understood what an unstoppable vine this alien is. Later, trees were added to keep the canyon from eroding further. Today they complement the drifts of wildflowers, plumleaf azaleas, and sculpted forms that make the canyon a scenic delight. Although Providence Canyon may not be completely natural, it shows how quickly and dramatically people can change a natural environment.

THE PIEDMONT

North on Route 27 and just east of I-185, the town of Pine Mountain is the gateway to **Franklin D. Roosevelt State Park❖,** the largest in the state park system. **Pine Mountain**, a series of long ridges at the southern edge of Georgia's piedmont region, is the backbone of the park

---

OVERLEAF: *Land-clearing practices in the 1800s first exposed the sedimentary rock that eroded into Providence Canyon. In this natural wonderland, the colorful cliffs are matched by a profusion of wildflowers.*

and the first mountainous area that travelers see as they drive north from the Florida flatlands. Lying between the inner piedmont and coastal regions, Pine Mountain supports an unusual mix of coastal longleaf pine and piedmont dry hardwoods. The reason for this odd-couple combination is the nearby Flint River, which cuts winding gorges into the mountain's eastern slopes and carries seeds of more northerly plants to this last bastion of the piedmont.

The Pine Mountain–Flint River area is one of the few places in Georgia where fiery flame azalea grows, along with such other rare plants as shoals spider lily, Georgia lead bush, fringed campion, and bluff white oak. The mix of animals includes ospreys and red-cockaded woodpeckers, rare freshwater mollusks, Barbour's map turtles, and eastern coral snakes.

The park is named for the thirty-second President, who first visited the area in 1924 hoping that the 88-degree waters of nearby Warm Springs would strengthen legs wasted from polio. He returned as often as he could and died in the modest house he built on Pine Mountain. Dowdell's Knob, a 1,395-foot spur off the main ridge, is where Roosevelt often came—as private citizen and president—to sit and contemplate. Surrounded by oaks and tulip poplars, Dowdell's Knob affords stately views of foothills spilling out to lowlands that extend to the south and east—a great and quietly green domain. Among the park's many miles of paths, the Cascade Trail, which passes a marshy pond and leads to a waterfall, provides a glimpse of the yin and yang of Pine Mountain flora. Lowland cane mixes with mountain laurel, bay trees grow alongside rhododendron, and longleaf pine shares space with the more northerly yellow buckeye.

Outfitters in Thomaston, about 25 miles east, offer canoe trips on the Flint River, which roars over such fearsome spots as Yellow Jacket Shoals and then meanders past **Sprewell Bluff State Park❖.** Glinting and winking where shiny mountain laurel clings to it, the bluff is a hanging garden of wildflowers and ferns.

Seventeen miles west of Atlanta, **Sweetwater Creek State Conservation Park❖** lies along Mount Vernon Road near Exit 12 of Interstate 20. In stark contrast to bustling Atlanta, this pleasant piedmont stream runs through woods full of river birches, small but lovely sourwoods, bigleaf magnolias, maples, oaks, and sycamores. Hawks soar above the canopy, where sparrows and finches hide among the leaves. In autumn, maples and oaks join asters and goldenrod in mounting a colorful spectacle.

Within view of Atlanta, off Route 155 southeast of the city, is the enormous granite dome that dominates **Panola Mountain State Conservation Park❖.** Although nearby Stone Mountain is probably the best-known of these rare-to-Georgia formations, Panola Mountain is doubtless the most pristine. Georgia's granite domes began forming when North and South America slammed into each other 350 million years ago. That earth-shaking event left cracks in the earth's crust where hot magma oozed through, sometimes erupting as volcanoes. Here the magma never made it to the surface, but was molded and metamorphosed into huge domes by pressure and heat. Slowly the rock and soil above the granite eroded, and some 16 million years ago Panola Mountain emerged.

Views from the top of the 220-foot dome are splendid. Smooth sweeps of granite form clean gray shelves touched here and there with shallow indentations full of colored lichen and ruby smears of small diamorpha. To the north and west, the rounded drop-offs overlook the Atlanta area and Stone Mountain; above, especially in the fall, red-tailed hawks soar effortlessly on the warm thermal air currents.

The miniature habitats nestled in the outcrops are home to rare plants with intriguing life histories. A plant succession begins when mosses and lichen colonize the bare rock. As they decay, they mix with water to make carbonic acid, which weathers the rock. Where the rock crumbles, potholes and shallow bowls form, where soil collects. Eventually tiny organisms, *Diamorpha smallii,* take hold in the thin soil. Their ruby stems and starry white flowers belying their tough constitution, these two-inch jewel-like plants can withstand fierce heat on the exposed rock, which sometimes rises to 180 degrees Fahrenheit in the summer. Their survival strategy is to stay low, out of the wind; bloom and set seed in spring, before the summer sun starts baking the rock; then hold their seeds on tiny stalks above the hot rock until autumn, when the seeds fall to the cooled soil.

Next to colonize the rock are white sandwort and Confederate daisies, which look like bright yellow paint spilled on the gray granite. Then come sedges, and finally pines and redcedars. Yuccas and persimmons grow on the outcrop, and although the persimmon fruits are

Above: *In a shallow bowl on Panola Mountain's granite dome, a natural rock garden mixes lichen, diamorpha, and broomsedge grass. Such tough plants colonize rock and begin the process of forest building.*

standard size, the plants are not. Hard conditions create bonsai plants. Not all the noteworthy plants take to rock. Deep-throated, flamboyantly white Atamasco lilies grow in colonies in the moist woods, as does blue spiderwort—both uncommon in these parts. Panola's Atamasco lily colonies are the largest ones on Georgia's granite outcrops.

Panola's woodland trails parallel a small stream and wind through pines and shrubs where deer hide and swallowtail butterflies flicker bright yellow. In spring, the white blossoms of serviceberry and dogwood lighten the shadows cast by the dark trunks of large hardwoods.

Southeast of Panola, bordering Oconee National Forest north of Macon, is the **Piedmont National Wildlife Refuge❖.** (Take Exit 61 from I-75 and drive east 18 miles on Juliette Road.) Set on Georgia's red clay hills, the refuge occupies former farmlands that produced cotton until the 1920s. As in many places in the South, ancient gnarled wisteria—an exotic Asian vine—now blankets the sites of old homesteads with dramatic purple blooms in spring. Seemingly wild clumps of daffodils mark where a garden was once planted. The rest of the 35,000-acre refuge is a mix of upland pine and upland and creek-bottom hardwoods. Many of the refuge's more than 200 bird species have been spotted in the upland pine habitats.

ABOVE: *In Panola Mountain State Conservation Park just outside Atlanta, tall pines and oak trees and an understory of dogwood, sweet shrub (calycanthus), fire pinks, and lilies surround a still, misty lake.*

Among the recreation areas in **Oconee National Forest❖**, Murder Creek Scenic Area, south of Eatonton on Route 129, is a showcase for some of Oconee's best features. Murder Creek and its falls are surrounded by about 300 acres of old-growth bottomland forest, unusual in the piedmont.

About 65 miles northeast, near the town of Appling, **Heggie's Rock Preserve❖,** a Nature Conservancy property, occupies an area just north of the fall line between mountains and piedmont. Singular plant communities have adapted to the extremes of rain and heat on this rare outcropping of granite flatrock, which rides high above the surrounding pines and hardwoods. Shallow rock pools support endangered plants, Spanish moss—unusual this far north—decorates cedar trees, and wild turkeys, deer, and beavers inhabit the preserve's creek.

EASTERN BLUE RIDGE

North along Routes 78 and 17, the foothills suddenly give way to forested peaks. One moment, the landscape is a soft roller coaster of low hills; the next, tree-mantled mountains interrupt the sky. By Route 441, which leads to **Tallulah Gorge State Park❖** and the most scenic series of waterfalls in the state, the commitment to mountains is complete.

97

LEFT: *After failing at business, George Cooke (1793–1849) found his true calling as an artist. He painted* Tallulah Falls *in the 1830s and 1840s, documenting the river's wild descent to the Chattooga.*

RIGHT: *Today torrents of water crash down the tiered rock-paved ravine of Tallulah Gorge only when Georgia Power opens a dam upstream. Views from the wooded canyon rims of the now-tamed river, however, are still spectacular.*

Millennia ago, the Tallulah River joined the Chattooga River to flow southward into the Chattahoochee River and eventually to the Gulf of Mexico. Nature is never static, however, and a gorge may well become a broad valley over time. Today the Tallulah and Chattooga make their way eastward to the Atlantic Ocean after what geologists call a tale of piracy.

The headwaters of the nearby Tugaloo and Savannah rivers were once farther south, but constant erosion slowly moved the headwaters northwest. Eventually the Tugaloo-Savannah migration met and captured the waters of the Tallulah and Chattooga. As the Tallulah raced down to the new lower riverbed, it cut a narrow rent through the rock about a thousand feet deep. This classic example of "stream capture" has produced one of the sheerest and most breathtaking gorges in the East. (Chattahoochee River tributaries are only ten miles from Tallulah. Their capture could eventually reshape the face of Georgia.)

The Cherokee called the Tallulah the terrible river because its waters roared and raged as they plunged over hard bedrock ledges. The first of the four great falls is Ladore, followed by Tempesta, Hurricane, and Oseana. Although it still flows, the river was tamed by a dam in 1913. Today the gorge is thrilling only intermittently—when the Georgia Power Company releases water. Some trails lead down to the bottom of the gorge and into the woods, but the North Rim Trail affords the best views of Tallulah Gorge. Near the lip of the gorge, the forest is a mix of pines: Virginia, slash, shortleaf, and white. Damp, shady spots by

streams nurture the rare lacy Carolina hemlock, and American holly and rhododendrons populate the understory along with white-tailed deer, raccoon, and other mammals.

Highbush blueberry carpets the understory on higher ground, and scalloped burgundy galax takes over in wetter areas. Every year the pink-and-white flower clusters of trailing arbutus announce that spring has arrived. Bluets, little brown jugs, rue and wood anemones, fringed polygala, yellow lady's slippers, and many other wildflowers pepper the woods and sunny banks. Among the abundant trillium is most of the world's population of *Trillium persistens*, earning its name because once established it flowers year after year, blooming white then fading to rose.

At cliff's edge, mountain-laurel limbs, twisted by wind into bizarre shapes, promise pink-and-white glory in summer. A serviceberry dangles giddily over the precipice, its white blossoms floating like careless pom-poms. Far below, the river runs along bare rock, pauses in pools of jade green, then flows on, breaking into glittering cascades between gorge walls that bulge as though they cannot contain themselves.

About 3.5 miles south of Tallulah Falls, the **Panther Creek Recreation Area❖** contains smaller falls and cascades and such rich plant diversity that part of it has been designated a "protected botanical area." The Panther Creek Hiking Trail traverses this area of Chattahoochee National Forest.

Panther Creek and Tallulah Gorge are the southeastern gateway to **Chattahoochee National Forest❖** and the southern Blue Ridge Mountains. On some highway maps, the national forest is a continuous swath of light green capping the entire northern tier of the state. Although national forest comprises 1,200 square miles of this green area, many of the coves, gentler slopes, and pocket valleys are a patchwork of small farms and towns—part of the Appalachian folkcraft country of Foxfire books now transformed into a recreational center. In the North Georgia mountains, intriguing names like Chunky Gal Mountain and Bagscuffle lure visitors along narrow two-lane roads that wind around loaf-shaped mountains and cross gaps into the next set of slopes and valleys.

At this southernmost end of the Appalachian Mountains, old metamorphic rock is overlain by thin, fragile soils that surprisingly support unparalleled floral diversity and out-and-out gorgeous flowers, fruits, and foliage. In the moist forests nature has produced extravagant displays: fringe trees with a creamy froth of scented petals among the hardwoods; purple-blossomed sweet shrub in damp coves; delicate silver bells in forest understories; fountains of leucothoe along streams; and rhododendrons in a rainbow of colors on the slopes. The wild-flowers are legion, including such rare species as pink lady's slippers, purple pitcher plants, and whorled pogonia, as well as the more famil-iar hepatica, bluebells, and violets. In autumn, oaks, maples, hickories, beeches, and other hardwoods paint the mountains in every glowing color in the red-to-gold spectrum.

Arguably the wildest, most scenic river in Georgia's Blue Ridge—and the entire Southeast—is the Chattooga, which thunders down from North Carolina in sprays of white water to form part of the boundary between South Carolina and Georgia. One way to see the river is on the **Chattooga River Trail,** whose southern terminus is at the Route 76 bridge in Chattahoochee's Tallulah Ranger District. Better yet, travel the river assisted by outfitters in Clayton and along Route 76.

A prime place to see the river's muscle is **Woodall Shoals,** just across the state line in South Carolina. (Cross the river on Route 76, turn right—south—almost 2.5 miles past the bridge, then right again at the first gravel road. The parking lot is about two miles from the turn.) When the river is high, Woodall Shoals becomes an adrenaline-charged challenge. When water is low, the shoals become a "dance-of-death" rock garden for river runners. In spring, the woods flanking the Chattooga are bright with purple trillium, chaste white bloodroot, and other wildflowers. Glossy-leaved holly reflects light more subtly than the river. Flowing south, the Chattooga sheets clean and unbro-ken towards the shoals, where it bursts into stars of light when it hits the rocks cobbling the riverbed.

The mountain town of Helen and neighboring **Unicoi State Park❖,** near the intersection of Routes 75 and 356, make fine centers for ex-ploring the southeastern Blue Ridge. The Smith Creek Trail leads to **Anna Ruby Falls❖,** a Forest Service scenic area off Route 356. Al-though it detracts from the gorge's natural beauty, the short paved trail to the falls makes the area accessible to all. Pouring off Tray Mountain from Curtis and York creeks, the double falls charges the gorge with its energy. The slopes leading to the falls are pricked with yellow, blue, and white violets. Below the cascading water, Smith Creek is framed by

leucothoe, whose arching limbs support tiny chandeliers of scented white flowers. The fluffy spikes of foamflowers cling to wet crevices on the rocky slopes beneath a canopy of soaring oaks, hickories, and yellow poplars. At the head of the gorge, 153-foot Curtis Creek Falls and 50-foot York Creek Falls make furious music.

About ten miles west of Anna Ruby Falls, Richard B. Russell Scenic Byway (Route 348) affords a visual entrée to the wilderness as it leads from Alternate Route 75 northwest to the parking area for **Raven Cliffs Falls❖** in Chattahoochee's Chattooga Ranger District. Raven Cliffs is the southernmost wilderness area along the Appalachian Trail, and Raven Cliffs Falls Trail offers one of the best hikes in this part of the Blue Ridge. Because it is accessible from a paved road, Raven Cliffs Falls Trail is extremely popular and crowded on weekends.

ABOVE: *Scarlet tanagers, which winter in South America and then migrate north, are best spotted in spring before the trees leaf out.*

LEFT: *Wild as a river can be, the forest-hemmed Chattooga gains tributary water at Dick's Creek Falls on the Georgia–South Carolina border.*

Most of the way, the trail winds along Dodd's Creek through pines, hemlocks, and hardwoods, passing an occasional open sun-soaked slope. Under an awning of rhododendron, the creek frequently plunges over rock as the moist slopes reveal their treasures—ferns, a sprinkling of violets, white-veined rattlesnake plantain, bellworts, trout lilies. Swallowtails and spring azure butterflies add more hues to the color-spangled scene. Approaching the falls, the trail becomes steeper, and a jumble of huge boulders line the sides of the creek. At the veiled falls, waters pour from unseen ridges, shoot from notches in the sheer rock cliffs, and finally braid into Dodd's Creek.

A few miles north of Raven Cliffs, scenic Route 348 intersects Route 180. About eight miles farther east, Spur Route 180 switchbacks up to 4,784-foot **Brasstown Bald,** the highest point in Georgia. The old igneous rocks have nothing to do with brass; the Europeans who named the mountain confused the Cherokee word for "new green place" with a similar-sounding one meaning "brass."

From the huge parking lot, a half-mile paved trail climbs 500 feet higher to the Brasstown Ranger District visitor center and observation deck atop Brasstown Bald. Crowding the path, dense rosebay rhododendron and mountain laurel turn it into a bower of white and pink blossoms in summer. About halfway up the walk, the peeled, curling bark of short yellow birch trees glows a dull gold. These trees of far northern hardwood forests reach their southern limit at Brasstown Bald, where the altitude and the moist cloud-forest climate enable them to survive, but as dwarfs. Somewhere a woodpecker hammers on a trunk. A black cherry tree rises above a rock slab layered with lung lichen. Springy beds of moss tucked between the cracks and a tease of trailing arbutus complete another exquisite tableau in the cloud forest.

Just below the open top of Brasstown Bald, a pygmy oak forest ekes out a meager living. The stunted oaks are centenarians at least; the harsh environment atop the bald keeps them small and gnarled. From the observation deck, visitors can see a few soft green valleys and a clutter of peaks: staircase slopes, sturdy shoulders, bosomy peaks, peaks beyond peaks beyond peaks from the Cohutta Mountains in the western part of the state to Rabun Bald in the east. Lending perspective to the scene, towhees pick at the scarlet berries of a mountain ash just below the observation deck while jays and juncos flit among dwarf willows.

Three trails radiate from the base of Brasstown Bald: Jack's Knob, Wagon Train, and Arkaquah. Beginning beside the bald's service road, Arkaquah Trail meanders along a ridge past overlooks, wildflowers, and Chimney Top Mountain, then descends 2,500 feet and 5.5 miles to Track Rock Gap. Enchanting and quiet, Arkaquah weaves among groves of rhododendron and laurel on a leaf-softened trail that opens to more fine views of the Blue Ridge.

Nine and a half miles south of Blairsville on Route 129 and two miles west on Route 180, the Brasstown District's **Sosebee Cove Scenic Area**

RIGHT: *Near Dodd's Creek along Raven Cliffs Falls Trail, hardwood trees leaf out above thickets of rhododendron sheltering ferns and wildflowers.*
OVERLEAF: *Seen from Russell Scenic Highway in the Raven Cliffs wilderness, Yonah Mountain shows why this range is called the Blue Ridge.*

is rich in wildflowers and the rare yellowwood tree, whose flower panicles cascade like cream-colored wisteria. A few miles south of the Route 180 intersection on Route 129, **DeSoto Falls Scenic Recreation Area** in the Chestatee Ranger District offers an array of floral beauty: rhododendron blossoms in purple, white, and pink; sourwood trees distinguished by vibrant red fall color and sprays of ivory flowers that resemble lilies of the valley; dogwoods whose perfect white blooms lie in horizontal tiers like those in an Oriental painting. A series of cascades and fine views complete the rich scenic mix. Located on Blood Mountain (the highest peak on the Georgia section of the Appalachian Trail), DeSoto Falls was named for Hernando de Soto because a piece of armor from his expedition was reputedly found here.

Still within the Chestatee Ranger District, take Route 60 northeast from its intersection with Route 19, turn right (east) on Forest Road 33, and follow it about half a mile beyond the paved section to **Cooper Creek Scenic Area,** which is bisected by Cooper Creek and etched by a number of its feeder branches. Here in the oft-logged Georgia mountains, the scenic area provides a rare look at huge old-growth hardwoods and virgin conifers. On foot, take the first logging road to the north, then the first one heading west, an old path that travels in the same direction as Cooper Creek and passes through more old-growth stands. Moist cove forests shade lavish displays of wildflowers, and farther on, the big trees begin to show themselves: red and white oaks and giant tulip poplars, massive with age and battered by circumstance.

At the other side of Cooper Creek Scenic Area, where Forest Road 236 heads north from Road 33, virgin hemlock and white pine groves reach their southern limit. These stately northern trees are probably relict communities from the last ice age, which forced northern species to migrate south.

WESTERN BLUE RIDGE

From the old mining town of Dahlonega, which means "golden color" in Cherokee and is said to be the site of America's first gold rush, turn west on Route 52 to **Amicalola Falls State Park and Lodge❖.** As a tributary of the Etowah River, Amicalola Creek is on the western side of Georgia's Blue Ridge. When North America and Africa collided, rock on the east took most of the heat, so the eastern Blue Ridge contains more metamorphic rock. The western Blue Ridge is the terminus of ranges that stretch from Georgia through the Great Smoky Mountains to the Iron Mountains of Virginia. The eastern Blue Ridge forms a solid bulwark from north to south, whereas the western Blue Ridge contains more discrete ranges.

Amicalola is an onomatopoeic word that in the Cherokee language means "tumbling waters." And these falls, the highest in Georgia, do indeed tumble and plunge dramatically down rocky ledges. The surrounding hardwood forest is ablaze in fall, and in spring white dogwood blossoms and red-purple redbud glow softly in the understory. On the ridges, pine mixes with oaks and hickories, which can tolerate drier soils. Because the park lies along the line where mountains and piedmont meet, species diversity is high.

From Amicalola Falls State Park, a rugged connector trail leads to **Ed Jenkins National Recreation Area❖,** the southern terminus of the famed Appalachian Trail, which snakes 2,000 miles along the top of the Appalachians from Georgia to Maine. Just north, the Toccoa River canoe trail, from Deep Hole Campground to Lake Blue Ridge, provides a view of the mountains from one of the Blue Ridge's loveliest rivers.

The fertile soils and lush growth of the **Rich Mountain Wilderness❖,** in the Toccoa Ranger District, lie on the east side of a huge trough in the landscape called the Murphey Syncline. Taking advantage of geology, engineers sited Route 76 within this long trench. On the other side of the syncline, the Cohutta District of Chattahoochee National Forest encompasses some of the wildest country in the north Georgia mountains.

Like the Rich Mountain Wilderness, the 38,000-acre **Cohutta Wilderness❖** has relatively deep, loamy soils compared to the eastern Blue Ridge. More ferns—and more black bears—live here than in other parts of the mountains. Because there are fewer paved roads, however, access to the area is more difficult. The parking area at Dally Gap is near the trailhead for Jack's River Trail, which winds through the eastern side of the wilderness. At nearly 17 miles, it is the longest hike and one of the muddiest—but also one of the most scenic.

Farther west is **Lake Conasauga Recreation Area❖,** centered on Georgia's highest lake. (Take Route 411 north from Chatsworth and turn east—right—at Eton. The county road becomes Forest Road 18.

At Forest Road 68, turn north—left—and continue ten miles to the recreation area.) Although created for recreation, the lake and surrounding area are home to a wide range of mammals and birds. The Songbird Management Area is planted to attract not only songbirds but also woodpeckers, grouse and turkeys, raptors, ducks, and others. Forest, beaver ponds, swamp accessible by a boardwalk, and other habitats attract crossbills, cuckoos, wood ducks, loons, and several species of warblers to Lake Conasauga Recreation Area.

CUMBERLAND PLATEAU REGION

As visitors drive west from the Cohuttas, geology presents itself with candor. First the land drops precipitously from the heights of the western Blue Ridge to the Great Valley, for centuries an agricultural enclave in a rocky region. Next comes a roller-coaster crossing of the longitudinal Armuchee Ridges and the Armuchee District of Chattahoochee National Forest.

The jewel of this district is **Keown Falls Scenic Area❖,** reached by taking Route 136 west. Just before Villanow, turn south (left) on Pocket Road (Forest Road 203) and go about five miles to Forest Road 702, the entrance to Keown Falls. Here rock bluffs, springs that give rise to small swamps, creeks that become waterfalls, and cove hardwood forests paint a shimmering picture. The Keown Falls Loop Trail winds up to a bluff overlooking the falls and connects with the John's Mountain Trail.

South of the national forest near Rome, in the Great Valley, the Nature Conservancy's **Marshall Forest Preserve** highlights some of northern Georgia's remaining old-growth forest. In addition to an intriguing mix of northern species, such as chestnut and red oak, and southern longleaf pine, here at the northern edge of its range, the preserve also harbors rare plants such as the endangered large-flowered skullcap. To visit the state's first national natural landmark, contact the Georgia office of the Nature Conservancy.

West of the high, narrow Armuchee Ridges, a collection of valleys striped with low ridges forms the Chickamauga Valley, which has long provided access to points south. Enclosing the valley on its western side is **Lookout Mountain** and a connected thumb of land called Pigeon Mountain, both actually flattop plateaus. Geologists speculate that the rocks that compose the landforms were once part of valleys or coastal plains when ancient shallow seas washed through North America. Layers and layers of sand, mud, and marine shells and skeletons

The Cohutta Wilderness near the Tennessee border blends rounded peaks, rich soils, and abundant wetlands (left). Wildlife ranges from bobcat and black bears to water-loving beavers (above), who sculpt the landscape with ponds and can fell young softwood trees in minutes.

were laid down to produce those broad plains of sandstone, shale, and limestone. Eventually rivers such as the Chickamauga carved through the ancient plains, creating plateaus and some spectacular scenery.

On Route 136, 18 miles west of La Fayette, **Cloudland Canyon State Park❖** lies at the western edge of Lookout Mountain. One of the most dramatic in the East, the canyon demonstrates its name in early morning after a rain, when rising mist fills it and the surrounding land with ethereal clouds.

Visitors standing at the lip of the canyon experience the enormous scale of the place. A thousand feet below, the silvery thread of Sitton Gulch Creek, which sculpted the view, winds north toward Tennessee. Across the broad wedge-shaped gap, ant-sized hikers make their way along the rim trail. Where the canyon opens up, trees stretch across the rolling country to the horizon. Yellow violets and bluets flanking the trail add touches of color, and in autumn, this quiescent view blazes with burgundy reds, bright yellows, and deep orange-golds.

Trails beside waterfalls allow visitors to descend through time as the canyon's rock provides a geology lesson of exquisite clarity. Near the top of the canyon, broad shoulders of hard sandstone form clifflike outcrops wet with dripping water and green with mosses and lichens. Ferns and the soft white spikes of foamflowers find footholds in crevices. Farther into the canyon, water has worn away softer shale in thin, flaky layers. In spring, where these sloping shales are covered with soil, the delicate blooms of rue anemone, wood anemone, bellwort, trillium, and other wildflowers set off the new green foliage. In the cool, damp recesses of the canyon bottom, hemlocks frame the tumbling waterfalls.

One of Georgia's westernmost natural areas is also one of the best. Although the **Crockford-Pigeon Wildlife Management Area❖** is not as easily accessible as a state park, it is worth the effort. The check station, where maps and other information are available, can be reached from La Fayette by heading west 2.5 miles on Route 193. Turn left on Chamberlain Road, follow it three miles to Rocky Lane Road, and then turn right and go a half mile farther to the check station.

The Crockford-Pigeon Wildlife Management Area encompasses the plateau connected to Lookout Mountain, coves nestled into the sides of the plateau, and an underground karst kingdom riddling the interior of **Pigeon Mountain.** Named for the tens of thousands of now-extinct passenger pigeons that once roosted on Pigeon Mountain, the area contains Caribbean-blue springs, strange tufa precipitates, even stranger sandstone formations, caves, flower-filled coves, hardwood forests, bogs atop the mountain, and rare plants and animals.

Blue Hole, lying at the base of the mountain and named for its aquifer-fed spring, is also the lower entrance to **Ellison's Cave,** at 1,062 feet the deepest in the eastern United States. Within the cave, Fantastic Pit (586 feet) and Incredible Domepit (440 feet) are the two deepest

112

Pigeon Mountain harbors myriad wildflowers: The stalkless red trillium (top left) appears directly above its mottled leaves; Virginia bluebells (top right) and the celandine, or wood, poppy (bottom left) are rare in Georgia; fragrant showy orchis (bottom right) prefers damp coves.

domed pits in the country. The superlatives of the Pigeon Mountain karst system include mineral formations as well. This filigreed mountain owes its existence to the hard cap of sandstone, which covers a thousand-foot-thick limestone layer—the thickest in the East above the water table. Sinks and other depressions atop the plateau allow water to percolate through the sandstone and into the limestone layer, where it creates domes, passageways, and other karst structures.

Over Dug Gap, on the western side of Pigeon Mountain, is the Pocket. A low-key parking lot marks the entrance to this moist low-walled cove. An unmarked trail hopscotches back and forth across the stream, and in spring, the short walk up the streambed is a trip into a flowery wonderland. The north slope of the Pocket is a mass of deep yellow

113

celandine poppies, which glow like a soft light in the narrow, shaded cove. Carpeting the Pocket's damp floor at the feet of the poppies are nodding bluebells, their clustered blue-purple blooms centered in bouquets of large, arching green leaves. Red trillium, white trillium, cocky long-spur red violets, pinkish purple native geraniums, and tall wild blue phlox are just a few of the wildflowers here. Endangered salamanders—protected within the wildlife management area—scurry for cover where walking fern stretches its long legs across a moss-covered boulder.

At the deepest recess of the cove, a stream adds its pleasant voice to the quiet place as it pours over a low ledge. Where the carbonate-rich water drops to the rocks below, piles of tufa have formed. A precipitate that resembles spongy rock, tufa is found nowhere else in Georgia.

Wild turkeys—the mottled white ones are an unusual genetic variation common on Pigeon Mountain—cross the road leading to the top of the mountain. In a few places on the flat top of Pigeon Mountain, depressions in the sandstone have helped create small peat-lined bogs, which become important wildlife watering areas in summer when the springs dry up. A coyote trotting through the hardwoods is a descendent of those that migrated into Georgia in the 1920s. Another carnivore, the golden eagle, is seen more often these days thanks to a program that has reintroduced these majestic bronze birds to the area.

Of all its unusual features, Pigeon Mountain is probably most noted for **Rock Town.** The signs to Rock Town are small and the last mile is dirt road—both measures to keep this remarkable sandstone labyrinth from being overrun. About a half mile down the trail from the small parking lot, wind and water have worn the sandstone caprock into a weird world populated by giant mushrooms, tall organ pipes, rocking horses, and jumbled pillows of stone. Visitors squeeze between rock slots that rise 20 to 30 feet. Highbush blueberries and mountain laurels add a bit of green to the sandstone floor, and the tops of the formations harbor tiny microclimates. Nearby is Hood Overlook, which offers a fine view of the valley below. To the west lies Alabama, where Lookout Mountain presents an equally attractive face.

RIGHT: *Hidden in a remote part of the Pigeon Mountain area, Rock Town is a 160-acre jumble of lichen-covered sandstone. Here wind and water have carved strange shapes, including these crevice-riddled slabs.*

ALABAMA

PART THREE

ALABAMA

In its broad lowland fields and moss-draped bayous, Alabama obligingly fits the image of a Deep South state. In the mountainous north, however, white-water rivers, dancing waterfalls, and steep gorges strewn with wildflowers add an unexpected dimension to the state's natural wealth. The plateaus and peaks that ripple across the northern tiers of Alabama and neighboring Georgia are the tail end of the Appalachians, a range that begins some 2,000 miles northeast in Maine. The mountains that dominate the north give way to low rolling hills in the middle of the state and then to a broad coastal plain that stretches to the Gulf of Mexico. Here the waters of Mobile Bay form a huge wedge in the center of the state's distinctive boot heel.

Sweeping into Alabama from the northeast, the thick sedimentary layers of the Cumberland Plateau jab a crooked elbow of land deep into the state's midsection. Lookout Mountain, Sand Mountain, and Little Mountain across the Tennessee River are part of these rocky uplands, which contribute so much scenic splendor to the state. Little River Canyon and adjoining De Soto State Park on Lookout Mountain—the jewels in Alabama's mountain crown—delight visitors with frothy waterfalls, rugged slickrock outcrops, and a canopied forest lush with myriad flowering shrubs and extravagant displays of wildflowers.

As it surges into the state from southeastern Tennessee, the Tennessee River cuts across Alabama's uplands and then angles north again on its way to a confluence with the Ohio River. No longer free-flowing after the transformations wrought by the Tennessee Valley Authority in the 1930s, the mighty waterway is now broadened by dams and thick with barges. Yet this working river is also fringed by flower-filled coves and—near high-tech Huntsville—flanked by primordial swamps that still harbor alligators and massive cypress trees.

PRECEDING PAGES: *Surrounded by sunlit live oaks and pines, a peaceful pond in Conecuh National Forest is home to egrets and alligators.*

The highlands of the Cumberland Plateau end in a confusion of choppy hills and ridges in Bankhead National Forest. Laced by gallant little untamed rivers such as the Sipsey, these rolling woodlands contain a wilderness area as pristine as any in the region. To the southeast lies the last thin finger of the Blue Ridge Mountains, a narrow forested ridge surrounded by Talladega National Forest, which encompasses Cheaha State Park, the loftiest point in the state. This high slice of mountain range is home to showy flame azaleas, scented silver bells, and vistas of lakes and rolling hills that invite restful contemplation.

The lower portion of the state occupies a complex coastal plain. From the fall line south to the Gulf, bands of black soil and red hills stripe the state from east to west. The Fall Line Hills arc through the midsection, cupping the mountains and piedmont to the north. South of those hills lies Alabama's legendary Black Belt, where a broad swath of rich black loam supported a cotton industry so successful that Alabama was called the Cotton State. The Red Hills supplied iron ore to the Confederacy and still feed the steel mills of Birmingham.

Today agriculture and industry so pervade the coastal plain that the few natural lands remaining are places with scant potential for development—marshes, infertile sandy areas, and barrier islands. Southern Alabama, which borders Florida's panhandle, does not lack scenic spots, however. In Conecuh National Forest, graceful longleaf pines tower over sandy wire-grass prairies. The lower coastal plain is replete with blackwater rivers, dazzling white-sand beaches, and a sparkling necklace of barrier islands, which attract a tremendous variety of birds.

Long the lifeblood of the state, a network of rivers—the Alabama, Coosa, Tombigbee, Chattahoochee, Black Warrior, and Tallaposa—pattern southern Alabama as they deliver their waters to the Gulf of Mexico. Except for the Tennessee River, all flow into the gulf, most through Mobile Bay. Second only to Chesapeake Bay in size, Mobile Bay was once a broad river valley and delta. Over the ages, as silt was carried out to sea and the land sank, the gulf claimed this now-drowned river valley. Today the edges of Mobile Bay are softly fringed with salt marshes, whose undulating grasses and warm estuarine waters provide a rich breeding ground for a multitude of sea animals and those that dine on them—from fish and mollusks to birds, amphibians, and people. Beyond lies the Gulf and a world of marine life.

ALABAMA:
END OF THE APPALACHIANS
TO MOBILE BAY

ven before the French arrived in 1699, countless cultures inhabited Alabama. As long ago as 7000 B.C., hunter-gatherers
occupied Russell Cave, in the state's mountainous northeast
corner. The great Mound Builder culture from a millennium
ago left a premier example of its civic centers in western Alabama near
Tuscaloosa and the Black Warrior River. The Cherokee, Creek,
Choctaw, and Chickasaw all lived within the borders of present-day
Alabama. (Indeed, the state name, which means "brush gatherers" in
Choctaw, referred to the Alibamu tribe, part of the Creek confederacy.)
By the mid-1800s, however, all these native peoples had been dispos-
sessed—largely relegated to the parched grasslands of Oklahoma—by
the inexorable advance of European settlement.

Europeans first visited the area in the mid-sixteenth century, and
Spanish explorer Hernando de Soto brought 500 warriors here with
him in about 1540. Over the next century Spain, England, and France
all tried to claim the region. During the early 1700s France made
Dauphin Island, just off the coast of southern Alabama, the capital of
its Louisiana Territory, which stretched to the Rocky Mountains.

Today pretty French courtyards enclosed by iron grillwork, Spanish-
ancestry shrimpers trawling nets behind their boats, and echoes of
English architecture recall the gumbo of European cultures that found
their way to the Alabama coast. Even pockets of landscape are still

LEFT: *Pink-and-white mountain laurel clings to a cliff overlooking Little
River Canyon, an area contiguous with the Cumberland Plateau in
northern Georgia and visited by Hernando de Soto in the mid-1500s.*

reminiscent of the scene that greeted early visitors: bayous bordering cypress swamps, marshlands where herons hunt, lofty pinelands that are home to rare woodpeckers and reptiles.

In the north, farmers descended from Welsh immigrants have long scratched hardscrabble livings from the high, rocky soils of Sand Mountain. Nearby, wild white-water rivers and surging waterfalls roil through rockbound gorges bright with mountain wildflowers. Despite Alabama's rich multicultural and natural heritage, however, its general image seems frozen in the Deep South of the plantation era, perhaps because agriculture, especially cotton, still dominates the vast midsection. Although coal and iron mining, oil drilling, space technology, and other industries play a substantial role in Alabama's current economy, the stereotype of lowlands planted in cotton along lazy brown rivers is hard to overcome. One difficulty in expanding the state's image is that natural Alabama lacks the superlatives—"largest swamp," "most tropical bog," "highest peak"—that stick in people's minds. Its mountains are modest and so are its rivers. Until recently the state has also suffered a dearth of stewardship for its natural resources, and today many state parks are primarily recreation centers rather than sanctuaries for its natural heritage. Nonetheless, Alabama harbors more natural beauty than most suspect; although admittedly too little has been preserved, the best of what remains is now protected.

The itinerary for this chapter begins on the Cumberland Plateau in northeastern Alabama, zigzags westward through mountainous country, and then swings east through Bankhead National Forest to the Blue Ridge. From the banks of the Chattahoochee River on the Georgia border, the route heads west again to the southernmost forests and then southwest to explore Mobile Bay, the coastal marshes, and the barrier islands.

NORTHEAST ALABAMA: THE MOUNTAINS
The most scenic approach to De Soto State Park, the state's crown jewel, is from the southwest via Route 89, part of the Lookout Mountain Park-

OVERLEAF: *Slipping over a cliff face of Cumberland Plateau sedimentary rock, Grace's High Falls—one of the tallest in the state—plunges into Bear Creek Canyon, a narrow side ravine of Little River Canyon.*

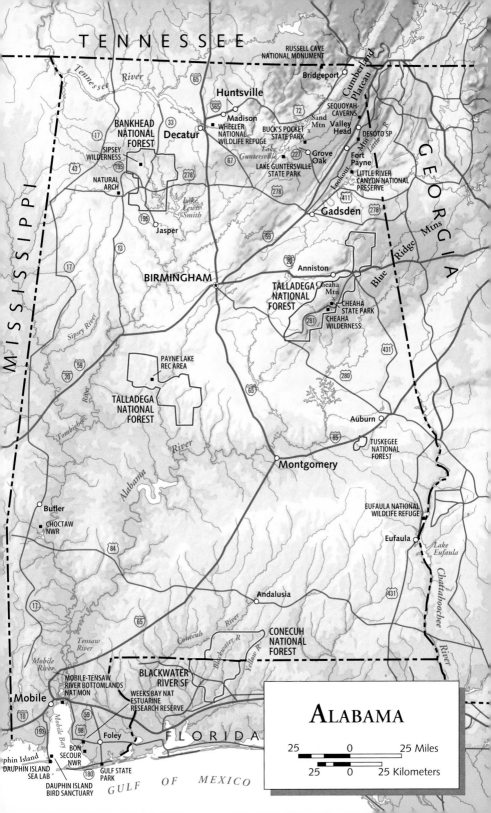

ALABAMA

25 0 25 Miles

25 0 25 Kilometers

way. Traveling northeast from Gadsden, Alabama, to Chattanooga, Tennessee, the parkway winds atop Lookout Mountain, the high southernmost section of the Cumberland Plateau. Extending diagonally through Alabama and Georgia to Tennessee, this hundred-mile-long sandstone-capped table of land is more a mesa than a mountain. Like Pigeon Mountain in Georgia, Lookout Mountain once lay at the bottom of an ancient sea. Rock layers preserve fossilized ripples from sea-bottom sands, as well as fossils of ancient corals and ferns from the Carboniferous Period, visual reminders of the area's fascinating geologic history.

ABOVE: *In De Soto State Park, a spicebush swallowtail perches on a rock; the butterfly uses its namesake plant as a home for its chrysalis.*

On the top of Lookout Mountain lies the spectacular **Little River Canyon National Preserve❖,** one of the deepest gorges in the East. The wild and scenic Little River is the only river in North America formed and flowing its entire length on top of a mountain. Where the canyon drops from one level of rock to another, the Little River spills over in luminous cascades. **Little River Falls** provides one of the best views of the tree-cloaked canyon. Here slabs of sandstone, similar to Utah slickrock, usher the rushing water to the lip of the rock where it plunges in broad white skirts to emerald pools below.

About 15 miles farther north along Route 89, the other Little River waterfall, **De Soto Falls,** is one of the highest in the state at 104 feet. Dashing through a chute carved by the water, the river plunges over a sheer cliff face framed by mountain laurel, pine, and cherry—a quiet backdrop to the watery tumult.

Between the two falls lies **De Soto State Park❖,** named for Hernando de Soto, the Spanish explorer who reached these parts in 1540. His expedition found a shaded hardwood forest dotted with rock outcrops and boulders and a sparkling river clasped between rocky banks draped with flowering shrubs. Passing pools decorated with yellow-tipped wands of golden club, the park's Yellow Trail hugs the Little River. In spring garnet-tinted redbud, layers of white-blossomed dogwood, and airy white serviceberry shade the trail. Each May, the extravagant purples and pinks of rhododendron and mountain laurel transform the forest into a festival of bloom.

The park supports an impressive roster of wildflowers, some 650 species. Pink lady's slippers bloom in large colonies. Yellow-trumpeted jessamine (jasmine) vine, with its clean, baby-powder scent, coils through wild hydrangeas and hollies. Reddish brown gingers and blue irises, magenta fire pinks and lavender cranesbill are among the blossoms brightening the forest floor. Small sphagnum peat bogs fill depressions atop the mountain, providing a congenial home for the federally endangered pitcher plant, a carnivorous species that traps insects within long tubular leaves. Also represented are hawks, herons, ducks, warblers, and all the usual residents of moist rich woods. Bald eagles winter in the canyon, and wild turkeys are often spotted scuttling across trails at dawn or dusk.

The river trail offers ringside seats for the highlights of the park. Here hikers can follow the fortunes of the Little River as it floats calmly in quiet pools or squeezes into a foam of white water between intruding rock walls. Visitors perched on an outcrop where the river burbles by can watch waxwings dash overhead or catbirds sample holly berries.

ABOVE: *Vividly tinted flame azalea—native only to the Appalachians—produces outstanding spring floral displays in Alabama.*

On other trails, such as Azalea Cascade, enormous moss- and lichen-covered boulders stand sentinel. Pine needles carpet the high trail, and where a small bridge crosses Laurel Creek, delicate mountain laurel, ranging from white to pink, brightens a secret garden.

The limestone and sandstone of Lookout Mountain and Sand Mountain have supplied northeastern Alabama with a vast network of caves, which attract spelunkers from all over the world. Several commercially owned caves are open to visitors, including **Sequoyah Caverns❖,** just off I-59 northeast of Valley Head. A 45- to 60-minute tour gives visitors a chance to appreciate the rock formations and the mirrorlike reflection of the underground pools, which inspired the cave's other name: Looking Glass Caverns.

127

One of the largest of the thousands of caverns in this region and one of the longest occupied, **Russell Cave National Monument❖** is close to the Tennessee border in the state's northeast corner. (Follow Route 72 north to Bridgeport, then take County Road 75 west to County Road 98 north through soft-featured farm country.) About 8,500 years ago, archaic peoples took shelter in the cave, flaking stone for spear points and fashioning fishhooks from bone. Native Americans of the Woodland Period (1000 B.C.–A.D. 500) farmed along the rivers but retreated to the cave in winter. Although the Cherokee and later European settlers made little use of the cave, archaeological evidence shows that habitation had continued unbroken for thousands of years prior to the Cherokee.

Wild hydrangeas frame the cave's mouth, and vines and ferns clinging to limestone ledges drape down in green hanging gardens. Inside, the floor of the cavern's upper level is paved with rock and dirt that have accumulated over millennia, and the lower level is split by a stream flowing from underground springs. Near the mouth of the cave water seeps around tumbled rocks covered by clouds of purple phacelia and then trickles down into a giant sinkhole—its size hints at the Swiss cheese–like porous limestone below.

The monument's Montague Mountain Trail overlooks dogwood and redbud trees whose white and pink spring blossoms brighten the sur-

rounding basswood, beech, and pine. Beneath tree trunks where red-headed woodpeckers hammer and branches where chickadees scold, wild blue phlox, wild ginger, pink oxalis, and other wildflowers quilt the slopes.

Southwest, across the Tennessee River, **Buck's Pocket State Park❖** sits atop **Sand Mountain,** a long, high plateau like Lookout Mountain. (Near the town of Grove Oak, go north off Route 227.) Sand Mountain is so unlike a rocky peak that meadowlarks trill from fence posts here. Point Rock, the highest spot in the park, affords a view of the "pocket" formed where South Sauty Creek and Little Sauty Creek cut through the sandstone. Like a crow's nest on a ship, the rocky point of land seems perched over open air. Along the sides, twisted pines and gnarled rhododendrons clutch thin-soiled cracks in the rock, giving the place the feel of a bonsai garden. From Point Rock a trail descends to the canyon floor 400 feet below, passing fragrant fringe trees, velvety purple and lavender bird's-foot violets, and dwarf irises. A connecting trail, Indian House, leads by overhangs that sheltered the Cherokee when they lived here.

At the bottom along Little Sauty Creek—which disappears into an upstream sinkhole during the dry summer months—a slope filled with flowers resembles a wildflower preserve, and near the base of the slope sweet shrubs bear blooms the color of port wine. Huge white bloodroots and unusual deep-red trilliums grow along the trail, along with small white-flowered saxifrages paired with lavender and pink wild phlox. Cascades of purple phacelia tumble over rocks and disap-

129

pear beneath the umbrellalike leaves of mayapples. At the feet of an old beech and black cherry that married as they grew, a variety of violets embroider the ground. The speckled foliage of trout lilies and silvery leaves of white phacelia cling to the slope with jack-in-the-pulpits, foamflowers, and white baneberry, which bears pale berries known as doll's eyes.

Just 18 miles south on Route 227 is **Lake Guntersville State Park❖,** which borders a dammed section of the Tennessee River. Overlooking the broadened river, Taylor Mountain at 1,300 feet is the park's highest point. Although geared toward recreation such as tennis and golf, the park also offers plenty of opportunities to experience the natural. Along Town Creek in particular grow such rare beauties as yellow lady's slippers and mountain stewartia, also known as mountain camellia.

ABOVE: *The pink lady's slipper, one of the largest native orchids, reaches its southern limit in Alabama.*

Taylor Mountain is the hard sandstone cap above the park's layers of limestone. At mid-mountain, blocks of gray limestone form steps on a slope pocked with nascent caves and covered with wild displays of white wood asters, ferns, and several types of mint. Hiking the three-mile Tom Bevill Interpretive Trail provides a good overview of the native flora.

Because five botanic zones converge in northeast Alabama, the park harbors cool-weather oaks and hickories as well as southern plants such as wild grape and azalea. The palmate leaves of the buckeye tree—the southerly red, the more northerly yellow, and a red-orange natural hybrid—flutter in the breeze. In autumn, various oaks, red and sugar maples, sweet gums, sumacs, and hickories glow on the Guntersville hills.

White-tailed deer bound through the

LEFT: *The shadowy recesses within Buck's Pocket conceal stewartia, sweet shrub, and other native flora.*

OVERLEAF: *A great blue heron, whose wings span seven feet, flaps slowly over a misty Town Creek in Lake Guntersville State Park.*

131

woods, and because the park lies along a songbird flyway, cerulean, Blackburnian, and other warblers serenade in the trees spring and fall. Guntersville has also become a wintering place for Great Lakes bald eagles. Although these raptors do not nest in the park, as many as 80 eagles roost in pines along Lake Guntersville and Town Creek. At dusk, from designated viewpoints along Route 227, visitors can watch dozens of eagles return to their nests after a day of hunting and fishing.

In an effort to reintroduce nesting bald eagles to Alabama, state wildlife biologists have been "hacking" eaglets in this area for a number of years. Hatched under chickens, then fed by eagle puppets so they never see humans, the young eagles are released throughout the state at about 12 weeks old, when they would normally be ready to leave the nest. Some of these birds are nesting at Lake Guntersville.

The North-Central Section: Wheeler and Bankhead

ABOVE: Bald eagles once again roost and some even nest at Lake Guntersville, thanks to wildlife biologists' efforts.

When the Tennessee Valley Authority remade the landscape of northern Alabama, part of the newly configured, dam-impounded Tennessee River became the first national wildlife refuge on man-made terrain. The 1938 experiment was so successful in attracting thousands of waterfowl and wading birds that the **Wheeler National Wildlife Refuge❖** soon became a prototype preserve. The best time to visit Wheeler NWR is midwinter, when throngs of waterfowl find sanctuary in its ponds and river bays. Tens of thousands of migrating ducks (wigeon, black, pintail, mallard) and geese (snow, blue, and Canada) ply the waters and browse adjoining fields planted in corn and winter wheat for them.

The 34,500-acre refuge edges the Wheeler Reservoir between Huntsville and Decatur. (Take the Madison exit from I-565 to Route 20 west and go south on County Line Road past the I-565 crossover where signs and a road west lead to a boardwalk.) The one-mile **Beaverdam Boardwalk** offers a close-up view of Alabama's northernmost tupelo-cypress swamp. Because the meandering Tennessee River and its bordering valley and associated wetlands are lower and warmer than the surrounding mountains, the **Blackwell Swamp** here even harbors Alabama's northernmost alligators.

The refuge's visitor center is across the river. (Take Exit 334 off I-65 and go 2.5 miles west.) An observation tower and a short boardwalk near the visitor center provide a glimpse of the larger habitat. Across Route 67, the Environmental Trail loops past a riverine inlet edged with pond cypress and winds through bottomland forest where ethereal pink azaleas float beneath silver maples and tulip poplars.

The Dancy Bottoms Trail visits an even more imposing section of Wheeler's bottomland forest. (Take Indian Hills Road south and Red Bank Road west to the parking lot.) Fishing is fine along the river, and the forest is buttressed with immense trees and poison ivy vines as thick as a thigh. The abundant flora and fauna attract both herbivorous and carnivorous mammals: deer, foxes, bats, weasels, moles and shrews, bobcat, and river otters. Two endangered bats—the Indiana and the gray—frequent the refuge's Blowing Wind Cave unit, which is located west of Huntsville and just west of Scottsboro on Route 72. In summer, visitors can observe dramatic twilight flights of more than 250,000 bats winging out of the cave to feed.

ABOVE: *White-tailed deer roam the Wheeler National Wildlife Refuge. They signal danger by flipping up their white tails.*

About 25 miles southwest of Decatur, Route 33 heads south into **Bankhead National Forest❖.** (Turn west at County Road 60 to the picnic area and a bridge overlooking the Sipsey River.) Here visitors enter the wildest area in Alabama, the 26,000-acre **Sipsey Wilderness.** Because it has no imposing peaks or craggy terrain, the Sipsey seems to welcome visitors and allow the natural world to work its magic on rattled human psyches. At this quiet southernmost end of the Cumberland Plateau, southern Appalachian forest is partitioned by the Sipsey River and its branches. Patches of virgin forest still grow here.

The state's only national wild and scenic river, the Sipsey purls

ABOVE: *More than 60 miles of the Sipsey River system crisscross the Sipsey Wilderness in Bankhead National Forest. Here old-growth trees flank graceful waterways that have never been confined by dams.*

ebulliently between sandy banks set with house-sized boulders. Above its narrow sand banks, forested bluffs rise to the top of the plateau. Along these slopes, trails parallel the contours of the river, passing from sun-dappled deciduous forest to shaded evergreen groves springy with fallen needles. Occasionally the path encounters one of the Sipsey's many branches, providing a pleasant excuse to wade through calf-high water.

Sidestreams have formed gorges flanked with massive rock outcrops and cavernous overhangs. Dark hemlocks and hollies as well as flowering oak hydrangeas and mountain laurels, guard the cool and moody recesses. Beeches, maples, and oaks, among the forest's mainstay trees, stage a fiery show in autumn, and at their feet grow a full range of southern Appalachian wildflowers. A quiet paddle on the river or a solitary perch atop a warm boulder affords the best views of deep green pools that reflect overhanging trees and conceal fish. Swallowtail butterflies flirt with the sun-fretted river as a hawk's shadow drives small birds back into the woods.

136

A tamer version of the Sipsey Wilderness awaits visitors at the **Clear Creek Recreation Area,** also within the Bankhead forest. Signs south of Double Springs on Route 195 direct travelers east on Lamon Chapel Road, then north on Fall City Road. Centered on Lake Lewis Smith, the area includes the Raven Trail, which passes rock outcrops and overhangs where Union sympathizers in Winston County holed up during the Civil War.

Some 15 miles northwest, off Route 278 a mile west of its intersection with Routes 13 and 5, is **Natural Bridge❖,** the longest natural rock arch east of the Rocky Mountains. This old-time private park charges visitors a modest fee, but despite the hokey wrought-iron entrance and souvenir sales, the forest and arch are essentially natural. Edging the small stream that bisects the park are hemlocks and two dozen species of ferns, botanical relics of the last ice age, when northerly plant communities retreated as far south as Alabama.

CENTRAL ALABAMA

South of Anniston, **Talladega National Forest❖** encompasses the last tongue of the Blue Ridge Mountains, which spill over the border from Georgia. The **Talladega Scenic Byway** follows Route 281, winding ever upward toward the crest of the long curving ridge that forms the spine of the national forest. Foothills and spurs extend onto the piedmont, where low, iron-rich red hills nourish Birmingham's iron ore industry. Views along the byway showcase this panorama from a number of perspectives.

The 92-mile Pinhoti Trail traverses both the Talladega and Shoal Creek districts of the forest, as well as the nearby **Choccolocco Wildlife Management Area.** Talladega's natural centerpiece, however, is the **Cheaha Wilderness❖,** where logging is banned (it is permitted in the rest of the national forest). Odum Scout and Cave Creek trails, which begin in the same parking lot a quarter-mile east of Cheaha State Park on Route 281, make a rewarding, if long, loop through the Cheaha Wilderness when combined with part of the Nubbin Creek Trail. Coaxed by warming temperatures, dwarf irises, trilliums, mayapples, and other wildflowers burst into bloom before the forest leafs out each spring. Hickories and chestnut, scarlet and blackjack oaks produce the forest canopy; in the fall, red maples and black gums set the hills ablaze with brilliant color. Pines—Virginia, loblolly, and long-leaf—flourish here as well.

Set in a diadem of bluets, lush clusters of bird's-foot violets thrive beneath a flowering serviceberry. A seductively scented silver bell tree makes an odd couple with a structured sumac. In summer, the fuzzy leaves of oak-leaf hydrangea flutter around fat domes of white blossoms. The flame azaleas that are Cheaha's great glory burnish the hillsides in colors that anticipate autumn. Besides botanical plenty, walks in the wilderness offer bubbling rivulets, waterfalls, and views of the great curving spine of the Blue Ridge.

Cheaha State Park❖, a good base for exploring Talladega National Forest, encompasses Cheaha Mountain, Alabama's highest point at 2,407 feet. The park's Bald Rock Nature Trail also provides fine scenery. Most of the place names in Talladega National Forest are derived from the language of its former occupants, the Upper Creek Nation. Talladega means "border town," because a Creek settlement occupied the border between their territory and that of the Natchez people. Pinhoti, also named for a town, is the word for "turkey house." And Cheaha may be derived from the Choctaw word meaning "high."

Although the natural areas of Alabama's midsection are more modest than those in the mountainous north or the coastal south, highlights include the mile-long nature trail at **Payne Lake Recreation Area❖,** in the Oakmulgee District of Talladega National Forest southwest of Birmingham, as well as the Reed Break Natural Research Area—an undeveloped area that harbors endangered red-cockaded woodpeckers. Periodic flooding at the **Choctaw National Wildlife Refuge❖,** southeast of Butler about 40 miles from the Mississippi border, attracts a fine diversity of wildlife: wintering ducks, wading birds, resident alligators in the sloughs, and warblers, songbirds, wood storks, bald eagles, and wood ducks in the woodlands. In the **Tuskegee National Forest❖,** off I-85 between Montgomery and Auburn, 8.5 miles of the Bartram Trail wind through both upland pines and rich hardwood bottomlands, where deer and wild turkey live. Never

---

RIGHT: *A Virginia pine grows on Bald Rock in Cheaha State Park, the highest area in the state. From here views sweep forth—from the southern Appalachians to rolling foothills and the broad coastal plain.*

LEFT: *In the early 1800s, Audubon set out to paint North America's birds; in 1821 he completed his portrait of the wood stork, a coastal denizen that breeds in cypress swamps and mangroves.*
RIGHT: *Now endangered, the wood stork occasionally ventures as far north as the Eufaula National Wildlife Refuge on the Chattahoochee River. Refuge wetlands, here dotted with withered yellow lotus leaves, support great flocks of migrating waterfowl.*

difficult to spot in Alabama's midsection, kudzu is an alien vine that has invaded large parts of the South, smothering wild shrubs and old fields in a thick blanket of green.

THE COASTAL PLAIN

Forming the Georgia–Alabama border for more than 150 miles, the Chattahoochee has always been an imposing and important river. During the plantation era, millions of cotton bales traveled down the Chattahoochee to Florida's Apalachicola River, where they began their transit to Europe. In the town of Eufaula, a center for the cotton trade, great white-columned mansions still reflect the antebellum era. Although now used mainly for recreation, the Chattahoochee is still an important flyway for eastern birds.

The **Eufaula National Wildlife Refuge❖** is a complex of managed fields, woods, seasonal impoundments, the Chattahoochee River (impounded as Lake Eufaula), and its wetland borders. (Take Route 431 eight miles north past **Lakepoint State Park,** then turn right on Route 165 to the refuge entrance.) Encounters with herons, gulls, and ducks—from shovelers and mallard to teal, wood ducks, and gad-

walls—reward quiet canoe excursions through waters populated by bass, bream, and crappie. Along the riverbanks turtles and alligators bask on sun-warmed logs. (Canoes can be rented at the park.)

Near the refuge entrance, 7.5-mile Wingspread Wildlife Drive meanders past forests and fields where a portion of the crop is left for wildlife. Dawn and dusk are the most likely times to see white-tailed deer and wild turkeys. Hawks and kestrels patrol the open spaces on the lookout for dinner as a flock of cattle egrets, spooked by a hawk, rise from a field and cartwheel across the sky. Red-winged blackbirds trill from the tops of dead stalks while a loggerhead shrike keeps a solitary vigil on a fence post. Blinds and an observation tower allow patient watchers to observe cardinals, chickadees, mockingbirds, nuthatches, and other forest dwellers. Eufaula NWR attracts close to 300 bird species, including endangered wood storks in summer and sandhill cranes in winter. Because the refuge is especially popular with migrating waterfowl, spring and fall are the best times to see the greatest number of birds and species.

About a hundred miles southwest, Andalusia is the gateway to **Conecuh National Forest❖,** contiguous with Florida's Blackwater

River State Forest. This 84,000-acre spread, whose broad canebreaks prompted the Muskogee to call the area "conecuh," looks much as it did before European settlers logged and cleared most of the coastal plain. Maintained by periodic natural fires, this area was the unchallenged realm of the longleaf pine, known as yellow pine to lumbermen who sold millions of board feet of the lofty, long-lived tree all over the world. An integral duo, longleaf pines and wire grass have colonized the higher, sandier soils in Conecuh, especially on the east side of the forest as well as on much of the west. Soggy bottomlands and bayheads are home to swamp communities of bald cypress, black titi, dogwood, sweet bay, and other bay-type trees.

Because this land is geologically new and not much above sea level, the water table often rises to soak the sandy soils. About two dozen bogs dot the forest. Bogs arise when an impermeable layer, such as clay, causes water to remain on the surface. Plants living in the poor soil of bogs must adapt to provide themselves with nutrients. Conecuh's bogs, for instance, abound with carnivorous plants—24 different species

LEFT: *In Conecuh National Forest, towering longleaf and slash pines and bright green swamp tupelo (or tupelo gum) trees surround Gum Pond.*

TOP RIGHT: *Although it smells like a violet, sweet pitcher plant acts like a predator, consuming insects in its tube-shaped leaves.*

BOTTOM RIGHT: *Part of the morning glory family, manroot is a white-flowered smooth-stemmed vine that climbs high up into Conecuh's forests.*

that lure and digest insects. In one hardwood bottomland bog, a rare red Wherry's pitcher plant emerges near a fat clump of parrot pitchers, whose clustered heads resemble the beaked heads of parrots.

Conecuh is also underlain with porous limestone, and in places the bedrock is packed with sinkholes where water—slightly acidic from organic matter—has eroded funnel-shaped holes in the limestone. Open, Blue, and Nellie ponds were formed when some of the larger sinkholes became ponds. The dark, tannin-stained Blackwater River has its origins in Conecuh, as does the clear-running Yellow River, the forest's other major waterway. The Conecuh River, the third major watershed, forms the northwest boundary of the forest.

Within Conecuh's strange and wonderful habitats live numerous rare and endangered species, such as the dusky gopher frog, gopher tortoise, Indiana bat, red-cockaded woodpecker, needle palm, and a number of orchids. The dusky gopher frog, one of the rarest amphibians in Alabama, was further threatened by anglers who illegally stocked Conecuh's ponds with largemouth bass and crappie, which devoured

143

the dusky gopher tadpoles. Forest managers are currently trying to restore the balance by eliminating the alien fish and collecting gopher frog eggs to hatch in labs and return to the ponds.

Because the dirt roads that crisscross the forest can be confusing, Open and Blue ponds provide the best introductions to Conecuh. Both are ringed with pines whose understories shimmer with fringe tree and dogwood blooms. A trail rings Open Pond, and others radiate out in loops to Five Runs Creek and Blue Springs. Along the way, signs warn of alligators, but a gangly great blue heron ignores the danger.

Longleaf pine is a highly desirable timber tree because its resins keep the wood from rotting. After loggers cleared most of the longleaf from the Southeast, however, people planted faster-growing slash pine, which ultimately does not do as well as longleaf in Conecuh's sandy, well-drained soils. The National Forest Service is now removing parcels of slash pine to replant with indigenous longleaf.

For years, land managers everywhere suppressed naturally occurring fires in the name of habitat protection. The shade-intolerant longleaf, however, depends on fire to clear out leafy hardwoods, thus opening up sunny areas where the pines can thrive. Under natural conditions, lightning-sparked fires sweep through the southern coastal plain regularly, destroying hardwoods and aggressive shrubs such as gallberry and saw palmetto.

Although the longleaf's outer bark and cascades of foot-long needles burn away, a cordon of inner needles protects the thick, waxy white candle of new needles. Even in a blackened and blasted landscape, the heart of the longleaf is tumid with new life. Because longleafs naturally space themselves widely, a longleaf forest is more like a sunny, grassy park with a scattering of tall pines than a thick, dark woodland. Once fire has cleared gallberry and palmetto, fresh green tufts of wire grass sprout almost immediately at the feet of the trees. Scattered through the tan-and-green carpet of arching wire grass are hundreds of other herbs, including a wealth of wildflowers. At Conecuh National Forest, prescribed burns are restoring this exceptional habitat.

RIGHT: *Just off Alabama's Gulf Coast, Little Dauphin Island provides welcome landfall for birds that migrate north each spring from South America. An offshore oil rig in Mobile Bay glimmers in the distance.*

THE BOOT HEEL, THE BAY, AND THE GULF SHORE

Just northeast of Mobile, the fecund Mobile delta has evolved where the Mobile and Tensaw rivers meet. Ten miles wide, the delta supports a rich variety of life ranging from black bears to alligators. This 185,000-acre area, called the **Mobile–Tensaw River Bottomlands❖,** was designated a national natural landmark in 1974 and is one of the largest deltas in the nation. Its swamps and marshes are best seen by boat. (Boat tours are available in the town of Saraland.)

Mobile Bay, which was added to the National Estuarine Reserve Program in 1995, is a drowned river delta about 35 miles long, 10 miles wide, and 10 to 12 feet deep. Along its edges, hummocks of longleaf pines struggle to make headway in spartina and juncus grass marshes, where mussels attached to the grasses help keep the marshes from eroding. The shellfish also filter a gallon of seawater per hour while feeding, fertilize marshes with their waste, and are food for crabs, birds, and mammals such as otters. All the flora and fauna within the marshlands are united in an exceedingly fertile web of life. Where marshes give way to narrow beaches, trembling fronds of sea oats catch the sunlight glittering on Mobile Bay. Dark cormorants wing

146

LEFT: *Tall pines rise above mounds of Florida rosemary, which help anchor Dauphin Island dunes. The short needlelike leaves of rosemary protect the plant by conserving moisture.*

TOP RIGHT: *Happy near both fresh and salt water, the dramatic yellow-crowned night heron is commonly seen during the day near such places as Dauphin Island's swamp pond.*

BOTTOM RIGHT: *A great egret hunts in shallow coastal waters; it snakes out its long neck like a whip to stab its aquatic prey, which ranges from fish to frogs.*

hurriedly above. Pelicans plane just inches above the bay, their necks tucked against their bodies in a perfect flying wedge, their movements smooth, their faces seemingly smug.

As travelers move south, French names on shops and street signs remind them that **Dauphin Island,** Alabama's largest Gulf Coast barrier island, was the capital of France's Louisiana Territory in the early 1700s. Sitting just offshore, the island is also the first landfall many migratory birds reach after an exhausting 500-to-600-mile flight from Central and South America over the Gulf of Mexico. As a result, it is one of the best birding areas in the Southeast.

Dauphin Island, which lies south of Mobile via Interstate 10 west and the Route 193 bridge, retains a sleepy charm despite crowds of vacation homes. More important, it encompasses a world-class bird refuge run by the Audubon Society. **Dauphin Island Bird Sanctuary❖,** on the east side of the island, is the best place to see Dauphin's nearly 350 bird species. The 164-acre preserve attracts a wide variety of avian species—from woodland to wetland—because its habitats include maritime forest, marsh, dunes and beach, swamp, and a lake. Although traveling the entire loop trail requires only a mile-plus of walking, ob-

147

ABOVE: *Not at all fussy about habitat, cardinals range from forest edges to sand scrub barrier islands such as Dauphin.*

RIGHT: *Like other beaches on the Gulf Coast, Bon Secour's white sands are colonized first by grasses.*

BELOW: *A red-breasted nuthatch clings to a tree trunk. Pines supply this short-tailed canopy dweller with its main winter forage, conifer seeds.*

serving all that the habitats contain can take a number of pleasurable hours.

Tall pines form a thin canopy above magnolias, live oak, tupelo, and yaupon in the maritime forest, where saw palmetto and conradina, with its purple flowers, dwell closer to the forest floor. Small flocks of cedar waxwings, uttering their telltale buzzing calls, flit among the high tops of the pines while mourning doves, cardinals, nuthatches, and yellow-rumped warblers busy themselves on lower branches. At Gaillard Lake, egrets rest in a bush above the water, a heron picks at unseen morsels in the mud, and a pig frog adds its throaty *blat* to the sounds of the surrounding forest.

At the edge of the dunes, prickly-pear cactus, sassafras, sumac, and oaks coexist in happy confusion. This area, where habitats overlap, attracts squirrels and brown thrashers, red-headed woodpeckers, and a prothonotary warbler with its brilliant orange-gold head and breast. A small tan lizard strikes, then works vigorously to swallow the captured dragonfly and its fan of protruding wings.

Farther out on the dunes, oversize pillows of scrub oak catch the light on their leathery leaves, and the papery yellow flowers of rock roses nestle in the sand. Rosemary and other herbs attract monarch and sulphur butterflies. When the sun and the incessant clamor of the mockingbirds become too overbearing, the overlook in the sanctuary's swamp provides welcome escape for hot and tired travelers. There dark waters conceal alligators and turtles,

and a sudden sound scares off a shy black-crowned night heron.

At the eastern tip of the island is **Dauphin Island Sea Lab❖,** established through the efforts of 22 Alabama colleges and universities. In addition to its Marsh and Dune Boardwalk, Sea Lab offers exhibits and classes on the importance of the Mobile Bay estuarine system, one of the largest in the United States.

Seen from the ferry that connects Dauphin Island with **Fort Morgan❖** on the mainland to the east, the squall-darkened waters of Mobile Bay are busy with commerce. Big shrimp trawlers plow majestically through the mouth of the bay like imperious dowagers holding up voluminous skirts on a dark, rainy day. Oil rigs perch on tall steel stilts above Gulf waters. Below, the bay and Gulf teem with sea life: red snapper, sheepshead, southern flounder, spot, sea urchin, mullet, calico crab, oyster, catfish, shrimp—hundreds of species fill every niche in the marine habitat.

On the east side of Mobile Bay, **Bon Secour National Wildlife Refuge❖** occupies bits and pieces of forest and shore along Route 180—precious wild space on the developed Gulf Coast. (The refuge office is about eight miles west of Gulf Shores at Mile Marker 13 on Route 180. To reach the beach by car, turn south at Mile Marker 12 off Route 180 on Mobile Street.) French for "safe harbor," Bon Secour encompasses maritime forest, beaches, dunes, marshes, lakes, lagoons, and the waters of the Gulf. At the height of the migration season, as many as two million birds visit Bon Secour at a time: mergansers, laughing gulls, cormorants, pelicans, terns, dowitchers, ruddy turnstones, lots of loons in the winter, and hundreds of other species.

Along the refuge's Pine Beach Trail, an accompanying trail guide helps identify live oaks, coral bean, purple beautyberry, feathery dog fennel, spicy-scented red bay, and other flora. Flanking the trail are a 40-acre freshwater lake and a lagoon where herons and egrets work the shoreline. The path ends at the beach, home to the endangered Alabama beach mouse, fiddler crabs, ruddy turnstones flipping over clamshells in search of food, a hermit crab wearing a whelk shell, and lines of cormorants and pelicans.

The one-mile Jeff Friend Trail, which begins at Mile Marker 15, provides a relaxed meander through a carpet of saw palmetto and ferns beneath tall pines, water oaks and live oaks, magnolias, and wax myrtles. An open, sandy area next to a lagoon is a good place to spot forest birds, edge birds, and waterbirds. Visitors can also see the refuge by water, on the Gulf or a lake. The focus at nearby **Gulf State Park** is more recreational than natural, but it too has a good beach.

To explore an estuary, take Route 98 west from Foley to **Weeks Bay National Estuarine Research Reserve✧,** just after the Fish River Bridge. The Environmental Protection Agency chose the Weeks Bay estuary to demonstrate how to protect wetlands, and it is one of the country's few interpreted estuarine reserves. The Weeks Bay visitor center provides exhibits and information on the workings and importance of estuaries. From the back door of the visitor center, a boardwalk winds out to Weeks Bay, where classic estuarine bottomlands are green with chain ferns and tall cinnamon ferns, sapsuckers drill holes in magnolias, and the long-spurred pink blossoms of wild azaleas light the dim forest. At the edge of the bay, marsh grasses grow thick, and boat-tailed grackles and red-winged blackbirds vie for position as terns wheel and dive over the water beyond. Along a wilder trail that also begins at the visitor center, informational markers explain what these wet woods have to offer. The trail ends at Weeks Bay itself, which is best experienced from the water.

Route 98 east leads toward Gulf Islands National Seashore and the incredible natural abundance of coastal Florida.

ABOVE: *Tiny fiddler crabs scuttle sideways, swarming the edges of brackish water. They eat decaying vegetation—and sometimes each other.*

151

FLORIDA

PART FOUR

FLORIDA

Florida is naturally extravagant. From tropical mahoganies to centuries-old cypress swamps, from American crocodiles and birds seen nowhere else in the nation to the endangered and elusive Florida panther, natural Florida amazes and delights. Although northern Florida harbors plants and animals that share characteristics with those of the Appalachians, southern Florida and the Keys sustain the only taste of the tropics in the continental United States. Florida's biological diversity encompasses such a broad range of habitats that it claims more tree species than any other state. Despite the rush of people and development to its warm beaches and forgiving climate, the state still contains more protected natural acreage than anywhere else in the eastern half of the country.

Only about 300 feet at its highest point, Florida barely rises above the waters that surround it: the Atlantic Ocean on the east, the Gulf of Mexico along the panhandle and west, and just south of the Keys, the Straits of Florida, which separate the state from Cuba by fewer than a hundred miles. Often the difference between land and water is subtle, one shading into the other imperceptibly at barrier islands and coastal salt marshes or in the low fringe of the largest mangrove swamps in the world.

Underlain with porous limestone, the northern part of the state is pitted with 3,000 sinkhole lakes. The southern tip is covered by hundreds of square miles of the extraordinary Everglades—saw-grass prairies that rise from glittering watery marl, striped here and there by ancient cypress strands. Only at its northern border, where it adjoins Georgia and Alabama, does Florida make a firm land connection with the rest of the continent.

In the Paleozoic era, Florida was part of Africa, but as continental plates drifted and shifted, it joined North America. Since then, coastlines have been in flux. During ice ages, when oceans were hundreds of feet lower, the Gulf of Mexico, for instance, lapped a shore dozens of miles to the west of Florida's present-day western shore. When the great glaciers

PRECEDING PAGES: *In Everglades National Park a brown pelican takes a break from fishing to perch on a channel marker in Florida Bay.*

melted and flooded the coasts, South Florida shrank, sometimes disappearing completely beneath the encroaching seas.

Today, although soils are often thin and sandy, lush vegetation fills every available niche thanks to warm year-round temperatures and nearly 60 inches of annual rain, most of it from summer storms. Glittering bays and barrier islands drenched in sun can be suddenly slashed by furious rains and world-class lightning—Florida is the lightning capital of the country. Long before settlement, natural fires, especially in the panhandle's longleaf pine forests, cleared underbrush and kept the ecosystem diversified and healthy.

Where northern Florida soils are richer, hardwood forests of magnolias, beeches, and oaks thrive. Where lowlands fill with water, cypress swamps dominate. Along parts of the coast and on the high central ridges, the terrain is dry and sandy. There shiny mounds of scrub oak and Florida rosemary reign in scrub communities that have waxed and waned for millennia. The vast sweep of the Everglades and exotic, sensuous tropical forests describe the landscape of southern Florida. Coral-island Keys are flanked by perhaps the nation's most gorgeous habitats: coral reefs colored with a rainbow of fish, corals, and other tropical marine life.

When Spanish explorer Juan Ponce de León came seeking the fountain of youth in 1513, he named the territory for the holiday on which he arrived: *Pascua Florida*—Feast of Flowers, appropriately enough. For the next 200 years, Europeans, Native Americans, and Americans fought for possession of this lush peninsula, where sovereignty passed consecutively from Spain to England to Spain and finally to the United States in 1819.

Viewed from the jumble of modern highways, much of today's Florida looks as though it has been bought and sold a few times. Visitors have difficulty imagining that the ibis and herons flying overhead live anywhere but golf courses, orange groves, or the manicured lawns of flamingo-pink housing developments. But natural Florida still claims pockets of breathtaking beauty. Ponce de León's serendipitously named Feast of Flowers thrives in the blooming wire-grass gardens beneath the longleaf pines of Apalachicola or Blackwater River national forests. And in the wet meadows of Paynes Prairie, where alligators sun themselves amid an ever-changing display of native flowers. And along the cypress strands of the Fakahatchee, home to more types of orchids than anywhere else in America. And in the Florida Straits, where corals and tropical fish create underwater gardens of unimaginable beauty.

NORTHERN FLORIDA:
SUGAR SAND BEACHES AND BLACK-WATER RIVERS

lthough few out-of-state visitors know the nontropical "other Florida," an abundance of relatively undiscovered natural beauty awaits those who tarry in the panhandle and the northern Florida peninsula. All three of the state's national forests—Apalachicola, Ocala, and Osceola—lie in the north, which also boasts Florida's highest point, only waterfall, and sole cavern. The region is home to most of the state's major rivers and contains its greatest concentration of bubbling crystal springs. Here the sugary white sands of Gulf Coast beaches dazzle the eye, and sunny pine forests awaken vestigial memories of nature's most graceful parkland.

Where the panhandle abuts neighboring Georgia and Alabama, the longleaf pine dominates the landscape and regional ecology. Blackwater River State Forest, in fact, protects more longleaf pine than any other site in the nation. Characterized by tufted whorls of wire grass, bogs teeming with carnivorous plants, sprays of wildflowers, and lofty old-growth trees, the longleaf habitat is also the only home of the red-cockaded woodpecker, an endangered bird whose greatest numbers are now found in Apalachicola National Forest.

As the panhandle edges into the Gulf of Mexico, broad white sand beaches slope gently down to brilliant blue waters. Just offshore, a necklace of barrier islands protects the mainland from devastating hurricane-force storms that periodically rip across the Gulf. Shining

LEFT: *At Saint Joseph Peninsula State Park, the setting sun tints the fine sands of one of the panhandle's least-crowded beaches. The park also encompasses some of the most pristine sand-scrub habitat in the nation.*

mounds of oak and rosemary as well as sand skinks and gopher tortoises make these islands superb examples of a flourishing sand-scrub ecosystem.

Some of the most pristine black-water rivers in the country etch the state's northern pinelands. Bubbling up from underground springs in Florida's limesink region or flowing from swamps like the great Okefenokee, rivers such as the Blackwater, Wakulla, Saint Johns, Steinhatchee, and Suwannee meander slowly to the coast. As they near the Gulf, they spread their watery wealth in broad salt marshes that attract myriad waterfowl to beds overflowing with shellfish, crabs, and fingerling fish. Florida's Big Bend, where the panhandle curves south into the peninsula, is one of the state's least populated areas and encompasses some of its most fecund marshes.

Between the pine flatwoods occupying the state's upland sandy ground and the cypress swamps filling the low, wet spots, subtropical hardwood forests shelter an astoundingly rich diversity of plants and wildlife. In lush Ocala National Forest, limpid springs form turquoise pools fringed with sabal palms and bay trees, black bears—at the southernmost extension of their range—bed down in titi thickets, and elegant swallow-tailed kites soar effortlessly above. Near Gainesville, wet prairies showcase the seasons' ever-changing palette of wildflower color, and alligators eye seemingly oblivious high-stepping herons. On higher ground nearby, reintroduced bison roam.

The journey through northern Florida begins at the western edge of the panhandle, travels east through longleaf and black-water country, and then heads south through the Big Bend toward the west coast. Turning northeast, the route then visits the state's north-central prairies and forests and culminates at the marshes and beaches of Florida's northern Atlantic coast.

THE PANHANDLE

Less than five miles offshore in the Gulf of Mexico, a string of long, narrow barrier islands stretch from the Mississippi coast east along the Florida panhandle. These islands begin as sediment, carried by coastal rivers and then deposited along the Gulf floor by westward currents and wave action. Eventually, some deposits grow into sizable sandbars, plants colonize them, and barrier islands are born. These strips of land, however,

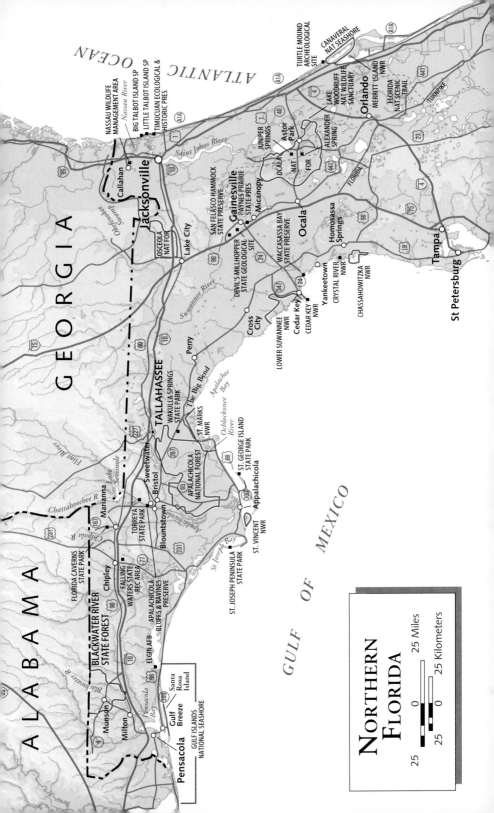

remain malleable: Currents constantly shape and remold them, and a fickle hurricane can instantly change their topography.

A classic barrier island ecosystem thrives at the Florida unit of **Gulf Islands National Seashore❖,** south of Pensacola. Begin with a visit to the seashore headquarters and visitor center in the **Naval Live Oaks** area near Gulf Breeze, across the Pensacola Bay Bridge (Route 98). In perhaps the federal government's first effort at resource conservation, this site was purchased in 1828 to preserve the region's live oaks, whose dense and decay-resistant wood was widely used in ship construction. From the visitor center a short walk passes through a still-magnificent stand of Spanish moss–draped live oaks growing among magnolias, hickories, cedars, and pines. Although the forest crowds the shore of Santa Rosa Sound, overlooks afford views of shiny mullet leaping from bay waters and brown pelicans fishing for lunch. Mergansers float past in pairs, and a lone loon points its beak at the sky. Below the surface, beds of sea grass protect redfish, speckled and white trout, crabs, oysters, and shrimp.

ABOVE: *Found at Gulf Islands National Seashore, glades morning glory lives only in the Southeast and flowers all year.*
LEFT: *Scrubland on the Gulf Islands features slash pines, grasses, and shrubs, including gallberry, wax myrtle, and greenbrier.*

Take Route 399 toward Pensacola Beach on **Santa Rosa Island** and turn west to the Fort Pickens unit of the national seashore. Although there is a daunting gauntlet of development on Santa Rosa Island, at the entrance to the Fort Pickens area the clutter vanishes. Beyond, the island looks much as it did when the Spanish first explored this pristine coastline in the 1500s. The Blackbird-Marsh Nature Trail loops around ponds and along the bay side of the island, which features the lavender-pink blooms of low, shrubby conradina and yaupon hollies loaded with red berries. A brown thrasher scours the white sand below. Palmetto and gallberry thickets surround ponds clogged with cattails and saw grass, where frogs sound their presence like small motors. Above, in tall slash pines, blue herons shuffle on their nests, and among the contorted limbs of a nearby live oak flit yellow-rumped warblers.

ABOVE: *Near Fort Pickens on Santa Rosa Island, the white, sugar-fine sand beaches support sea oats, sea rocket, and beach elder and are home to sandpipers, terns, laughing gulls, and other shorebirds.*

On the other side of the island, trails lead over low dunes toward the Gulf of Mexico. Among the sun-dazzled dunes nestle broad clumps of shiny-leaved scrub oak, pruned low by salt spray and wind. Grouped in tight mounds, Florida rosemary forms a light green counterpoint to the darker oaks. Evening primrose and yellow rock rose dot the blinding white sands, and mockingbirds maintain a constant chatter. Spires of sea oats, their seed heads fluttering in fragile beauty, anchor the last line of dunes before the beach.

Where the broad sweep of the beach meets the mild waters of the Gulf, a tide line ripples with shells and small clear jellyfish. Clouds of laughing gulls rise, hover above the sand, settle, then rise again. Willets hurry along the tide line, stopping frequently to probe the sand for tasty morsels. Small flocks of sanderlings dart as one out to the waterline, then scurry back en masse. As they plummet into the sun-slicked sea, terns flick long swallowtails. Rolling in again and again, the sound of the surf turns the scene into a waking dream.

To the west, occupying a vast, largely undeveloped expanse between Route 98 and I-10, **Eglin Air Force Base** encompasses one of the state's most diverse natural areas. Here terrain ranging from coastal barrier islands to high sand hills supports colonies of red-cockaded woodpeckers and numerous other species, old-growth longleaf pines near Roberts Pond, and more than 120 species of native reptiles and amphibians. Camping is allowed, and some 55 miles of canoe trails beckon paddlers. Permits are required for all visits and hunting and fishing. (They are available on a walk-in basis at the Natural Resources branch of the base, at the Jackson Guards sign off Route 85N in Niceville.)

From Pensacola, take Route 90 northeast through the charming historic town of Milton, and then Route 191 north to Munson and headquarters for the **Blackwater River State Forest❖,** Florida's largest. Combined with the **Conecuh National Forest** (see chapter 3) just across the border in Alabama, the Blackwater River forest forms the largest longleaf-pine ecosystem left in the world. These fire-dependent forests are now maintained by controlled burns.

The two most accessible areas of the forest are the **Krul Recreation Area** and **Bear Lake,** both home to alligators and waterbirds. The trail around Bear Lake presents a range of Blackwater River's singular features. Past the picnic area, an airy longleaf forest slopes gently up from the trail. Beneath the tall well-spaced pines—home to about 70 endangered red-cockaded woodpeckers—is a bed of wire grass dotted with bright spots of yellow star grass, white daisies, and numerous other flowers.

Longleaf pine saplings also appear among the wire grass clumps. To survive the lightning-caused fires that regularly swept the southeastern coastal plains, longleaf pines developed a clever plan. For the first four to ten years of life, longleaf saplings—which in their grasslike stage resemble the swirls of wire grass that surround them—stay low, out of the range of high, hot-burning fires. Low-intensity fires are less threatening because the trees' long needles protect a thick waxcovered core of new growth. In addition, during their early years longleaf pines concentrate their energies underground, developing deep, tenacious roots. When their roots are long and strong enough, the saplings race for the sky, growing like proverbial beanstalks to get above fire height before the arrival of the next conflagration.

Closer to the lake, where the land is low and the water table high, carnivorous plants that grow in boggy, nutrient-poor soils have had to develop a taste for insects to survive. Cheery yellow butterworts trap their prey in the greasy film that coats their shiny, low-growing leaves. Jewel-like pink sundews glitter with sticky liquids that serve the same purpose. Exotic-looking pitcher plants, the stars of this strange floral world, raise foot-high trumpet-shaped yellow leaves containing wells of liquid that attract and then digest insects; above, the huge yellow chandeliers of their flowers droop from stalks. Poking up among the trumpets are rarer red pitcher plants and their gaudy flowers. Farther along the trail, where a stream feeds into the lake, magnolias, red bays, and other hardwoods line the water. Scented white orchids and blue butterworts rise from the soft sphagnum peat moss. At the far end of the lake, beavers have created ponds where cormorants and great blue herons fish.

Weaving through the state forest are four main waterways: the Blackwater River and Coldwater, Juniper, and Sweetwater creeks. In the past, Creek, Choctaw, and Yuchi peoples all lived or traveled along these riverbanks, which were called Okalusa—"black water"— even then. Today the Blackwater is one of the world's last undisturbed sand-bottom rivers, and its side streams are even more pristine. Although it looks black, the river water is among the purest in the nation. Tannins from forest plants stain the water dark, disguising the white sand of the riverbed.

Just off Route 191 are lovely views of Juniper Creek and banks lined with Atlantic white cedars. Coldwater Creek, to the west off Route 4, is edged with titi and tall, lustrous-leaved blueberries against a backdrop of Atlantic white cedars and red maples. Where the creek curves, tall bald cypresses shade the water. Oxbow lakes and picture-pretty sand beaches lie along the creek, and green herons wing above water populated by bream, bass, and catfish. Adventures Unlimited and other outfitters are located near Milton.

Take Interstate 10 about 75 miles east to Chipley and then Route 77A south to **Falling Waters State Recreation Area❖,** which preserves prime examples of Florida's limesink region. Here boardwalks skirt a number of deep funnel-shaped holes, or "sinks," which form when

---

RIGHT: *At Blackwater River State Park, the river appears inky and tea-colored. Although stained by tannins that leach from forest trees, the waters flow over white sand bottoms and are famous for their purity.*

weak acids from rainwater mix with plant material and then percolate through the porous underlying limestone. The acids eat away at the stone, eventually eroding the bottom. Falling Waters Sink is 100 feet deep and 20 feet wide. A stream running into the sink cascades over a long waterfall and disappears—no one knows exactly where.

ABOVE: *White spider lilies light up the swamp edges in the Apalachicola National Forest.*

In the moist woods surrounding the sinkhole area, mockernut hickories, farkleberry, white oaks, and magnolias share space with beech trees whose smooth gray bark is scarred with heart-shaped declarations of love. In autumn, the brilliant reds of sweet gum set the woods ablaze; in spring, the long-throated pink flowers of wild azaleas color the landscape. Yucca and goldenrod are companions in the open areas above the sinkholes, and the highest, driest parts of the park belong to longleaf pines above a wire-grass understory studded with violets.

An even more dramatic example of the Southeast's limestone karst topography lies just to the east in **Florida Caverns State Park❖** (take I-10 east to Marianna and then Route 166 three miles north). The state's only cave system open for public tours, the cavern was discovered in 1937 when a falling tree revealed a sinkhole into the cave. Where water bubbles up from the Chipola River to form pools, blind albino cave salamanders and crayfish feed on isopods. The salamanders navigate with extra-sensitive nerve endings, and the crayfish employ unusually long antennae.

On the ceiling, hollow soda-straw formations follow cracks where surface water has leaked through the rock. Stalactites, stalagmites, and columns stand sentinel in the caverns, and graceful stone drapes and pipe-organ formations decorate the walls. Resembling the edge of a giant fluted clamshell, rimstone holds shimmering pools of water. Where the ceiling is low, visitors can discern the ancient chambered nautiluses, sea urchins, and other fossils that were embedded in a sea bottom eons ago and are now preserved in the park's underlying limestone.

Above ground, wildflowers dapple the park each spring. Extravagant white Atamasco lilies grow in clusters among the rocks, and open areas are brilliant with rose-purple phlox and bright yellow butterweed. Red-and-gold native columbine, delicate white rue anemone, early-blooming bloodroot, and lace-leaf squirrel corn dot the woods. Many of these plants are native to the Appalachian Mountains, but when ice-age glaciers pushed south, these species migrated ahead of the walls of ice. Beavers and rare Barbour's map turtles, found only in the adjacent Chipola River and in the Apalachicola River, live here as well.

THE BIG BEND REGION

A quiet Eden that offers a truly unspoiled view of northern Florida awaits visitors at **Torreya State Park❖,** one of the most remote and natural in the Florida system. (Take Route 12 south from I-10 through Greensboro to C-1641 northwest to the park.) Here shady pine and hardwood forests follow the contours of the rugged ravines that etch the park. This singular incised landscape sustains the torreya tree and the Florida yew, plants found nowhere else in the world. Hiking trails ramble over hill and vale, here passing a soaring loblolly pine grove, there winding along a small stream.

ABOVE: *The spring-blooming white Atamascos are popularly called Easter lilies.*

The Apalachicola River is responsible for most of Torreya's highlights, particularly its soaring bluffs, which are among the highest points in the state and a perfect setting for shedding the stresses of daily life. Flowing quietly below the bluffs, the broad brown river is the domain of cormorants and other waterbirds. A red-shouldered hawk glides overhead, and a breeze ruffles the lacy, creamy white flower caps of nearby oakleaf hydrangeas.

OVERLEAF: *In the Nature Conservancy's Apalachicola Bluffs and Ravines Preserve, the sedimentary rocks of Alum Bluff rise above the dark Apalachicola River as it twists south through Florida's highlands.*

In the 1800s, the Apalachicola, which begins at Lake Seminole where the Flint and Chattahoochee rivers meet on the Georgia border, was one of the South's main transportation routes, conveying cotton and other raw materials from Alabama and Georgia to the Gulf of Mexico. Still part of the inland waterway, the river also carried treasures of another sort—seeds from the Appalachians that washed down from the highlands and found purchase in Torreya's cool, shaded ravines. Relicts from the last ice age—baneberry, hound's-tongue, and leatherwood, which retreated south ahead of the glaciers—still thrive in the cool gorges.

ABOVE: *In Apalachicola's boggy, infertile soil, yellow trumpet pitchers grow among native wire grasses.*

The park is also the last refuge of the highly endangered torreya tree, *Torreya taxifolia,* named for American botanist John Torrey. A midsize tree in the yew family, the Florida torreya is one of only a handful of species in its genus. Researchers believe that the genus was widespread during the Tertiary Period and that the remaining species—now found in California, Japan, and China—are far-flung relicts of the time when most of the world's land mass was one supercontinent, Gondwanaland. In Florida, the torreya is an understory tree that grows along ravine slopes near the Apalachicola River. Hugging the banks of Rock Creek, a small torreya glistens in the sun, its pointed green needles so shiny that they seem freshly waxed. Unfortunately, this bright little tree will probably never reach to its potential height of 40 to 60 feet. The torreya was heavily logged in the 1800s for its rot-resistant wood, and the concurrent destruction of its habitat posed a dangerous strain for the species. Pathogens that a healthy population of torreya could resist are killing the species today as scientists struggle to understand and halt the decline.

Although the torreya is no longer abundant, the woods are filled with luminous white clumps of Atamasco lilies shaded by amethyst-hued redbud trees. Beeches and huge magnolias occupy the moist lower slopes of the ravines where trillium and wild blue phlox bloom. In the towering pines on the higher, drier slopes, a red-bellied woodpecker clings to the side of a tree while an unseen owl hoots nearby. Still as stones, tiny tree frogs are hard to spot, but the site is so rife with amphibians and reptiles that Torreya State Park is known as a "herp hot spot." Occasionally, the peace is broken by the roar of enormous man-made birds—camouflage-colored bombers from nearby Elgin Air Force Base.

Head south from the park on County Road 270 (Dr. Martin Luther King Jr. Road), and after Sweetwater—just past the gas pipeline—look for signs announcing **Apalachicola Bluffs and Ravines Preserve❖.** This Nature Conservancy area protects the largest exposed geologic formation in the panhandle, Alum Bluff, and remarkable wildlife diversity. A three-mile trail that starts beyond the office shows off the steep bluffs and ravines.

ABOVE: *Pitcher plants trap insects in their hollow tubular leaves, where enzymes speed digestion.*

Nine miles south of Bristol begins the **Apalachee Savannahs Scenic Byway,** which winds south along Route 12 and onto Routes 379 and 65. The byway crosses **Apalachicola National Forest❖,** at more than half a million acres the largest national forest in Florida and home of the largest population of endangered red-cockaded woodpeckers in the United States. From the bayheads—low, wet areas crowded with magnolias and red bays—that edge swamps of cypress and titi to the airy stands of longleaf pine that tower over savannas carpeted with wildflowers and wire grass, the byway presents an overall view of the forest.

In the past, national forests have served primarily as suppliers of wood products; lumber companies work the sites and sell the stock. The team at Apalachicola is pursuing a different goal by actively managing the forest, especially the western half, to protect the endangered red-cockaded woodpecker and its specialized longleaf pine habitat. The red-cockaded is the only woodpecker that is able to excavate a cavity in old-growth longleaf pine. The bird prefers mature trees because they are more likely to have red-heart disease, which softens the core and makes the trunk easier to excavate.

Northern Florida

TOP RIGHT: *Among the hundreds of native plant species that grow in Apalachicola National Forest—including 44 listed as rare and sensitive—is toothache grass, which numbs the mouth when chewed.*

BOTTOM RIGHT: *Flames destroyed the lower original needles on this longleaf pine seedling. Because it was protected by a thick, fire-resistant waxy "candle," new growth has burst forth, fresh and healthy.*

FAR RIGHT: *Longleaf pines rise from a wire-grass prairie studded with wildflowers—yellow trumpets, meadow beauties, and orchids. This airy ecosystem once dominated the Southeast's coastal plain.*

To maintain stands of mature longleaf, managers must burn the forest regularly. The longleaf seedling needs plenty of sun to flourish, and without fire, magnolias and other leafy hardwoods shade it out. Before settlement, lightning-caused fires cleaned out hardwoods and thickets clogged with palmetto and kept gallberry shrubs at bay while the fire-dependent longleaf pine merely shed its burnt layers and rose phoenixlike from its own ashes. These days the Forest Service sets and controls the fires that enable this quintessentially southeastern ecosystem to thrive.

Fire also maintains the wire-grass prairie that dominates the understory of the longleaf pine forest. Periodic ranger-set conflagrations—especially roaring, searing summer fires like ones that occur naturally—insure that fire-tolerant wire grass produces viable seeds and fresh clumps. Among the green mops of wire grass grow a fascinating array of wildflowers, many of them rare: blue-eyed grass, violas, irislike xyris, false indigo, lilies, and orchids. Where the longleaf–wire-grass system dips to low points, boggy savannas are bright with banks of yellow and white pitcher plants, sundews, blue and yellow butterworts, and other carnivorous plants.

Wildlife at Apalachicola is equally intriguing. Residents include 21 species of wood warblers, 9 species of bats, rabbits, squirrels, foxes,

bobcat, and deer—as well as many types of salamanders, tree frogs, turtles, tortoises, terrapins, and snakes (upland and water). The most unusual inhabitants are the red-cockaded woodpeckers, which construct their nests about 26 feet above the base of a longleaf. Because the birds spend most of their day foraging, their young are exposed to such predators as rat snakes, which can wriggle up the tallest tree and raid a hole. To protect their offspring, the woodpeckers have developed a primitive security system. Every day they peck at the pine, creating resin wells to maintain a steady flow of sticky sap, a gummy sludge that acts as an effective deterrent to snakes. (Sap buildup also identifies an active red-cockaded woodpecker tree, making the longleaf shine like a white candle.) After the red-cockadeds abandon the nest, the hole is often colonized by red-bellied woodpeckers, bluebirds, southern flying squirrels, or red rat snakes.

On the ground, the endangered gopher tortoise also has a better chance of survival when the wire-grass prairies are protected. The long tunnels that these tortoises dig in the open sandy soils become veritable apartment complexes shared with 120 other species (not all at the same time), including endangered eastern indigo snakes. Although the savannas along the scenic byway are perhaps the most interesting areas of Apalachicola National Forest, intrepid canoeists may

173

Red Cockaded Woodpecker
Picus Querellus.

Males 1, Female 2.

Drawn from Nature by J.J. Audubon
Louisiana July 29th 1821.

174

want to consider a trip through the New River Wilderness in the southwest section; Wright and Camel lakes west of the Ochlockonee River are wooded and include campgrounds.

From Route 65, backtrack west along Route 98 toward the city of Apalachicola; just before the John Gorrie Memorial Bridge, take Route G1A south to the bridge and causeway to Saint George Island and **Saint George Island State Park❖** at the eastern end. Black skimmers, least terns, and other shorebirds make regular appearances at this barrier island, and snowy plover and gray kingbirds nest here. Trails and boardwalks allow visitors to explore a sizable portion of the park, which also boasts the largest number of nesting loggerhead turtles in the northern Gulf of Mexico.

West of historic Apalachicola, follow routes 30A and 30E to **Saint Joseph Peninsula State Park❖,** a thin fishhook of land that curves to enclose Saint Joseph Bay. The 14-mile-long peninsula, which would be a barrier island without its narrow land bridge to the mainland, protects one of the nation's oldest and most intact pine-scrub habitats. Tall, thin slash pines, live oaks, and sabal palms rise from the interior; scrub oak and Florida rosemary anchor rolling dunes edging the peninsula; and long pristine beaches sparkle beside the brilliant blue waters of the Gulf.

Although a classic pine-scrub habitat usually cycles no more than 50 years before fire wipes it clean, Saint Joe has been lucky. Somehow this extensive pine-scrub habitat has escaped both fire and major hurricanes for nearly 200 years. Except for the park's pleasant bayside cabins, marina, campground, and boardwalks to the beach, Saint Joe remains an isle of unusual natural tranquillity at the end of a line of burgeoning beachfront communities stretching east from Pensacola. In fact, the entire north end of the Saint Joe Peninsula has been designated a wilderness area.

Beginning in a natural archway of pines and shrubs draped with muscadine grape, the Bay Trail circles under the shade of venerable live oaks and magnolias. At bay's edge, yaupon holly, heavy with red-orange berries, attracts catbirds and warblers. Crowding the hollies are

---

LEFT: *When Audubon painted red-cockaded woodpeckers in the early 1800s, the birds were as plentiful as their longleaf pine habitat. Once the longleaf was logged off, the woodpeckers became endangered.*

At Saint Joseph Peninsula State Park, a blue crab (left), whose paddle-shaped back legs help it move in the water, makes a meal of a smaller fiddler crab. With its 14 miles of wide white beaches (right), this park has become a premier rest stop for hawks and butterflies on their annual migrations.

wax myrtles, whose blue-gray berries are coated with the substance used to make bayberry candles. Among the sea-washed marsh grasses thrives a world in miniature: Fiddler crabs scuttle in and out of their holes, winkles creep along marsh leaves, and shrimp wave spindly antennae in the shallow water. Saint Joe's bay side is tangled with secret hammocks as well as mini-marshes, where herons stalk and raccoons wash.

Because it is along a hawk migration route, the peninsula is one of the best places in Florida to see peregrine falcons, and spectacular waves of orange and black monarch butterflies migrate past as well. The sand-scrub area is a sun-bright puzzle of mounded scrub oak and Florida rosemary on a field of white sand. At first this low maze seems a monochrome, but closer inspection reveals numerous flowering plants, including rare endemics such as large-leaved jointweed, which puts on a red show, and a particular blazing star. Threatened sand skinks "swim" across the hot sand, leaving telltale serpentine trails. In autumn, deer feast on scrub oak acorns. Bobcat prey on a myriad of small mammals, including a beach mouse that is endangered, but not as a result of bobcat predation.

Topping 60 feet, Saint Joseph's dunes are among the tallest in the state, and Florida offers no finer beaches. On white sands stretching to the horizon beside startlingly clear blue waters, sandpipers, ruddy turnstones, sanderlings, gulls, and other shorebirds are more numerous than people.

Southeast of the peninsula, **Saint Vincent National Wildlife Refuge❖** is an undeveloped barrier island accessible only by private boat. Its diverse habitats provide sanctuary for many species, including

176

Many birds migrate through the Saint Vincent National Wildlife Refuge, including occasional raptors such as peregrine falcons (above left). Oystercatchers (above right) patrol the beaches of the uninhabited island, where sabal palms and pine trees line the shore (right).

a nesting population of endangered loggerhead turtles and endangered red wolves in a breeding program.

WAKULLA SPRINGS AND SAINT MARKS NATIONAL WILDLIFE REFUGES

Just east of Apalachicola National Forest and about 16 miles south of Tallahassee, **Wakulla Springs (Edward Ball) State Park❖** encompasses one of the world's largest and deepest freshwater springs. A private commercial venture until the state bought it in 1986, Wakulla, just off Route 267, also offers the park system's only resort accommodations—a large Civilian Conservation Corps–era 27-room lodge, built in 1937.

At Wakulla the river flows not from a collection of streams but from an enormous hole in the ground, where an average 400,000 gallons per minute gush from the source of the springs in the limestone bedrock below. When the water is clear, visibility extends about 120 feet down, and the springs drop even farther—to about 360 feet—where they angle back under the land. Professional diving teams doing research have found a watery cavern 16 stories high and have explored 6,000 feet of passages in this largest of U.S. freshwater springs. A tour along the river

in a glass-bottom boat is de rigueur, and canoes are available as well.

Not surprisingly, the abundant natural resources of this area have attracted humans for some 12,000 years, and wildlife probably frequented the springs even earlier. Researchers have found the remains of extinct giant sloths, giant armadillos, and camels at Wakulla and have removed three complete mastodon skeletons from the springs.

Diverse wildlife still inhabits the park's nearly 3,000 acres. In winter, thousands of wigeon, cormorants, pied-billed grebes, and wood ducks ply the waters of the Wakulla River. Male moorhens proclaim their territories with flamboyant fantail dances, and little blue herons stake out fishing areas while anhingas, perched on waterside shrubs, spread their dark, iridescent wings to dry. Ospreys and bald eagles roost near a yellow-crowned night heron trying unsuccessfully to shoo its overgrown youngster from the nest. In its search for a mate, a limpkin, a long-legged brown wading bird related to cranes and rails, cries all

---

OVERLEAF: *Saint Marks National Wildlife Refuge occupies 100,000 acres on Florida's Big Bend. Each year its marshes attract graceful wading birds (herons, egrets, ibis) as well as thousands of migrating waterfowl.*

night long. Found solely in Florida and a tiny part of Georgia and in the greatest numbers at Wakulla, limpkins eat apple snails and must stay near spring-fed rivers where the rare mollusks live.

Mullet, bass, carp, gar, and bluegill inhabit the river. Along shore-lines lush with wild rice, muscadine grape, and spider lilies, alligators and Suwannee cooter turtles (related to snapping turtles) emerge from waters edged with eelgrass to bask in the sun. Although the eelgrass is native, the Brazilian elodea is not. Park managers suspect that the elodea, which is clogging riverbanks, was a castoff from a home aquarium. They are investigating biological controls to remove the in-vader because herbicides could damage natural vegetation and get into the food chain.

White-tailed deer spring through the 1,500 acres of lush woodlands surrounding Wakulla, which includes huge state champion basswood, magnolia, beech, and sassafras trees amid the native hardwood and pine forests. Nature trails allow visitors to explore.

On its way to the Gulf, the first section of the ten-mile Wakulla River flows within the park; the last few miles cross **Saint Marks National Wildlife Refuge❖,** one of the oldest (1931) and best preserves in the national system. Located south of coastal Route 98 on Route 59, Saint Marks contains an excellent visitor center. Beyond lie 70,000 acres of salt marshes, hardwood swamps, pine flatwoods, and up-lands, as well as nearly 32,000 acres in Apalachee Bay, which lies in the Gulf of Mexico where Florida makes its Big Bend from the pan-handle to the southern peninsula.

Although the refuge is crowded with waterfowl during the winter, fall and spring are when the greatest numbers of different birds mi-grate through—nearly 300 species. The seven-mile wildlife drive from the visitor center to the historic Saint Marks lighthouse on the bay pro-vides a good overview of the refuge. Here life is seen on the horizon-tal. Pools, marshes, and pine flatwoods all seem oversize, expanding beyond view. Even the sky appears extraordinarily large.

Surveying its domain from a large dead tree, a bald eagle at Mound Pool One begins to harass a flotilla of black coots, which skitter hysteri-cally across the water. The eagle buzzes them again and again, seeming-ly for amusement. The noise brings great blue herons and great egrets to wing, inspiring them to seek more placid spots to fish. In an adjacent

ABOVE: *Widespread and abundant, white-tailed deer (left) wander the sultry marshes at Saint Marks. The flowers of* Sagittaria **lancifolia,** *a type of arrowhead (right), brighten the refuge's swampy waters.*

pool, pied grebes, shovelers, and a little blue heron keep a low profile. The dikes between pools make good trails, allowing visitors without boats to wander farther into the refuge's backwaters. Paths traverse the woods, where forest birds sing, and crisscross the refuge's Panacea Unit. The lighthouse levee is a good spot for seabirds. A long line of pilings provides perches for an equally long line of brown pelicans, cormorants, and laughing gulls, which gaze back at visitors.

After curving quietly through the Big Bend, two-lane Route 98 becomes bigger and busier at Perry. Here at the heart of Florida timber and cattle-ranching country, log trucks roar down the road and billboards advertise cowboy hats. Just beyond Cross City the road passes over the Suwannee River. Farther north, where I-10 crosses the Suwannee as it meanders down from the Okefenokee Swamp, a sign announces the river with a few musical notes to remind travelers of the Stephen Foster song. Foster was reportedly thinking of the Carolinas' Pee Dee River, but because the name was not euphonious, he took the Suwannee's name.

Although Foster never visited the river, he would have found the mouth of the Suwannee a good choice. Here a diverse ecosystem in

183

ABOVE: *At Manatee Springs State Park—named for the endangered manatees that sometimes appear here—the blue-green needles of bald cypresses edge crystalline spring waters flowing into the Suwannee River.*

the state's most pristine salt marshes is preserved within the **Lower Suwannee National Wildlife Refuge❖.** (From Route 98, take Route 24 west, then Route 347 north about 10 miles.) A walking trail from the office follows a boardwalk and includes an observation point overlooking the Suwanee River. In the Shell Mound area, two short trails give a good sense of this delta and estuarine area. The large mound of cast-off oyster shells is the remains of meals eaten by tribal people living along this coast hundreds of years ago.

Just to the south is **Cedar Key National Wildlife Refuge❖** (backtrack to Route 24, then proceed to the western end of the road). The picturesque resort town of Cedar Key draws visitors, and the town's environs attract the wildlife. Just off the mainland, small tropical islands (keys), marshes, and the sea form one of Florida's largest nesting areas. More than 50,000 birds—including cormorants, white ibis, brown pelicans, herons, and egrets—nest here each year, coexisting peacefully with a large population of poisonous cottonmouths. To protect these species, except for Cedar Key all islands and parts of the refuge are accessible only by boat, and only the beaches are open to the public.

Those restrictions hardly limit wildlife viewing, however. The bridges and road leading to Cedar Key pass pools thick with birds,

184

easily seen from a car pullout. Hundreds of red-billed skimmers float in a crush; dowitchers, sanderlings, and sandpipers crowd together by the dozens. On the town's high wooden pier, great blue herons and brown pelicans, from immature youngsters to portly males in breeding plumage, await handouts from local anglers while less supplicant relatives scour mudflats and marshes for food.

Between Cedar Key and Yankeetown to the south lies **Waccasassa Bay State Preserve❖,** 27 miles of marshy, largely undisturbed coastline designated a national natural landmark. Here hammocks, savannas, tidal creeks, tidal flats, and freshwater swamps are home to a rich mix of wildlife including black bears, manatees, shellfish, birds, and reptiles. South of Homosassa Springs, where Florida's west coast finally points straight south, **Chassahowitzka National Wildlife Refuge❖** preserves a similar habitat. Both areas are accessible only by boat.

About 15 miles north via Route 98/19, the **Crystal River National Wildlife Refuge❖** was set aside to protect the Florida manatee, and

today the warm waters in and around Kings Bay and Crystal River support Florida's greatest concentrations of these zeppelin-shaped mammals. Because manatees graze on coastal sea grasses and prefer relatively shallow water, their greatest threat is human water-related activities, especially boat propellers and well-meaning but disturbing swimmers. Endangered Florida manatees number approximately 2,000. Gentle and slow-moving, they are thought to have inspired the mermaid myth among sailors. Although Florida manatees are native to peninsular Florida, they have been found as far north as Rhode Island and as far west as Texas during summer migrations. They congregate in warm waters such as Crystal River in winter, which is the best time to see them. Boat rentals and tours are available in the town of Crystal River.

NORTH-CENTRAL FLORIDA

The southernmost—and only semitropical—national forest in the 50 states lies directly east of Ocala, a city better known for its horse farms. **Ocala National Forest❖** is the southern limit of the American black bear and a place of exquisite spring-fed pools. Except for the Suwannee River, north-central Florida's drainage system is wholly internal. The region's underlying limestone layers are a Swiss cheese of sinkholes and springs: Rain percolates into these spongy aquifers, and water bubbles up in pools, burbles for a while, then plunges back into the earth through sinkholes. Some of Florida's most pellucid azure springs rise in Ocala National Forest.

Alexander Springs Recreation Area❖, in the southeastern part of the forest south of Astor Park off Route 445, forms a small lake bordered on one side by a sand beach. The 77 million gallons of crystal-clear water flowing daily from the spring exit the lake by way of a small river that is a favorite of canoeists and kayakers. Looping past the springs, the Timucuan Trail visits four habitats: aquatic; bottomland with cypress and water oak; higher, drier oak hammock; and dry pine scrub. In general, Florida soils are quite sandy, and bedrock lies close to the surface because the land is relatively new. Lower spots, where water cannot readily percolate through the bedrock, tend to be swampy; in contrast, higher sand ridges, home to xeric species such as scrub oak and pine, drain quickly.

Unfolding its feathery blue-green needles amid clumps of cane, a swamp cypress hugs the shoreline. Yellow jessamine twines over the emerging leaves of red maples—a study in burgundy and yellow. A rain-polished redcedar trunk leans into the water, where water lilies, water poppies, and pickerelweed create a luxurious water garden. Nearby, archaeologists unearthed a clay pot with the remains of an aboriginal stew made from freshwater snails, mussels, gar, catfish, speckled perch, largemouth bass, turtle, bird, white-tailed deer—all spiced with sabal palm berries.

Otters, freshwater eels, and ospreys all live in Ocala National Forest, along with black bears, which are seldom seen because they

ABOVE: *A limpkin, a long-legged wader related to the crane, hunts along the shallow waters of Alexander Springs Creek.*

LEFT: *Alexander Springs is edged by lush subtropical vegetation—sweet bay magnolia, swamp laurel oak, and sabal palm.*

BELOW: *A protective mother raccoon and her young offspring forage at the edge of a stream at Alexander Springs.*

189

make their dens in almost impenetrable titi thickets. Also found within the forest's boundaries are fernlike coonties, members of the cycad family and the world's most primitive seed-producing plants. Native peoples and European-American settlers used their starchy roots so extensively that today coonties are protected plants. A sabal palm, the state tree, presses in upon a trail as woodpeckers work at prizing insects from its smooth gray bark. On the dry ridges, leathery scrub oak and holly glisten in a light rain.

About ten miles northwest off Route 40 lies **Juniper Springs❖,** one of the oldest national forest recreation areas in the East. Here a stone-walled pond, a quaint mill, and shredded-bark paths make the site less natural than Alexander Springs, but no less appealing. At the entrance rufous-sided towhees scrabble in the dirt, and pines and palms shade pathways edged with white violets and ferns. Swallowtail butterflies flit above, resplendent in their sophisticated black-tie plumage. From a footbridge the floor of **Fern Hammock Springs** is clearly visible, the water so crystalline that the shadows of turtles swimming at the surface are sharply delineated on the bottom of the pool. Also visible on the bottom are swirling sand vortexes through which spout 20 million gallons of water a day.

Canoe rentals are available for both Alexander and Juniper springs and their associated wilderness areas. The Salt Springs Trail, off Route 19, winds through hardwood hammock and bayheads to wetlands where alligators and wading birds dwell. Flanking Forest Road 79, the Lake Eaton Trail and Sinkhole highlight dry scrubland and an 80-foot sinkhole. In the area known as the Big Scrub is one of the best tracts of old-growth sand-pine scrub left in Florida. Near Ocala National Forest are **Rice Creek Sanctuary❖,** a privately owned hardwood hammock open to the public, and **Lake Woodruff National Wildlife Refuge❖,** which offers nearly 20,000 acres of streams, freshwater and timbered swamps, and open water best explored by boat or canoe.

Florida's first state sanctuary, **Paynes Prairie State Preserve❖,** is

RIGHT: *Northern Florida's diverse habitats ensure rich birdlife (clockwise from top left): Seaside sparrows prefer saltwater marshes; eastern kingbirds fearlessly defend their forest-edge territory; red-winged blackbirds sing from cattails in freshwater marshes; and purple gallinules, with their long yellow toes, cross swamps on floating plants.*

about 10 miles south of Gainesville off I-75. Take the exit for historic Micanopy and follow Route 441 about a mile north of town to the main entrance to the preserve, which looks like an open meadow from the interstate. The 20,000 acres here represent the best and largest of Florida's remaining wet prairies. Although the popular vision of the state—beaches, palm trees, and cypress swamps—does not usually encompass prairies, the broad sweep of grasses visible from the observation tower is prairie indeed—especially when bison wander past. Probably never as abundant here as on the Great Plains, bison lived in Florida until the early 1700s. Human population pressures caused their numbers to decline in the Southeast, and the animals at Paynes Prairie have been reintroduced. Not long ago coyotes arrived on their own, possibly filling the predator niche left by extirpated red wolves.

What the view from the observation tower does not reveal is the thin layer of water covering the feet of the lush vegetation, mostly maiden cane, rushes, cattails, and sedges. In this large "solution prairie," weak natural acids are slowly eroding the limestone bedrock, creating an ever-broadening low area where the water table lies at the land's surface.

Behind the observation tower, trails visit pine flatwoods, scrub sandhills, and mixed forest communities; but the best of the prairie lies

Wet meadows (left) and wooded hammocks at Paynes Prairie State Preserve yield great botanic diversity. Shrubby swamp mallows (above) bear flowers up to eight inches wide; trailing vines produce exotically fringed purple passionflowers (right).

near the preserve's North Rim Interpretive Center. In this northern section, cattle ranchers tried to drain the wet terrain by crisscrossing it with dikes, which preserve managers are now removing to restore the natural water flow. The alligators are unperturbed by the changes. As William Bartram wrote of resident alligators during his eighteenth-century travels: "They are so abundant that, if permitted by them, I could walk over any part of the basin and the river upon their heads, which slowly float and turn about like knotty chunks or logs of wood."

Although alligators are not quite as abundant today, a few of the several thousand at Paynes Prairie are always visible. Obvious too are the anhingas, great blue herons, egrets, and moorhens. Huge flocks of white ibis turn and bank, their wings fluttering like flowers in the wind. In late autumn, 10,000 sandhill cranes migrate through the preserve from their upper Midwest nesting grounds, and some 2,000 winter here, making Paynes Prairie the major wintering ground of the eastern sandhill. In addition, pairs of threatened Florida sandhill cranes live at the preserve year-round.

Starting in early spring, a succession of colorful wildflowers—including blue spiderwort, fat yellow thistles, purple-and-white toadflax, and on the forested hammock, pink phlox, yellow hawkweed, pink oxalis,

193

and wands of lacy green ferns—make Paynes Prairie a botanical wonder. Within protective sinkholes live sugarberry, soapberry, endangered buckthorns, and other rare plants.

Visitors can travel through time at **Devils Millhopper State Geological Site❖,** two miles northwest of Gainesville off Route 232. Descending to the bottom of an enormous 120-foot-deep 400-foot-wide sink-

ABOVE: *For protection, the viceroy butterfly (top) mimics the coloring of the unappetizing monarch. The bright orange longwing Gulf fritillary (bottom) often travels long distances over water.*

RIGHT: *Seen from above, a lush hardwood hammock at Paynes Prairie features tall live oaks hung with gray-green Spanish moss and sweetgum trees with deep green, starlike leaves.*

hole, stairways pass layers of stone revealing fossil shark teeth, marine shells, and remains of extinct animals from Florida's past. Along the way, natural hanging gardens festoon the rock walls, and numerous waterfalls and rivulets tumble to the stream at the bottom. These wet environs make good homes for salamanders and crayfish, as well as other water-loving animals.

Protected by the sinkhole from extremes of weather, a singular blend of plants—from southern Appalachian to semitropical—coexists at Devils Millhopper. (Local lore dubbed the sinkhole a funnel-shaped "hopper" leading to a devil's mill deep within the earth.) About two miles from Devils Millhopper is **San Felasco Hammock State Preserve❖,** which includes wildlife, rare plants, swamps, sinkholes, prehistoric sites, and one of Florida's best examples of a climax hardwood hammock.

Northeast of Lake City via Route 90, **Osceola National Forest❖** encompasses a mix of longleaf and slash pine forests, cedar and gum swamps, and bayheads. Ocean Pond, with its beaches and campsites, forms the recreational center of the forest and includes a hookup with the **Florida National**

In Osceola National Forest, alligators (above), cold-blooded reptiles that like a sun-warmed bank, cruise the murky swamps while sandhill cranes (below) stick to the shallower wetlands to do their stalking.

Scenic Trail❖, which ranges in segments from the panhandle to the southern part of the state near the Everglades. Because much of the terrain here is boggy, the Osceola section of the scenic trail contains 20 boardwalks.

The one-mile **Mount Carrie Wayside** along Route 90 provides an interpretive overview of the longleaf pine–wire-grass community. At the northern edge of the forest, **Pinhook Swamp** is contiguous with Georgia's Okefenokee, and the **Big Gum Swamp Wilderness** poses a daunting challenge to those intrepid enough to venture into a swampy, trackless wetland where white lotuses glow on muddy ponds like diamonds in a coal bin. Alligators and black bears, sandhill cranes and wild turkeys, endangered gopher tortoises and red-cockaded woodpeckers are just a few of the wildlife species that inhabit the forest.

EAST COAST

Just south of the Georgia border, Route A1A leads northeast above Jacksonville. Near Callahan, the **Nassau Wildlife Management Area❖** preserves a swatch of wildness at the edge of the city. Route A1A then circles south toward **Timucuan Ecological and Historic Preserve❖,** on the coast at the eastern edge of Jacksonville, and the associated **Big Talbot Island❖** and **Little Talbot Island❖** state parks. Like the vast spartina salt marshes that soften land's end along the Georgia coast just to the north, these marshes are the legacy of big lazy rivers and some of the best wetland habitats on Florida's ocean coastline. Where the Saint Johns and Nassau rivers, carrying loads of enriching silt, meet the Atlantic, sea life is fecund. Contemplating the vast estuaries with their wealth of shellfish, mollusks, and birdlife, visitors can understand how the Timucuan peoples lived before European explorers arrived in the sixteenth century. Trails within Timucuan's Theodore Roosevelt Area pass freshwater ponds and high-ground hammocks on the edges of the marsh, and Big and Little Talbot islands are ideal settings for relaxed study of beaches, dunes, marshes, and offshore waters.

Coastal Routes 1 and A1A south give travelers a sense of South Florida's eastern coastline before a crush of development hid the state's native beauty behind strip malls and high-rises. Often sleepy and low-key, these northern Florida towns offer affecting glimpses of a less frantic past. About a hundred miles farther south, the roads reach New Smyrna Beach, the northern gateway to **Canaveral National Seashore❖.** Although the seashore is cheek-by-jowl with the Kennedy Space Center, spacecraft make unobtrusive neighbors for the seashore's 24 miles of pristine beach.

At the northern edge of the seashore, **Turtle Mound Archaeological Site** reveals long human habitation: a high mound of discarded oyster and other shells representing 600 years of Timucuan meals. Turtle Mound also marks the start of entirely new habitats: Nakedwood, with its thin, "muscled" tan trunks, reaches its northern limit here; the shiny corrugated leaves of wild coffee appear; disturbingly red coral bean flashes flowers concealing poisonous black seeds with come-hither color. The tropics begin here.

On Canaveral's long wind-burnished beach, ruddy turnstones wheel along the tide line, showing off intricately patterned brown-and-ocher wing markings. A stiff breeze swirls the black crown feathers of royal terns around their heads like aureoles. Other shorebirds race ahead of the incoming tide, poking long beaks into the wet sand for bits of food; each species' bill is specialized to harvest a particular food community. Unlike the sugary white sand of Gulf Coast beaches, Canaveral's is coarser, yellower, easier to sink into. Away from the water, morning glories and sea oxeye daisies grow near the dunes.

The Castle Windy Trail leads from the Atlantic coast side through an

OVERLEAF: *Canaveral National Seashore offers miles of deserted wilderness beach where thousands of sea turtles—loggerheads, greens, and occasionally leatherbacks—come ashore each year to lay their eggs.*

ABOVE: *An endangered gopher tortoise emerges from its burrow on Merritt Island; during fires this reptile will let other animals share its long tunnels.*

LEFT: *On the wing, black skimmers use their lower jaws to dip for fish. Because it wears down quicker, the lower mandible grows faster than the upper one.*

RIGHT: *Spiky saw palmetto thrives among the scrub oak on Merritt Island; this common understory plant often blankets the floors of pine forests.*

inviting tunnel of green to Mosquito Lagoon. The overarching vegetation is a mix of scrub oak, sabal palm, redcedar, and red bay, whose spicy leaves are still used in cooking. Along their horizontal branches, thick-limbed live oaks support colonies of resurrection fern. In dry times, the ferns conserve energy by shriveling up as if they were dead, but after one good dousing, they rise again in fresh green ranks. At the end of the cool, shaded path, wild red salvia and painted poinsettia frame the lagoon, as does a verge of mangrove—another indication that Canaveral is the beginning of southern Florida. A canoe trail winds through Mosquito Lagoon, providing closeups of mangroves and marsh grasses that harbor crabs, oysters, shrimp, young fish, and baby sea turtles.

Abutting Canaveral National Seashore and sharing an island with NASA is **Merritt Island National Wildlife Refuge❖,** a tapestry of fresh-water ponds and brackish marshes, pine woods and hardwood hammocks (the visitor center is on Route 402). The refuge is home to an astonishing variety of wildlife—330 species of birds, 31 mammals, 117 fishes, 65 amphibians and reptiles—and many residents are visible in abundance. Along Black Point Wildlife Drive, one of the best ways to see Merritt Island, lines of sabal palms and pines delineate the vast watery edges of marshes and pond impoundments, which are thick with

fishing herons—great blue, little blue, tricolored, even reddish egrets. Reddish egrets are particularly wily hunters, spreading their wings to create what fish believe are shadows of safety. When the fish fall for the ruse, the herons strike. Long Vs of white ibis cleave the sky, and coots by the hundreds blacken the water's surface. Shovelers, pied-billed grebes, and other waterfowl search the borders of the wetlands as a light-colored marsh hawk cruises low, a stealth hunter looking for prey.

A black racer sidewinds across the road while an osprey soars above. Long lines of laughing gulls and royal terns squat on thin sandbars that part the waters. Nearby, a tiny island is crowded shore to shore with white pelicans. One stop in the self-guided auto tour leads to Cruickshank Trail, which affords an even closer view of the refuge. Black skimmers give new meaning to the term *fly-fishing* as they continually dip their long red bills into the water while flying just inches above a pond. The lower bill, a third longer than the upper, dips in and scoops without the skimmer ever missing a wing beat.

At day's end, pink clouds streak the sky and huge flocks of gulls, terns, and sanderlings seem to explode from refuge waters, whirling and turning against the sunset like the grand finale of a fireworks display— an appropriate introduction to the natural opulence of southern Florida.

201

SOUTHERN FLORIDA:
EVERGLADES AND THE KEYS

Once southern Florida seemed a land of dreams—a place where palms swayed gracefully against a matchless sunset, coral islands glittered like gems in an aqua sea, and lavishly plumaged birds preened in exotic trees. Today, however, this vision of a semitropical utopia is increasingly difficult to realize as car-clogged highways and store-flanked residential developments impinge more and more on the region's shimmering and incredibly fragile natural beauty.

Visitors traveling a torrid highway have trouble imagining the cool beauty of Jonathan Dickinson State Park or the lush delicacy of the Loxahatchee River, which lie just beyond the road. Yet most of natural southern Florida seems to follow a similar pattern: Quiet jewels are hidden at the edges of mint-green mini-malls. In fact, southern Florida supports three dozen state parks and recreation areas, more wildlife refuges than any other state, and more national park acreage than any other state east of the Mississippi. In the lower 48 states, only Yellowstone is larger than Everglades National Park.

Because southern Florida has so recently emerged from the sea, water is never far away. At only 200 feet, the region's central ridge— about halfway between Tampa and the eastern shore—is the highest land around; east, west, and south, the terrain slopes gently toward the sea. On both coasts, the blurry segue of mangrove swamps and

LEFT: *Sabal palms, Florida's state tree, line the bank of Myakka River State Park. This hardy New World palm, also called a cabbage palm for its edible buds, grows as far north as the North Carolina coast.*

barrier islands makes the transition between land and ocean hard to distinguish. On high ground, the land is canopied by hardwood hammocks, tree islands that rise—if only a few feet— above surrounding lowlands. South Florida hammocks harbor progressively more tropical species such as mahoganies, gumbo-limbos, and other trees found nowhere else on the United States mainland. Beyond the hammocks, pine flatwoods hug thin sandy soils, and cypress swamps, festooned with orchids and other epiphytes, populate low water-logged areas.

ABOVE: *The critically endangered and rarely seen Florida panther is a cougar subspecies that has been reduced to a few dozen animals.*

Rivers such as the lovely Loxahatchee and the languorous Myakka drain slowly toward the coasts. Most noteworthy, however, is the watercourse that flows 100 miles south from Lake Okeechobee, a magnificent—and ecologically threatened—"river" some 50 miles wide but less than a foot deep. Often described as the River of Grass because of the broad saw-grass prairies it nourishes, this shallow, seasonal flow of freshwater is the key to the delicate ecosystem that dominates the southern tip of Florida. Pervading millions of acres that encompass sanctuaries such as the Fakahatchee Strand State Preserve, Big Cypress National Preserve, and Everglades National Park, this water represents the most complex and endangered hydrologic system in the United States. And the habitats the water supports shelter increasingly rare and threatened plants and animals—the Florida panther, snail kite, American crocodile, and many others.

Below these fragile wetlands, the famous Florida Keys curve toward the setting sun. This linked chain of coral islands is home to flora and fauna that straddle the line between the tropical Caribbean Basin and temperate United States. The waters around the Keys—bright with rainbow-tinted fish and exquisite corals—are yet another dimension of southern Florida's incredible natural abundance.

The chapter begins with a coastal tour of refuges along the Atlantic,

swings northwest to the pinelands of the central ridge, and then angles over to the sanctuaries along the west coast. Next come the lush sloughs, strands, and swamps known as the greater Everglades, and the itinerary concludes on the sun-drenched coral islets of the Keys.

EAST COAST

Just east of the coastal town of Sebastian lie two national wildlife refuges—**Pelican Island** in the waterway and **Archie Carr** along the Atlantic coast beaches—established to preserve endangered species. In

1903 Theodore Roosevelt issued an executive order designating Pelican Island the nation's first national wildlife refuge to protect nesting populations of eastern brown pelicans. The Archie Carr sanctuary, named for a longtime Florida conservationist, was included in the system in 1989 specifically to shelter endangered sea turtles.

Also a wilderness area, **Pelican Island National Wildlife Refuge❖** now encompasses the original 5.5-acre island, as well as nearby waters and mangrove islands. Accessible only by boat, Pelican rises just a few feet above water level. In January and February, however-

ABOVE: *In 1903 Theodore Roosevelt established the first national wildlife refuge at Pelican Island to protect this large coastal bird from hunters. Today thousands of pelicans nest here again.*

er, 10,000 birds may return here within an hour's time: dark, undulating lines of cormorants; white wood storks carrying nesting material; great blue herons flapping slate-colored wings; and brown pelicans by the score, clacking their great bills and waddling on mangroves weighed down by nests. Then the small, unprepossessing island seems to disappear under flurries of wings. Toward dusk the view is unparalleled (evening tours of Pelican Island depart from docks in Sebastian).

At the turn of the century, few roads crossed Florida, and most travelers journeyed along the coastal waterway right by this spot. Bored passengers on passing boats shot the pelicans for sport, and hunters gathered their feathers, used in the fashion trade and to make quill pens. By the early 1900s, this island—now about half its original size—was the only pelican rookery left on Florida's East Coast, supporting about 8,000 to 10,000 nesting brown pelicans. Although the number of nesting birds is much lower today, the brown pelican population is finally rebounding, and the bird's East Coast population was taken off the federal endangered list in 1985. Now the threat is not gun-toting sportsmen, but increasing development, which is transforming pelican nesting habitat on coastal lands and islands into resort communities.

A bridge at Wabasso connects the mainland to the barrier island and the **Archie Carr National Wildlife Refuge❖,** which occupies a narrow strip of sand running 20 miles along the Atlantic Ocean. Archie Carr protects habitat so perfect for nesting turtles that 25 percent of the loggerheads that nest along America's coastal beaches make their way here each summer. Signs along the beach warn visitors to keep lights turned off between May and October, when females come ashore to lay eggs: The turtles need natural light reflecting off the breakers to direct them back to the sea. Artificial coastal lights disorient them, sending the ponderous reptiles farther inland, where they starve or perish beneath cars.

ABOVE: *Threatened loggerhead turtles, whose heart-shaped carapace may reach four feet long, crawl onto the beach at the Archie Carr refuge starting in early summer to lay their leathery eggs.*

Although each female may lay 120 eggs up to four times during a season, fewer than a handful of the hatchlings reach adulthood. The rush from nest to sea leaves the tiny turtles vulnerable to hungry gulls, crabs, and raccoon. Once in the water, they become prey for fish. Few humans witness the largely nocturnal turtle-nesting drama, but during daylight hours the refuge presents a display of its own—long sea- and sun-washed beaches populated only by shorebirds and edged with

OVERLEAF: *On Florida's populous eastern coast lies an untamed oasis of calm: Jonathan Dickinson State Park. With its mature sand-pine-scrub habitat, the park features sand pines, saw palmettos, and oaks.*

ABOVE: *The Atlantic Ocean lines the horizon near Jonathan Dickinson State Park; hidden among the thick vegetation, the Loxahatchee River makes its way to the sea through scrublands and tangles of mangrove.*

sea daisies, palmettos, prickly-pear cacti, and the polished bronze-and-green leaves of huge sea grapes.

Just west of Route 1 between Hobe Sound and Jupiter, **Jonathan Dickinson State Park❖** provides a glimpse of Florida's Atlantic seaboard as it all appeared before the development that straggles south from here to Miami began. The park's 11,000-plus acres include some of the most mature sand-pine scrub in South Florida, airy groves of tall slash pine bedded with saw palmetto, and the state's only national wild and scenic river, the Loxahatchee—still an unimpeded waterway.

Within the park two self-guided nature trails interpret distinctly different habitats. The short Sand Pine Nature Trail, part of the 1,300-mile **Florida National Scenic Trail❖,** introduces visitors to plants and animals that eke out a living in the sandy, sunbaked scrub habitat, an

ABOVE RIGHT: *A prickly pear cactus (top) at Jonathan Dickinson State Park is ringed by reindeer moss. When young, low-growing saw palmettos (bottom) resemble sabal palms, trees that can reach 50 feet.*

ecological community that once dominated the Florida seaboard but has become increasingly rare. Flourishing here are lavender-flowered conradina, tight-needled Florida rosemary, and gopher apple, a low shrub whose fruits are food for gopher tortoises, raccoon, and other wildlife. Sand pines, with short, water-conserving needles, tower above an understory richly populated with scrub oaks, whose shiny, leathery leaves reflect light and preserve moisture.

The Kitching Creek Trail circles through flatwoods of tall slash pines so well spaced that each week the sun brings a new group of wildflowers into bloom, including irises, ground orchids, yellow hypericum, and goldenrod. The blossoms attract scores of zebra butterflies. Fat fish lurk in Kitching Creek, where tall swamp cypresses trace the course of the creek as it flows to meet the Loxahatchee. At Wilson

Creek a verdant fern garden—containing plants ranging from lacy royal to ten-foot-high leather varieties—attests that Florida is home to more types of ferns than any other state. Although woodpeckers are easily located, resident deer are harder to spot.

Nearby, the **Loxahatchee River,** accessible in the park by rental canoe and tour boat, slowly winds through mangrove swamps on its

ABOVE: *A fairly common sight in Florida's wetlands, the red-shouldered hawk spots prey from on high.*

way to the sea. In this brackish water, river otters float by on their backs, rolling, diving, and scaring basking turtles off a sunny log. Bass live in the river, and tarpon and blue make their way from the sea into the river's lower reaches. Tall sabal palms break the line of the low green horizon of mangroves; atop dead cypresses, ospreys have built broad nests.

Upriver, where the brackish water turns fresh, mangrove gives way to tall cypress crowded by pond apple and other shrubs. Leaping, silver-sided mullet slap the water surface without arousing the somnolent alligators sunning along the banks. At water's edge, delicate white swamp lilies bend and bob in a graceful ballet. Great blue herons with six-foot wingspans wade in the shallows along the narrowing river while red-tailed hawks soar above. Resembling small pineapples with long red flower spikes, fat bromeliads adorn the trees. Both Spanish moss and bromeliads are epiphytes, plants with aerial roots that trap moisture and nutrients from the atmosphere. Reflecting the lush green of overhanging cypresses and palms, the narrow waters of the upper river become aquatic gardens. The exotic blooms of huge bromeliads hang over the water like suspended flower baskets, and the corrugated gray-green leaves of water lettuce form large floating bouquets among the waxy, scalloped leaves of pennywort, strung across the surface like shiny green coins. (Canoe rentals are available in the River Picnic Area and at Riverbend Park, on Indiantown Road—Route 706—off I-95 a few miles south of the park.)

About five miles north of Jonathan Dickinson, just across Route 1, **Hobe Sound National Wildlife Refuge✦** includes a sand pine nature trail, as well as mangrove swamp and beach. Three types of endangered sea turtles—green, leatherback, and loggerhead—nest along its beaches. Some 25 miles south, **Loxahatchee National Wildlife Refuge❖** encompasses the northernmost section of Florida's Everglades, a vast natural wetland that once covered most of the state south of Lake Okeechobee. Off Route 441 between Boynton Beach and Delray Beach, Loxahatchee provides a cypress boardwalk, a marsh trail, an observation tower, and opportunities to see myriad wildlife by canoe. Because more than 250 species of birds have been recorded here, the refuge is a must for birders.

CENTRAL RIDGE

From Loxahatchee, Route 441 heads northwest toward the state's central ridge. Where the highway meets Route 78, **Parrot Avenue Wayside Park** affords a brief view of giant Lake Okeechobee—only the Great Lakes boast larger surface areas. In addition to harboring waterfowl, the lake helps water the Everglades.

ABOVE: *State-protected Florida scrub jays, crestless cousins of blue jays, inhabit the increasingly rare scrublands.*

The hinterlands of Florida's central ridge are a mix of orange groves, cattle ranches, and golf courses. Surrounded by agriculture and development is one of the small jewels of the Florida state park system, **Highlands Hammock State Park❖.** West of Sebring off Route 27, the park features exquisite natural habitats: one the quintessence of a hardwood hammock, another a cypress swamp, yet another a small but fine pine flatwoods.

The low, flat state of Florida is literally dotted with hammocks, raised islands of fertile land set among the more common lowlands. Here in the park, the high ground was once Florida's shoreline. After one of the great ice ages, when the earth was inundated with meltwater, the force of the Atlantic's waves piled sand up along the ancient seashore. The resulting dunes—or hammocks—are now far inland and covered with hardwood trees.

Of the nine or so short paths, the figure eight formed by the Lieber and Fern Garden trails presents one of the most scenic sections of Highlands Hammock. Within the woods, only the rhythmic clunk-

Above: *At Caladesi Island State Park, numerous young fish and shellfish swarm among the arching roots of red mangrove. This aquatic nursery proves good fishing grounds for these two tricolored herons.*

clunk of acorns dropping from live oak trees aflutter with Carolina wrens breaks the silence. Farther along, the persistent sound of wood-chopping can be traced to a large pileated woodpecker, its red comb quivering with noisy effort. Laurel oak, sweet gum, and sabal palm flourish among the hammocks. On red maple branches, wild pine epiphytes sprout like hairs on a witch's wart. Below, tropical wild coffee shrubs grow alongside beautyberry, whose arching branches are sheathed in dazzling amethyst berries. Carpeting the scene are soft beds of lacy green ferns.

Bayheads form the transition between hammock and swamp. Along the Cypress Swamp Trail, boardwalks traverse shadowed wetlands, and alligators glide by silently. Dominating the watery landscape are bald cypress trees, so called because their red-brown bark appears denuded after they lose their feathery blue-green needles each winter. Spikes of blue pickerelweed and moonglow-white swamp lilies brighten the dank waters. On other trails, young hardwoods are invading pinewoods where fire has been suppressed; elsewhere, longleaf and slash pines are returning to claim ground originally theirs.

About 25 miles farther north, just east of Lake Wales, the Nature Conservancy's **Tiger Creek Preserve❖** protects inland scrub that is

214

ABOVE: *On the Gulf side of Caladesi, one of Florida's last undeveloped barrier islands, coastal flora such as sea oat grasses, sea purslane, and seashore elder anchor dunes behind beaches crowded with shells.*

among the most ancient habitats in the United States. Some of the state's rarest species—scrub jay, scrub lizard, sand skink—are sheltered here.

GULF COAST

Like its Atlantic coast, the state's Gulf coast is bordered by low-lying barrier islands, or keys, many now transformed into resort communities complete with pricey homes, golf clubs, and marinas. Here hundreds of acres of native mangroves have disappeared so that property owners might have better views or access to the sea. Because so many acres of mangroves were cut, stiff laws now safeguard the trees, which help create keys and protect coastlines from erosion.

The most pristine island surviving on the west coast is **Caladesi Island State Park❖,** within the Tampa metropolitan area. (Ferries leave regularly from **Honeymoon Island State Recreation Area❖,** west of Dunedin via Route 586.) In the shallow waters around the marina, the ferry moves gingerly through a slow-wake zone where many marine species live and feed on dense beds of sea grass. Endangered manatees, the large serene-looking cows of the sea, are among the grazing animals most at risk in these zones. Once ashore, take a ramble through Caladesi's varied habitats. Profoundly peaceful fairy-tale tableaux along the Island Trail tempt visitors to remain right here and fantasize about adding a house, a store, maybe two—a telling insight into the progression that probably transformed every other island on this coast.

Luckily Caladesi remains unspoiled. The spangled white sand seems artfully set with clumps of palmetto, blue lupine, and prickly-pear cactus sporting fluorescent yellow flowers. Yellow-and-orange lantana and beach pea add their cheerful colors. Sabal palms, miniaturized by the effects of sea winds and salt, provide a counterpoint of height but scant shade. Deeper in the interior, a hammock of high ground supports one of the area's few remaining virgin stands of South Florida slash pine. Here pines and live oaks create cool green gardens where woodpeckers peer from holes in the trees. Atop a dead pine, an osprey balances confidently, pulling apart a newly caught fish to feed its young. A bluebird darts past. On the way to the beach, a small pond fringed by blue-eyed grass and white-topped sedge provides freshwater for a pair of mergansers and a tricolored heron.

West of the hammock, small semitropical trees such as marlberry and white stopper grow at the northern limit of their range. Nearby, a tree bedecked with clusters of flashy red berries flourishes far beyond its natural range. Brought to this country as an ornamental, the Brazilian pepper tree escaped to the wild and has prospered all over Florida, displacing native plants. Brazilian pepper is now one of the alien plants that managers at Caladesi, the Everglades, and many other natural areas are trying to eradicate.

Near the beach, hundreds of terns, gulls, and sandpipers rest on a thin sand spit breaching the Gulf. The spit and a small island are recent additions, the latter formed when a ferocious storm piled sand in shallow waters. Then mangroves and other plants colonized the nascent island. Caladesi's beach is idyllic—a good place to daydream, watch shorebirds, or play beachcomber. Thousands of shells wash ashore here, including turbans, whelks, scallops, horns, conchs, and slipper shells.

Even more remote and fragile than Caladesi, **Anclote Key State**

RIGHT: *Because endangered manatees graze on sea grasses in shallow water, no-wake boating zones at Caladesi and elsewhere in Florida protect these mammals from their greatest danger: motorboat blades.*

ABOVE: *At Myakka River, Florida's largest state park, a great blue heron stands four feet tall on legs designed for wading. Behind, a group of roseate spoonbills feeds by "threshing" water with their spatulate bills.*

Preserve❖ is the northernmost of the 320-mile chain of barrier islands that protect Florida's west coast. Lying west of Tarpon Springs, Anclote Key is accessible only by private boat.

A journey south over Tampa Bay via the remarkable Skyway Bridge reminds travelers that Florida is as much about water as about land. At the lower ends of the bridge, brown pelicans hover above the bay until they spot a large fish. Then, folding back their wings, they hit the water head-on, like a torpedo, stunning their prey before scooping it up and dining. Eventually, this jackhammerlike fishing technique can blind a pelican. At the mouth of Tampa Bay lie several tiny preserves—**Egmont Key, Passage Key,** and **Pinellas** national wildlife refuges. Islands of wildness in a tamed area, these sanctuaries are designed not to attract people but to safeguard species whose habitats are dwindling.

Southeast of Sarasota along Route 72, **Myakka River State Park❖** is Florida's largest at about 45 square miles. A brief drive down the park road gives the false impression that Myakka is composed of

218

ABOVE RIGHT: *Two snowy egrets fluff out their breeding plumage in an eye-catching mating display. Hunted nearly to extinction early in the century, snowies have staged a comeback at refuges founded to protect them.*

moody live oak forests draped with veils of Spanish moss. The true glory of Myakka, however, is its broad prairie and riverine habitats. Flowing 12 miles within the park, the state-designated wild and scenic Myakka River widens into marshes and lakes, then narrows again as it meanders toward Charlotte Harbor and the Gulf. On the upper lake, red-shouldered hawks, marsh harriers, and ospreys soar above the coots, blue-winged teal, pintail, shovelers, and other winter-resident ducks below. Perched on branches overhanging the water, belted kingfishers wait to strike any small fish that swims by.

In the early morning, when mist rising from the sinuous river obscures the far banks in a hazy dream, the scene is primeval. Canoeists glide silently along as herons squawk, ruffling flotillas of clucking moorhens. A wood stork, its glossy white wings tipped with black, probes the muddy water with its bill. Farther downstream, oblivious to an alligator headed its way, a white ibis also works the banks. Although alligators generally avoid humans, they are swift and power-

ful and can be dangerous when habituated to associating people with food. To keep confrontations to a minimum, the state imposes stiff fines on anyone caught feeding an alligator.

In southern wetlands, American alligators play a critical role. At Myakka's Deer Prairie Slough, a dozen foot-long baby alligators crawl over and around their mother as she snoozes in the shallow sun-warmed water. When people pass, the babies issue urgent little grunts. They might well be alarmed. Although female alligators are protective, few youngsters live to adulthood. Eight feet long on average, the largest reptile in North America is this ecosystem's top predator; but its offspring occupy the bottom rung of the food chain—a choice meal for wading birds, turtles, fish, and even other alligators.

Between the late 1800s and 1970 people killed more than five million alligators, leaving the species in danger of extinction. Since federal protections were enacted in 1970, the alligator has been reclaiming its place as a vital member of the wetland community. The deep holes that

LEFT: *Alligators, which can reach 17 feet in length, inhabit the Myakka River and nearby sloughs; they prefer fresh rather than salt water.*

RIGHT: *Cockles, arks, and dozens of other shells line Sanibel Island, which Spanish explorer Ponce de León named "Coast of Seashells" in 1513.*

gators dig in shallow swamps provide turtles, fish, and wading birds with water in the dry winter months.

During the breeding process, a mother gator piles mounds of vegetation along the edge of a hole she has dug, then lays several dozen eggs and covers them with more natural materials. As the vegetation rots, it produces heat, which determines the sex of the babies. The higher, warmer eggs will become male, the cooler eggs at the bottom of the nest female.

Beyond Deer Prairie Slough are Myakka's dry prairies. Traditionally these grasslands, like many other similar sites in Florida, were cleared by yearly fires ignited by Florida's extraordinarily high number of lightning strikes. Native plant communities and wildlife depend on these yearly conflagrations. To preserve this specialized ecosystem, which supports more than 250 plant species, park managers set carefully controlled fires. Plants such as pine lilies (*Lilium catesbaei*, also called leopard lilies) are making a comeback, and as fire nurtures the prairies, caracaras (a species of falcon) and other animals are returning as well.

West of Fort Myers on crescent-shaped **Sanibel Island** is the nation's most-visited national wildlife refuge. Named for a Pulitzer Prize–winning cartoonist who also headed the forerunner of the U.S. Fish and Wildlife Service, **J. N. "Ding" Darling National Wildlife Refuge❖** lives up to its reputation for avian abundance. And the birds are apparently indifferent to the tourists on Sanibel, a popular resort destination. At daybreak countless species go about their business along five-mile

Wildlife Drive: Pink roseate spoonbills are finishing up a night of shallow-water fishing; a wood stork is intent on nabbing a fish. An anhinga, drying its outspread wings, displays an opulent silver-and-black pattern of bars and squares while a cormorant and a little blue heron compete for the same fish, and a yellow-crowned night heron hunches in the bushes. Pelicans and a variety of ducks congregate on sand spits and in ponds. And the vegetation around the series of pools and marshes is alive with warblers, vireos, and other forest birds.

The visitor center is a good place to start because it displays some of the lesser-known indigenous plants and suggests the best way to see the refuge. Intoxicatingly sweet jacquinias—small shrubs with panicles of red, yellow, and white flowers—grow next to more tropical gumbo-limbo trees, distinguished by their peeling bark. Wild olives and the exotic hibiscuslike flowers of thespesia (also called the portia tree) compete with showy red Christmas berry shrubs for visitors' attention. The refuge trails afford close-up views of butterflies, as well as moonflowers, asters, and other plants. In addition, the preserve protects some 50 reptile and 32 mammal species.

ABOVE: *Common along the coast, a double-crested cormorant dries its dark plumage in a spread-eagle pose.*
RIGHT: *Young cypress trees thrive at Corkscrew Swamp, which protects some of the nation's oldest cypresses.*

Sanibel is probably best known as the seashell capital of the country because shells from whelks to nutmegs and scallops to conchs all wash up on its beaches. To keep beachcombers from depleting sea life, laws prohibit collecting live shells. A walk along the shore to observe the bounty deposited by a single tide provides a glimpse of the sea's incredible diversity.

SLOUGHS, STRANDS, AND SWAMPS
South Florida is the realm of the Everglades, not only the national park but the far-reaching and complex Everglades ecosystem. South Florida

was also once home to the Calusa tribes, and the Miccosukee and Seminole still live here.

From Fort Myers take I-75 south to Exit 17, then Route 846 east and north to **Corkscrew Swamp Sanctuary❖.** Managed by the National Audubon Society, this 10,000-acre preserve contains the largest remaining old-growth bald cypress forest in the world. Some of these mammoth trees are 700 years old—they were saplings during Europe's Middle Ages. More than two miles of boardwalk loop through swamp, wet prairies, marshes, and pine flatwoods, affording views of birds, orchids, showy hibiscuses, reptiles, and snails. Corkscrew was established to protect wood storks, which breed in cypress swamps—and these rare birds are still an excellent reason to visit. Hundreds of pairs of the wading birds, endangered throughout their United States range, nest in large colonies here between November and March. Unfortunately, development beyond the borders of the preserve drastically affects their numbers, and populations vary greatly from year to year.

The heart of Corkscrew is the swamp, anchored by the old-growth cypresses, whose "knees" poke through the dark waters. (Experts believe that the knees help the trees breathe in waterlogged anaerobic conditions and also help stabilize the shallow-rooted cypresses, which are often at the mercy of hurricanes.) Among the cypresses live numerous ferns, red maples, and the tropical pond apple, a favorite of aerial orchids and other epiphytes. Over millions of years, species have evolved to fit every biological niche. Because flowering plants in a swamp have little land base, species here have learned to live in the trees, absorbing nutrients and moisture from the air. Wild pine, yellow catopsis, cigar orchids, and clamshell orchids are just a few of Corkscrew's many epiphytes.

Due south of Corkscrew lies **Fakahatchee Strand State Preserve❖,** within the large area generally called the Big Cypress Swamp—a region not easy to know but well worth the effort. A porous limestone plain covers the tip of southern Florida, sloping gently toward the Gulf of Mexico. Here the landscape is dominated by

LEFT: *Wood storks nest in large rookeries, whether cypress trees at Corkscrew or this crowded mangrove in the Everglades. Since humans began disturbing their habitat, wood stork numbers have declined.*

saw-grass prairies slicked by a thin glaze of water draining south from higher ground around Lake Okeechobee. Within the Big Cypress system, higher ground supports pine flatwoods. In places, water has cut channels called strands, and along these strands grow dense cypress swamps. The largest and most diverse is Fakahatchee Strand, which is 20 miles long and 3 to 5 miles wide.

The easiest way to see Fakahatchee is from the boardwalk at Big Cypress Bend, seven miles west of the junction of Routes 41 and 29, northwest of Everglades City. Jays, woodpeckers, catbirds, and black-and-white warblers are among the birds darting through the understory of this pristine cypress swamp. Some of the lofty cypresses are caught in the destroying embrace of strangler figs, whose vinelike branches form captivating patterns even as they slowly choke the life from their hosts. Scattered among the cypresses is the world's largest concentration of royal palms, their smooth gray trunks and striking green crown shafts making them the sophisticates of the palm world. At the far end of the boardwalk, an alligator shares her huge hole with three broods of her young, as well as some red sliders and yellow-bellied turtles.

Another way to see Fakahatchee is to meander along Jane's Scenic Drive, a dirt road just beyond the ranger station off Route 29 northwest of Copeland. Hiking is allowed on the gated tracks that line the road, and a walk here surrounds visitors with aural mysteries: plops, plunks, and splashes behind thick walls of shrubs and trees. As visitors approach, lizards scatter like blown leaves, ibis rise from a half-hidden pond, and a box turtle, pulling in its head and tail, pretends to be a patterned rock. Cleaning itself in the crotch of a tree, a raccoon pays no attention to the zebra longwing and tropical orange sulphur butterflies floating past. Like tiny star sapphires, blue lobelias line swampy ponds where poppylike white duck potato and carnivorous yellow bladderwort grow. Although poachers took thousands of bromeliads and orchids before protections were instituted in the 1970s, Fakahatchee still harbors the largest number of orchid species in the nation, some of which grow nowhere else.

RIGHT: *Vast, spongy wetlands in Big Cypress National Preserve convey water to the Turner River. This infusion of freshwater draining into the Gulf keeps coastal habitats healthy and rich with marine life.*

The leaves of water lettuce (above), a floating aquatic plant, provide purchase for a little blue heron; at Fakahatchee Strand, a strangler fig vine (right) slowly garrotes a venerable bald cypress tree.

Bordering Fakahatchee to the east and Everglades National Park to the north and west is **Big Cypress National Preserve✧,** a vast 1.5-million-acre patchwork of wet prairies, swamps, hardwood hammocks, and pine flatwoods—the essence of the southern Florida landscape. The preserve's visitor center lies midway between Miami and Naples along Route 41, the Tamiami Trail. Constructed during the 1920s to connect the east and west coasts of southern Florida, the roadway was a monumental undertaking over daunting terrain. This engineering marvel, however, exacted a steep hydrologic price: The road blocks the flow of a vast but shallow sheet of water that once coursed slowly south across the face of the southern Florida peninsula. Although water gates allow water to pass under the highway, this artificial configuration hardly duplicates the natural flow.

Hikers can experience the preserve close-up via a 7-mile section of the **Florida National Scenic Trail✧,** which runs 1,300 miles from Big Cypress to the Gulf Islands National Seashore; begin near the Oasis Visitor Center off Route 41 and wind south to the education center. From a car, the best way to see the preserve is to drive along Turner River Road (Route 839), stopping at the side to view wildlife. Alligators, wading birds, fish, wild turkeys, deer, and armadillos (migrants from Texas) all appear frequently; present, but less visible, are Everglades

In South Florida wetlands, bromeliads cling to trees, gathering sustenance from the air (left); lacy bracts on white-topped sedge (above) brighten the marsh edges.

mink, black bears, and the rare and elusive Florida panther—a close cousin of the West's mountain lion. Panthers ranged throughout the Southeast until commercial development and efforts to eradicate them reduced their numbers and drove them into inaccessible areas of southern Florida. Now only 40 to 50 of the big honey-colored cats are left, barely enough to make a healthy breeding population. As one of the nation's most endangered species, solitary, wide-ranging Florida panthers are now monitored as well as protected. The health of the panther population has become a bellwether for the health of the wild.

EVERGLADES NATIONAL PARK

Adjoining Big Cypress to its north, **Everglades National Park❖** at 1.5 million acres is the third-largest national park in the contiguous United States and the largest east of the Mississippi. More important, it is one of the world's premier wild places. Because it shelters both tropical and temperate plants and wildlife, the Everglades has been designated a United Nations world heritage site as well as the first international

OVERLEAF: *Vast watery plains of saw-grass—a sharp-edged sedge that can top nine feet—stretch across the Everglades. Feathery bald cypresses, with deciduous blue-green needles, punctuate the flat terrain.*

biosphere reserve in the United States. Its landscapes are both subtle and unique: In the east, seemingly endless flat expanses of saw-grass prairie—not quite land and not quite sea—are dotted here and there by islands of trees; dense mangrove swamps edge its western Gulf coastline; stands of old-growth slash pine and hammocks of hardwoods occupy its higher areas; and the vast reaches of Florida Bay stretch away to the south. A huge roster—some 900 species—of plants grow in the Everglades. More than 600 types of birds and reptiles, mammals, amphibians, and fish of every sort make their home here as well, including such endangered species as the American crocodile, manatee, wood stork, snail kite, and hawksbill turtle.

Overall, the vast majority of the park is America's only subtropical wilderness, and 40 percent is water. Although the wilderness appears expansive and water seems abundant, the Everglades is no longer the pristine island of wildness it once was. Since the turn of the century it has been drastically affected by human efforts to change or control its natural rhythms.

ABOVE: *At Cape Sable, coastal prairie flanks Florida Bay. A natural water-delivery system feeds freshwater through the Everglades into Florida Bay, where the brackish mix helps keep the coral reefs healthy.*

LEFT: *Lake Okeechobee, with a surface area exceeded only by the Great Lakes, once spilled all its waters south, nourishing the Everglades. Today a network of locks and channels draws off water for human use; here at Port Mayaca, lake water is funneled into Saint Lucie Canal.*

The crux of the problem is water—the park's lifeblood. In its natural state, the Kissimmee River to the north long meandered through the uplands of central Florida, its wildlife-rich oxbows and sloughs absorbing summer's pelting storms. The river's plentiful waters then fed into Lake Okeechobee, which acted like an overfilled bathtub, spilling summer's excess in a vast, shallow sheet of water over the Everglades lowlands beyond. This slow-moving river, 50 miles wide but little more than six inches deep, stretched from the east side of the Florida peninsula to the Big Cypress Swamp on the west and flowed sluggishly 100 miles south to Florida Bay. Each winter, in a millennia-old natural cycle, the Everglades and its plants and animals survived dry spells.

The 1960s, however, brought an acceleration of big engineering projects ranging from social to hydrologic engineering—and southern Florida got its share. In the name of flood control and agricultural efficiency, the Army Corps of Engineers straightened the Kissimmee River. More than 1,400 miles of canals and dikes channeled Okeechobee's freshwater away from the natural environment and agricultural fields, to Miami and the expanding urban areas to the east. Roads crossing the region blocked the remaining natural flow, and water gates regulated volume on a human schedule.

As a result, Everglades water—now filled with pollutants—began arriving at unnatural times and places and in lesser amounts. The most telling of many consequences was that the wading bird population declined by more than 90 percent. In the 1930s colonies of more than 250,000 birds nested together; today these rookeries number between 2,000 and 3,000. Without its annual flush of freshwater, Florida Bay began to suffer from hypersalinity, and today fish populations and native vegetation have been severely affected. Realizing that the health of the Everglades is in jeopardy, state and federal government agencies are trying to return the Kissimmee River to a more natural course, building more water gates into the park, and acquiring more land to buffer the complicated ecosystem. All agree, however, that the road to recovery will be long and complicated.

Its vast and watery topography makes the Everglades difficult for humans to negotiate. As elsewhere in subtropical Florida, the winter months, especially at dawn and dusk, are the best times to observe wildlife—and to avoid mosquitoes and summer's oppressive heat. The Everglades' planar majesty can be approached via three gateways: in the east, from Miami and Homestead through the Main Visitor Center along Route 9336 to Flamingo, at the southernmost tip of the Florida mainland; off the Tamiami Trail (Route 41) at Shark Valley; and in the northwest, along the Gulf Coast at Everglades City and the Ten Thousand Islands. The 1.4 million visitors each year can follow self-guided walks along the main park road and rent canoes and motorboats; tram tours, concession-boat tours, and ranger-led excursions provide on-site expertise.

The heart of Florida's mangrove swamps—the most extensive in the world—is the **Ten Thousand Islands.** Hundreds of mangrove islands transform the park's west coast into a maze of green puzzle pieces on a sea-blue background. Distinguished by its low evergreen profile, the

---

OVERLEAF: *Most of the Everglades' Ten Thousand Islands developed when mangrove seedlings rooted in the shallow water off Florida's west coast, trapping sand and other seedlings as each island slowly grew.*

ABOVE: *Tree snails in nearly 60 different color variations graze on trees in the Everglades hammocks.*

RIGHT: *Black vultures are more southern and sociable than turkey vultures.*

BELOW: *Dolphins often play (with boats and each other) in the warm waters of Everglades National Park.*

red mangrove is the preeminent island-builder. Because storms destroy what mangroves build, however, the islands are always in flux. Dispersed by tides and winds, cigar-shaped red mangrove seeds are ready-to-root plant packages. The seeds float vertically until they lodge in shallow water; within 48 hours, roots and leaves have sprouted. As the mangroves grow, their arching roots trap more sand and detritus, creating soil. Red mangroves alone drop 20,000 pounds of leaves per acre per year. Seeds of black mangrove, white mangrove, buttonbush, and others find their way onto the growing mass, and eventually the islet becomes an island. At the island's edge, intertwined mangrove roots create havens for young fish, shellfish, and mollusks.

Above water, Ten Thousand Islands is a bird wonderland. Regal and serene, a bald eagle stands on the rim of her enormous nest until a kamikaze peregrine falcon—the fastest creature alive—dive-bombs her. Flocks of ibis flap like white handkerchiefs in water's-edge shrubs, and dozens of osprey nests top dead trees throughout the islands. A great blue heron spreads six-foot wings to lead the tour boat on a zigzag course. Ruddy turnstones, pelicans, and cormorants are among the most obvious residents. Manatees loll below the water's surface, and dolphins arching through the swells make sea life seem irresistibly appealing.

ABOVE: *At its northern limit in the Everglades, the endangered American crocodile has a more tapered snout than an alligator does.*

LEFT: *In Everglades National Park, saw-grass-edged Eco Pond is home to a mangrove island and a stalking great egret.*

A male swallow-tailed kite follows a female to her perch atop a tall pine. With their long elegant lines and black-white-gray plumage, the mating birds, their wings undulating, resemble one sumptuous many-armed Hindu goddess. On a remote sandbar at the far reaches of the islands, hundreds of royal terns, sanderlings, and oystercatchers stand with backs to the wind. Bauhaus birds with black heads, white bellies, and bright red bills, oystercatchers have become increasingly rare. Few but alligators and birds venture into the 100 miles of watery wilderness

Above: *Along the Anhinga Trail in Everglades National Park, a name-sake bird perches above swampy waters. Because it lacks oil glands, this long-necked fish eater must spread its wings to dry in the sun.*

farther south along the western coast of the Everglades, where Ponce de León was reportedly murdered by native Calusa more than 500 years ago.

Most visitors approach the park from the east on Route 9336, just west of the Florida Turnpike and Homestead. From the eastern entrance and main visitor center to Flamingo (which includes restaurants, lodgings, and a marina and overlooks Florida Bay) is 38 miles, a distance studded with overlooks, roadside exhibits, and short trails.

Although modern eyes have been schooled to find mountains and other vertical vistas sublime, the Everglades turns that view of beauty on its side. Like the Great Plains, the horizontal planes of southern Florida are vast and subtle, requiring more contemplation than a viewfinder moment. A good place to appreciate the breadth of the Everglades' undulating saw grass is **Pa-Hay-Okee Overlook** (13 miles from the eastern entrance), where at sunset the saw grass shimmers tan, green, bronze, and gold, and colossal mountains of rose-colored clouds fill the canvas of the sky. Gliding silently above the grasses, an endangered snail kite keeps a sharp eye out for apple snails, its main food, which are now rare because water delivery has changed drastically. In shallows of saw grass, pig frogs snort deep, throaty messages.

240

ABOVE: *One of North America's most common herons, the great egret stands about three feet high; its fluffy breeding plumage is so attractive that hunters nearly extirpated the species early in the 1900s.*

Except for them and the calls of barred owls, all is quiet.

Dusk and dawn in the winter are also the best times to visit **Eco Pond,** which lies within walking distance of Flamingo and attracts the full range of Everglades birds. Snowy egrets with gold-slippered feet, coots, gallinules, grebes, white and glossy ibis, anhingas, and a variety of herons crowd the water where alligators and rubbery Florida softshell turtles cruise. The forest edges of the pond are busy with cardinals and catbirds, yellow-throated warblers and red-shouldered hawks. Resplendent in its plumage of dazzling green, red, and indigo, a painted bunting—the most brightly colored bird in America—creates a spectacle as it turns its best side to a half-dozen cameras poised 20 feet away. Behind the line of trees, palmetto prairies are home to deer, marsh rabbits, and foxes.

Flamingo's marina is one of the few places on the United States mainland to see American crocodiles—and southern Florida is the only place in the world where alligators and crocodiles coexist. The territories of these large reptiles overlap only slightly because alligators prefer freshwater, and American crocodiles live in more brackish waters.

The National Park Service has developed a number of specialized trails and boardwalks that interpret the park's major ecosystems.

241

During winter's dry months, the short but well-known **Anhinga Trail** attracts so many species that the half-mile walk can take half a day. Bream, Florida gar, bass, and turtles are visible in open pools. Alligators doze on sunbaked banks edged by lipstick-red coral beans as least bitterns, yellow-crowned night herons, and other wading birds stab at prey near the shore.

The **Pinelands Trail** loops through some of the largest remaining stands of Dade County slash pine, an endangered subtropical species. The open understory harbors the largest number of endemic herbaceous species in the park—many found nowhere else. Garish orange-red butterflies hover over starry blue flowers as the wind creates a chorus in the tops of the pines. Occasionally, tree trunks are decorated with estivating tree snails. (Estivation is akin to hibernation but takes place during hot months rather than cold ones.) These large, colorful snails have become rarer as they have been plundered by collectors.

Mahogany Hammock features a profusion of tropical hardwood trees that introduce visitors to the plant world of the Caribbean Basin, which reaches its northern limits in southern Florida. Mahogany trees, gumbo-limbos (called tourist trees because their peeling red bark resembles sunburned skin), pigeon plums, paurotis palms, and satinleaf crowd the boardwalk, and ferns of every sort fill the understory. Where the boardwalk crosses the wet saw-grass prairie, a blue-gray marl covers the Everglades limestone base; the nutrient-rich algal mats that lie atop the marl form the base of the food chain.

The **Westlake Trail** provides a tour of mangrove swamps, and the **Nine-Mile Canoe Trail** affords an easy insider's view of the magnificent saw-grass prairie. This clearly marked canoe route twists and turns through a brief mangrove maze and then opens into the saw grass, one of the largest of the sedges. Although canoes glide across water here, the arching grasses all around imply otherwise, stretching the definitions of land and water. The park also encompasses many primitive camping areas, which are best accessed with knowledgeable local guides.

Leaving the Everglades headed east toward the coast highway to Keys, the park road passes **Rock Reef Pass,** elevation three feet. This ancient reef, which hugs Florida's eastern shore and then curves west, used to be the coastline. Now a line of trees defines the ridge, which seems adrift in a sea of undulating grasses.

ABOVE: *Bromeliads decorate a mahogany tree in the Everglades. A tropical species that reaches its northern limit here, this hardwood is rare in its U.S. habitat because it has been logged for its valuable lumber.*

THE KEYS

Nine miles east of Homestead on Southwest 328th Street (North Canal Drive) is **Biscayne National Park❖,** the portal to Florida's tropical necklace of coral islands called, simply, the Keys. Because nearly 95 percent of the park is underwater, most visitors view the marine wilderness splendors on glass-bottom-boat tours. In the park's clear blue waters, averaging eight to ten feet deep, manatees graze in beds of sea grass, and a kaleidoscope of colorful fish dart between living monuments of coral.

Corals are small animals—soft-bodied polyps—that excrete a protective casing of calcium carbonate. Over thousands of years these small limestone cells, built one atop another by billions of polyps, become coral reefs, which serve as breakwaters and protect the southern tip of Florida. Biscayne's reefs are home to more than 200 species of fish, many more colorful than any land animal. Eels, angelfish, parrot fish, wrasses, and sponges live in glorious profusion among corals of every sort: grooved brain coral, branching elkhorn coral, mountainous star coral, tube coral. Because coral is sensitive to pollution—even the touch of a human hand can halt its growth for years—the health of Florida's coral reefs hangs in the balance.

Although the underwater world is the focus of Biscayne National Park, islands such as Elliott Key contain a wealth of subtropical variety.

243

Behind red mangroves at bay's edge are black mangroves surrounded by a sea of sticklike vertical structures that help the plants absorb air. Wild morning glories and opalescent moonflowers drape themselves over shrubs such as wild lime and tamarind. Pigeon plum trees are striped by the telltale scratches of raccoon, which climb the trees to eat the plums. Sapodilla trees produce fruit so sweet that the sugar in them is partially crystallized.

About 35 miles south, just off Route 1 on Key Largo, is the entrance to **John Pennekamp Coral Reef State Park❖.** The nation's first under-water park, Pennekamp still protects the best examples of coral reef life in the continental United States. Concessioners work with park inter-preters to show this underwater world to visitors via glass-bottom boat, snorkeling, and scuba tours. Together, Pennekamp and the adjacent **Key Largo National Marine Sanctuary❖** cover 178 nautical square miles of coral reefs, sea-grass beds, and mangrove swamps within the Straits of Florida. State waters extend 22 miles along the shore and 3 miles out; from 3 miles to 6 miles are national sanctuary waters.

As one boats out to Grecian Rocks, Molasses Reef, or another patch

Underwater at John Penne-kamp Coral Reef State Park on Key Largo, a yellow-tailed snapper (left) swims past a giant brain coral; a redband parrot fish (right) takes cover near a mustard hill coral and lacy sea plumes.

of reef, the sea and sky present a seemingly two-dimensional blue monotone that sweeps to the distant horizon. Underwater, however, lie incomparable gardens overflowing with breathtaking color and form. At the feet of star coral mountains, lacy sea fans wave their purple arms. Small boulders of brain coral nestle against soaring branches of elkhorn coral. The romaine lettuce growing on the seafloor is a type of fire coral, whose sting can irritate for days. When the polyps that create coral reach out their arms to feed, the coral changes color. Brain corals become red. Sea fans, usually purple, turn brown when they are feeding.

Approximately 45 types of coral create an exuberant three-dimensional water world of caves, hollows, and ledges. Darting among the crevices are Matisse-colored parrot fish, whose luminous powder-blue bodies are striped with lavender; they graze on algae-covered coral, in the process chewing bits of coral and recycling them as sand. Blue and yellow wrasses lurk within crevices, waiting for a chance to munch off algae that have accumulated on the scales of other fish. A variety of fish come to these wrasse "cleaning stations"—a fine example of a commensal relationship.

French angelfish with soigné black-and-gold bodies drift like ele-

---

OVERLEAF: *Boats navigate carefully off the limestone coast of Florida's Indian Key State Historic Site because the shallow tropical turquoise-blue Florida Straights conceal many dangerous underwater coral reefs.*

ABOVE: *Tropical gumbo-limbo trees, typical Caribbean flora, grow on Lignumvitae Key. They are related to African trees that produce frankincense and myrrh; their unusual name is from the African Bantu language.*

gant grandes dames past a school of bright blue tangs flicking even brighter yellow tails. In appropriate ranks, military-striped sergeant major fish swim above a group of grunts, a species near the bottom of the food chain. In narrow sandy valleys between crags of coral, long silver barracuda lie in wait for a prey to wander too close. Clever predators, they strike with lightning speed or play dead, flopping near the surface until some foolish fish comes to investigate. Larger fish among the hundreds of species that live in or near coral reefs include tarpon, moray eels, snook, groupers, even sharks—although no shark attacks have ever been recorded in these waters. On land, the park includes a botanical site full of cocoa plums, huge mahogany-red sea grapes, and a variety of other plants, as well as lizards, birds, and endangered Key Largo wood rats.

Nearby on North Key Largo, in the waters of the **Crocodile Lake National Wildlife Refuge❖,** wading birds take their chances by fishing in the only U.S. federal crocodile preserve. The refuge (closed to the

ABOVE: *Now rare in the Keys, the lignum vitae tree (top) is protected on Lignumvitae Key, where its blue flowers (bottom left) create a show. The lumpy tamarind fruit (bottom right) is pungent and high in sugar.*

public) protects habitat for the American crocodile, whose numbers have plummeted to about 500, mostly because of habitat destruction.

Hopscotching along the small coral islands of Florida's long, curving tail, Route 1 leads south to **Lignumvitae Key State Botanical Site❖** between Upper and Lower Matecumbe keys, one of America's last pristine examples of a tropical hardwood hammock. Lignumvitae Key can be reached only by boat and seen only on a ranger-led tour; visitors to the **Long Key State Recreation Area** a few miles farther southwest can reserve a spot on the three-hour round-trip boat tour. A restored 1919 mansion and grounds, once the home of a wealthy chemist, occupy a small part of Lignumvitae Key; the rest of the island is a natural botanic garden. Because the coral of the Keys is extremely hard, the soils here are thin and poor and the forests fragile.

The key was named for the rounded lignum vitae tree, whose fragrant blue flowers are followed by orange seed capsules. The native lignum vitae population has languished, however, because of a dearth of

249

hurricanes in the past few decades. Just as longleaf pines require fire to flourish, lignum vitaes developed as slow-growing, hurricane-dependent trees. The yellow fruit of the mastic, one of the hammock's canopy trees, hangs over a natural pool on the island. Mosquitoes breed here, but so do gambusia—small fish that dine on them.

In the top of a pigeon plum tree, a white-crowned pigeon, native only to southern Florida and the Keys, flies off with a startled look. Farther on, a hawk has left the remains of a less fortunate pigeon. Ospreys live here, along with raccoon and marsh rabbits. Among the most colorful inhabitants are crab spiders, some tinted like Navajo blankets, others looking as though a child had dropped splotches of chrome-yellow paint on their backs.

ABOVE: *An orb weaver found mainly in the tropics, the silver argiope spider prospers on Big Pine Key.*

RIGHT: *Slash pines rise above lush palmetto scrublands at the National Key Deer Refuge on Big Pine Key.*

One of the hammock's loveliest trees is the satinwood, whose leaves sport shiny green tops and velvety undersides that form copper-colored canopies. Poisonwood trees are plentiful; if touched, they cause the same itchy blistering as poison ivy. With their smooth shiny red bark and artful branching pattern, gumbo-limbos are standouts. Like many other tropical trees, gumbo-limbos' drip-tip leaves allow the frequent summer rains to roll off rather than linger and nurture fungus and mold. During the dry winter months, most of the forest's "evergreen" trees lose up to a third of their leaves to conserve moisture. Although the key looks lush in winter, summer produces an even greener and shadier canopy.

On lists of the nation's best beaches, the southernmost park in Florida's state system, **Bahia Honda State Park❖,** appears regularly. (Bahia Honda flanks Route 1 on Bahia Honda Key, just southwest of Seven Mile Bridge.) Here warm golden sands meet tropical blue waters as tall, feathery palms arch out over the water. A pair of pink roseate spoonbills wing overhead. Visitors who can tear themselves away from the warm, soothing waters discover that Bahia Honda also has a num-

LEFT: *The endangered Key deer, related to the white-tailed variety, grows only to about the size of a large dog.*

ber of habitats to explore: beach dune, mangrove, hardwood hammock, and the marine world. The Silver Palm Nature Trail showcases one of the state's largest populations of silver palms.

Big Pine Key, the largest Key and the only one with a permanent supply of fresh-water, is the home of the **National Key Deer Refuge** (headquarters is in the Big Pine Shopping Center on Key Deer Boulevard). The island features stunted pinewoods, dense mangroves, and mudflats alive with wading birds, as well as **Blue Hole,** an observation pool in an old quarry supporting in-teresting aquatic life, and the pinelands of **Watson Nature Trail.** Like the pines, the endangered Key deer have been miniaturized by the is-land's harsh conditions. A distinctive subspecies of the white-tailed deer that has been in residence since prehistoric times, adult Key deer are about the size of a large dog; the current population totals only around 300. They often graze along Key Deer Boulevard at dawn and dusk and can also be spotted on the beach, strange companions to white ibis and godwits. Feeding the deer is illegal because it discourages nat-ural foraging and upsets the animals' nutritional balances.

Visitors with access to a boat can explore **Great White Heron** and **Key West** national wildlife refuges, which together encompass more than 600 nautical square miles and about 10,000 acres of land along the lower Keys. The refuges protect dozens of coral keys and 22 endangered species among thousands of mostly marine species. Agricultural runoff from the mainland and urban runoff from the Keys have caused the water quality in all national wildlife refuges in the Keys to deteriorate. Seeing porpoises breach in the light of an incomparable Keys sunset or a great white heron glide over the silky surface of the sea is a powerful reminder that such places are precious.

At the end of the Keys, 70 miles beyond the town of Key West, lies **Dry Tortugas National Park❖.** Accessible only by boat and seaplane, the park protects the most pristine coral-reef habitat within the continental United States. When Ponce de León came upon these seven islands in 1513, he called them *tortugas* because of the numerous turtles he found there. Until the late 1800s, Garden Key was the site of strategic Fort Jefferson, part of the country's coastal fort system and the largest brick and masonry structure in the Western Hemisphere. (Dr. Samuel Mudd, who set John Wilkes Booth's broken leg, was imprisoned here.) Now the fort's massive walls surround only silence, and biological rather than military matters are paramount.

The Dry Tortugas are arid, austere, even bleak; they have no boat moorings, no supplies, and no freshwater (visitors must bring their own). Tiny and exposed, these coral islets have accumulated little soil and support few indigenous plants—mostly coastal species such as sea grapes and mangroves. What the islands lack in floral abundance, however, they supply in bird and marine diversity. In addition to pelicans, cormorants, gulls, migrating songbirds, and other familiar avian species, these remote keys attract birds rarely if ever seen on the mainland. Beginning in March, among tens of thousands of sooty terns that nest here are a few thousand brown noddies, the only brown terns. Man-o'-war, frigate bird, and magnificent frigate bird are all names for the large bird with deeply forked tail that is magnificently adapted to soaring over the ocean. Many frigate birds choose the peacefully undeveloped Dry Tortugas for their nesting site.

Below the surface of exceptionally clear waters, sometimes in only three to four feet of water, coral reefs teem with life—conchs, lobsters, sea urchins, a variety of corals, and tropical fish splashed in blue, yellow, purple, pink, and green. Their colors provide camouflage in the sun-dappled water, help attract the right mate, and delight the eye of the observer in this wild, remote outpost of natural America.

OVERLEAF: *Seemingly afloat on the translucent water, Upper Harbor Key is a small spot of land in the vast Great White Heron refuge—a world of fish and birds, sea and sky, between Florida and the Caribbean.*

FURTHER READING ABOUT THE SOUTHEAST

ALEVIZON, WILLIAM S. *Beachcomber's Guide to Florida Marine Life.* Houston: Gulf Publishing, 1994. How do beaches develop? What animals live in a reef and why? This guide answers questions concerning everything from back dunes to the deep sea with accompanying drawings and photographs.

BARTRAM, WILLIAM. *Travels and Other Writings.* New York: Library of America, 1996. These journals, written in the 1770s by America's first home-grown naturalist and first published in 1791, present the best view of the natural Southeast and native peoples before development. Bartram's knowledge, his sense of adventure, and his drawings are equally astonishing.

BELL, C. RITCHIE, AND BRYAN J. TAYLOR. *Florida Wild Flowers and Roadside Plants.* Chapel Hill, NC: Laurel Hill Press, 1982. Well organized, with color photographs and a key to plants, this useful book covers most of the vegetation travelers see throughout the coastal plain region, not just in Florida.

BROWN, FRED, AND NELL JONES, EDS. *The Georgia Conservancy's Guide to the North Georgia Mountains.* Atlanta: Longstreet Press, 1990. Complete with drawings and topographic-map close-ups, this guide encompasses every part of the wild North Georgia mountains. It provides directions, natural history lore, and enough places of interest to keep a traveler occupied for years.

CARR, ARCHIE. *A Naturalist in Florida: A Celebration of Eden.* New Haven: Yale University Press, 1994. These engaging essays by a noted writer and conservationist who spent 50 years in Florida combine careful scientific observations with eloquent, poetic descriptions of the state's abundant wildlife and fascinating ecosystems.

DOUGLAS, MARJORIE STONEMAN. *The Everglades: River of Grass.* New York: Rinehart, 1947. More than any other person, Marjorie Douglas made the nation aware of its unique natural legacy—the Everglades—and the need for its protection. The undulating sawgrass plains serve as the focus, but the people and the future of the Everglades are an integral part of this classic book.

DUNCAN, JULIA COLEY, AND ED MALLES. *Alabama.* Portland, OR: Graphic Arts Center Publishing Co., 1983. A large-format photographic journey through Alabama, with essays and captions focusing equally on natural and cultural sites.

GREENBERG, IDAZ, AND JERRY GREENBERG. *Guide to Corals and Fishes of Florida, the Bahamas, and the Caribbean.* Miami: Seahawk Press, 1986. This book belongs with scuba or snorkling gear: It's waterproof, and the clear drawings and succinct text allow marine visitors to quickly identify whatever fish, coral, or turtle has come into view.

HIASSEN, CARL. *Tourist Season.* New York: Warner Books, 1986. Hiassen, a novelist and *Miami Herald* columnist who knows his territory, takes the clash between the natural and unnatural in Florida to deadly—and hilarious—extremes in one of the best of his inventive mysteries.

HOFFMEISTER, JOHN EDWARD. *Land from the Sea: The Geologic Story of South Florida.* Coral Gables: University of Miami Press, 1974. This slim, engaging book uncovers the mysteries of the United States's youngest lands, what they are made of, and how they have evolved.

LEIFERMANN, HENRY. *South Carolina.* New York: Fodor's Travel Publications, 1995. Part of the Compass guide series, this volume explores South Carolina's natural and cultural past and present in full-color detail and informative prose. Includes maps, addresses, and phone numbers.

MANNING, PHILLIP. *Palmetto Journal: Walks in the Natural Areas of South Carolina.* Winston-Salem: John F. Blair, 1995. Each of these 15 walks visits a distinctive natural environment found in South Carolina. Includes maps, mileage, and degree of difficulty for each walk, as well as essays on the natural and cultural history of the areas.

MCGUANE, THOMAS. *Ninety-two in the Shade.* New York: Vintage, 1973. One of America's finest contemporary writers takes readers into the world of the Keys. The story is fictional, but the descriptions of the feel of the islands, the smell of the sea, the look of the sky, the heat, and the light are dead on.

MCKEE, GWEN, ED. *The Georgia Conservancy's Guide to the Georgia Coast.* Savannah: The Georgia Conservancy, 1984 (revised 1993). Similar to the Conservancy's mountain guide, this book's drawings, maps, and directions allow travelers to explore the vast watery mazes of Georgia's coastal areas.

MYERS, RONALD L., AND JOHN J. EWEL, EDS. *Ecosystems of Florida.* Orlando: University of Central Florida Press, 1990. From pine flatwoods and maritime forests to coral reefs, this is the complete guide to Florida's ecosystems and all that lives within each, written in lay language with accompanying black-and-white photographs.

RAWLINGS, MARJORIE KINNAN. *Cross Creek.* New York: Scribners, 1942. No one has more vividly and caringly portrayed the culture and people of northern Florida—and the natural riches that filled their lives—better than this Pulitzer Prize–winning writer.

TEAL, JOHN, AND MILDRED TEAL. *Life and Death of the Salt Marsh.* Boston: Little, Brown, 1969. The Teals tell the fascinating story of this most mysterious, seductive, and fecund of coastal ecosystems, overlaying the narrative with human and natural history.

WIGGINTON, ELIOT, AND STUDENTS, EDS. *Foxfire.* New York: Anchor/Doubleday, 1977–93. This series of books was born in the north Georgia mountains, when Wigginton and his students at Rabun County High School began collecting the lore of Appalachia. From plant remedies to snake handling, ghost stories to cabin building, these books give readers a genuine feel for the life and the land of the southern Appalachians.

GLOSSARY

aquifer underground layer of porous, water-bearing rock, sand, or gravel

barrier island narrow island of sediment—sand, silt, and gravel—that protects the coast from direct battering by storm waves and wind

bog wetland, formed in glacial kettle holes, common to cool climates of North America, Europe, and Asia; acidic nature produces large quantities of peat moss

brackish referring to salty or briny water, particularly a mixture of fresh and salt water found in estuaries

coastal plain large area of low, flat land lying next to an ocean; wetlands may develop in such low-lying areas

delta flat, low-lying plain that forms at the mouth of a river as the river slows and deposits sediment gathered upstream

dike vertical sheet of rock formed when molten rock cools on its way to the earth's surface and surrounding rock later erodes

endemic having originated in and being restricted to one particular environment

epiphyte plant that grows nonparasitically upon another plant, deriving its nutrients and water from the rain and air; also known as an air plant

escarpment cliff or steep rock face, formed by faulting or fracturing of the earth's crust, that separates two comparatively level land surfaces

estuary region of interaction between ocean water and the end of a river, where tidal action and river flow mix fresh and salt water

floodplain flat area along the course of a waterway subject to periodic flooding and deposition of the sediment the stream has been carrying

hammock small raised area of fertile soil supporting hardwood habitat

hogback sharply defined ridge produced by the erosion of highly angled rock layers, one of which is more resistant than the others

igneous referring to rock formed by cooled and hardened lava or magma

karst area of land lying over limestone that is dotted with sinkholes, underground streams, and caves formed by the erosion of the limestone by rainwater

magma molten rock within the earth that becomes igneous rock when it cools and hardens

metamorphic referring to a rock that has been changed into its present state after being subjected to heat, pressure, or chemical change

oxbow lake that forms where a meandering river overflows and forms a crescent-shaped body of standing water; called an oxbow because its shape looks like the U-shaped harness frame that fits around an ox's neck

piedmont area at the base of a mountain or range; in the eastern United States, the piedmont area stretches from the base of the Appalachian Mountains to the Atlantic coastal plain

plates thick rock slabs making up the earth's outer shell, including the ocean floor and the continental land masses; the movement and interaction of these plates is known as plate tectonics

sedimentary referring to rocks that are formed from deposits of small eroded debris such as gravel, sand, mud, silt, or peat

sinkhole funnel-shaped hole formed where water has collected in the cracks of limestone, dissolved the rock, and carried it away; also formed when roofs of caves collapse

slough swampy, backwater area; inlet on a river; or creek in a marsh or tidal flat

sphagnum moss that grows in wet, acidic areas; decomposes and compacts to form peat

stalactite icicle-shaped piece of drip-stone on the roof of a cave formed when water containing dissolved limestone drips and evaporates, leaving the mineral formation

stalagmite spires formed on a cave floor when water drips and deposits minerals dissolved in the water

tufa porous, sedimentary rock formed from calcium carbonate deposited around a spring or along lake shores; resembles a sponge

wetland area of land covered or saturated with groundwater; includes swamps, marshes, and bogs

ABOVE: *Automobiles opened up many remote natural areas; here a couple enjoys a deserted—if chilly—outing at the beach in the 1940s.*

259

LAND MANAGEMENT RESOURCES

*The following public and private organizations are among the important adminis-
trators of the preserved and protected areas described in this volume. Brief explanations of the various legal and legislative designations of these areas follow.*

MANAGING ORGANIZATIONS

Alabama Department of Conservation and Natural Resources
Administers some 100,000 acres of state parks, wildlife management areas, and un-
used lands. Regulates hunting and fishing licensing. Includes Divisions of State Parks
and Game and Fish.

Florida Division of Forestry
Manages 630,574 acres in 36 state forests for multiple uses including recreation and
timber production. Part of Department of Agriculture and Consumer Services.

Florida Division of Recreation and Parks
Manages 451,751 acres within 141 state parks. Part of the Department of Environmental Protection.

Florida Division of Wildlife
Manages 5,603,748 acres within approximately 75 wildlife management areas and
wildlife environmental areas. Regulates hunting and fishing licensing. Part of Game
and Fresh Water Fish Commission.

Georgia Parks, Recreation, and Historic Sites Division
Manages approximately 72,000 acres within 52 state parks and 14 historic sites. Part
of the Department of Natural Resources.

Georgia Wildlife Resources Division
Manages more than 1,500,000 acres of wildlife management areas, natural areas, and
fish hatcheries. Also regulates hunting, fishing, and boating licensing. Part of the Department of Natural Resources.

National Audubon Society (NAS) Private Organization
International nonprofit conservation, lobbying, and educational organization. Owns
a private network of wildlife sanctuaries.

National Ocean Service (NOS) Department of Commerce
Administers the National Geodetic Survey, Nautical and Aeronautical Charting, estuarine reserves, and national marine sanctuaries. Part of the National Oceanic and At-
mospheric Administration.

National Park Service (NPS) Department of the Interior
Regulates the use of national parks, monuments, and preserves. Administers historic and national landmarks, national seashores and lakeshores, wild and scenic
rivers, and the national trail system.

The Nature Conservancy (TNC) Private Organization
International nonprofit organization that owns the largest private system of nature
sanctuaries in the world, some 1,300 preserves.

South Carolina Division of Wildlife and Freshwater Fisheries
Manages more than one million acres of wildlife management areas and individually
leased tracts of land. Regulates hunting, fishing, and boating licensing. Part of the
Department of Natural Resources.

South Carolina Heritage Trust Program
Manages 69,616 acres within 50 preserves for protection of habitats for endangered
species. Part of the Department of Natural Resources.

South Carolina State Park System
Manages 48 state parks totaling 72,611 acres. Part of the Department of Parks, Recreation, and Tourism.

U.S. Fish and Wildlife Service (USFWS) Department of the Interior
Federal agency responsible for conserving, protecting, and enhancing the country's fish and wildlife and their habitats. Manages national wildlife refuges, fish hatcheries, and programs for migratory birds and endangered and threatened species.

U.S. Forest Service (USFS) Department of Agriculture
Administers more than 190 million acres in the national forests and national grasslands and manages their resources. Determines how best to combine commercial uses such as grazing, mining, and logging with conservation needs.

LAND DESIGNATIONS

Heritage Preserve
Natural area with habitats for endangered species designated for conservation and protection. Managed by individual states.

International Biosphere Reserve
Protected area set aside to help solve problems associated with human impact on natural ecosystems. Managed by the U.S. Man and the Biosphere Program.

National Forest
Large acreage managed for the use of forests, watersheds, wildlife, and public recreation. Managed by the USFS.

National Marine Sanctuary
Coastal waters protected for their natural, cultural, or historic resources. Restricted fishing, boating, and diving allowed. Managed by the NOS.

National Park
Spacious wilderness area with scenery and natural wonders so spectacular it has been preserved as a primitive area by the federal government. Managed by the NPS.

National Preserve
Area that protects specific natural resources. Hunting, fishing, and mining may be permitted. Managed by the NPS and local or state authorities.

National Recreation Area
Natural area designated for recreation; hunting, fishing, camping, and limited use of powerboats, dirt and mountain bikes, and ORVs permitted. Managed by the NPS.

National Seashore
Area of pristine undeveloped seashore designated for conservation and public recreation. Camping and ORVs allowed with restrictions. Managed by the NPS.

National Wild and Scenic River System
Program to protect and preserve selected rivers in their natural free-flowing condition; stretches are classified as wild, scenic, or recreational. Also develops hydropower projects. Management shared by the NPS and USFWS.

National Wildlife Refuge
Public lands set aside for wild animals; protects migratory waterfowl, endangered or threatened species, and native plants. Managed by the USFWS.

Wildlife Management Area
Natural area owned, protected, and maintained for recreation; hunting, fishing, trapping, and cross-country skiing permitted. Managed by each state's wildlife division.

Nature Travel

The following is a selection of national and local organizations that sponsor nature-related travel activities or can provide specialized regional travel information.

NATIONAL

National Audubon Society
700 Broadway
New York, NY 10003
(212) 979-3000
Offers a wide range of ecological field studies, tours, and cruises throughout the United States

National Wildlife Federation
1400 16th St. NW
Washington, D.C. 20036
(703) 790-4363
Offers training in environmental education, wildlife camp and teen adventures, conservation summits with nature walks, field trips, and classes

The Nature Conservancy
1815 North Lynn Street
Arlington, VA 22209
(703) 841-5300
Offers a variety of excursions from regional and state offices. May include hiking, backpacking, canoeing, horseback riding. Call to locate state offices

Sierra Club Outings
85 2nd St., 2nd floor
San Francisco, CA 94105
(415) 977-5630
Offers tours of different lengths for all ages throughout the United States. Outings may include backpacking, hiking, biking, skiing, and water excursions

Smithsonian Study Tours and Seminars
1100 Jefferson Dr. SW, MRC 702
Washington, DC 20560
(202) 357-4700
Offers extended tours, cruises, research expeditions, and seminars throughout the United States

REGIONAL

Alabama Bureau of Tourism and Travel
401 Adams Ave., Ste. 126
Montgomery, AL 36103
(800) ALABAMA (252-2262)
Publishes maps and brochures. Answers recreation and accomodations questions

Earthwatch
680 Mount Auburn St., PO Box 9104
Watertown, MA 02272
(800) 776-0188
Nonprofit organization sponsors volunteer environmental research expeditions. Destinations include projects throughout Florida and the southeast coast

Florida Tourism Visitor Inquiry Services
PO Box 1100
Tallahassee, FL 32302
(904) 487-1462
Call for Florida Vacation Guide listing maps, attractions, events, hotels, and camping information

Georgia Tourism Division
PO Box 1776
Atlanta, GA 30301
(800) VISITGA (847-4842) for specific questions
(404) 656-3590 for brochures
Provides Georgia travel literature and maps and answers travel questions

South Carolina Department of Parks, Recreation, and Tourism
1205 Pendleton St.
Columbia, SC 29201
(803) 734-0122
Distributes travel brochures and maps and answers specific travel and recreation questions

How to Use This Site Guide

The following site information guide will assist you in planning your tour of the natural areas of Alabama, Florida, Georgia, and South Carolina. Sites set in boldface and followed by the symbol ❖ in the text are here organized alphabetically by state. Each entry is followed by the mailing address (sometimes different from the street address) and phone number of the immediate managing office, plus brief notes and a list of facilities and activities available. (A key appears on each page.)

Information on hours of operation, seasonal closings, and fees is often not listed, as these vary from season to season and year to year. Please bear in mind that responsibility for the management of some sites may change. Call well in advance to obtain maps, brochures, and pertinent, up-to-date information that will help you plan your adventures in the Southeast.

Each site entry in the guide includes the address and phone number of its immediate managing agency. Many of these sites are under the stewardship of a forest or park ranger or supervised from a small nearby office. Hence, in many cases, those sites will be difficult to contact directly, and it is preferable to call the managing agency.

The following umbrella organizations can provide general information for individual natural sites, as well as the area as a whole:

REGIONAL

National Park Service
S.E. Field Area
75 Spring St.
Atlanta, GA 30303
(404) 331-5185

U.S. Forest Service
Region 8, Suite 800,
1720 Peachtree Rd., N.W.
Atlanta, GA 30367
(404) 347-4177

U.S. Fish and Wildlife Service, Region 4
1875 Century Blvd.
Atlanta, GA 30345
(404) 679-4000

ALABAMA

Alabama Dept. of Conservation and Natural Resources
64 N. Union St.
Montgomery, AL 36130
State Parks Div., Rm. 538
(334) 242-3334
Game and Fish Div.
Room 567,
(334) 242-3465

FLORIDA

Florida Div. of Recreation and Parks
3900 Commonwealth
Blvd., Mail Station 500
Tallahassee, FL 32399
(904) 488-6131

Florida Div. of Forestry
3125 Conner Blvd.
Tallahassee, FL 32399
(904) 488-4274

Florida Div. of Wildlife
620 S. Meridian St.
Tallahassee, FL 32399
(904) 488-3831

GEORGIA

Georgia Parks, Recreation, and Historic Sites Div.
205 Butler St., S.E.
1352 East Tower
Atlanta, GA 30334
(404) 656-2770

Georgia Wildlife Resources Div.
2070 Rte. 278
Social Circle, GA 30279
(770) 918-6401

SOUTH CAROLINA

South Carolina Dept. of Natural Resources
PO Box 167
Columbia, SC 29202
Heritage Trust Program
(803) 734-3894
Div. of Wildlife and
Freshwater Fisheries
(803) 734-3889

South Carolina Div. of Marine Resources
PO Box 12559
Charleston, SC 29422
(803) 795-6350

South Carolina Dept. of Parks, Recreation and Tourism
State Park System
1205 Pendleton St.
Columbia, SC 29201
(803) 734-0122

South Carolina Forestry Commission
PO Box 21707
Columbia, SC 29221
(803) 869-8800

ALABAMA

BANKHEAD NATIONAL FOREST
U.S. Forest Service
PO Box 278
Double Springs, AL 35553
(205) 489-5111   **C, F, H, HR, MB, PA, S, T**

BON SECOUR NATIONAL WILDLIFE REFUGE
U.S. Fish and Wildlife Service
12295 Rte. 180
Gulf Shores, AL 36542
(334) 540-7720   **BW, CK, F, H, IC, MT, PA, S, T**

BUCK'S POCKET STATE PARK
Alabama Div. of State Parks
393 County Rd. 174
Groveoak, AL 35975
(205) 659-2000   **BT, BW, C, CK, F, H, I, MB, MT, PA, RA, RC, T**

CHEAHA STATE PARK
Alabama Div. of State Parks
Rte. 281, 2141 Bunker Loop
Delta, AL 36258
(205) 488-5115   **BW, C, CK, F, H, L, MT, PA, S, T**

CHEAHA WILDERNESS
Talladega National Forest
Talladega Ranger District
1001 North St.
Talladega, AL 35160
(205) 362-2909
  Motorized vehicles and bicycles prohibited; map available at office
    BW, C, F, H, MT

CHOCTAW NATIONAL WILDLIFE REFUGE
U.S. Fish and Wildlife Service
PO Box 808
Jackson, AL 36545
(334) 246-3583
  Day use only; tours by prearrangement
    BT, BW, CK, F, H, I, MB, MT, PA, T, TG

CONECUH NATIONAL FOREST
U.S. Forest Service
Rte. 5, Box 157
Andalusia, AL 36420
(334) 222-2555
  Day use fees in developed recreation or picnic areas   **BT, BW, C, CK, F, H, HR, MT, PA, S, T**

DAUPHIN ISLAND BIRD SANCTUARY
Friends of the Dauphin Island
Audubon Sanctuary, Inc.
PO Box 1295
Dauphin Island, AL 36528-1295
(334) 861-2120   **BW**

DAUPHIN ISLAND SEA LAB
Marine Environmental
Science Consortium
PO Box 369-370, Dauphin Island, AL 36528
(334) 861-2141
  Educational programs by reservation
    BT, BW, GS, I, MT

DESOTO STATE PARK
Alabama Div. of State Parks
Rte. 1, Box 210, Fort Payne, AL 35967
(205) 845-5075
  Cabins available   **BW, C, CK, F, GS, H, I, L, MT, PA, RA, RC, S, T, TG**

EUFAULA NATIONAL WILDLIFE REFUGE
U.S. Fish and Wildlife Service
Rte. 2, Box 97-B, Eufaula, AL 36027
(334) 687-4065
  Canoe rentals and other facilities available at adjacent state park
    BW, CK, F, H, HR, I, T

FORT MORGAN
Alabama Historical Commission
51 Rte. 180 West, Gulf Shores, AL 36542
(334) 540-7125
  Admission fee; tours on request
    BW, F, GS, I, PA, T, TG

GULF STATE PARK
Alabama Div. of State Parks
20115 Rte. 135, Gulf Shores, AL 36542
(334) 948-7275   **BW, BT, C, CK, F, GS, H, IC, L, MT, PA, RA, S, T**

LAKE GUNTERSVILLE STATE PARK
Alabama Div. of State Parks
7966 Rte. 227, Guntersville, AL 35976
(205) 571-5445   **BW, C, CK, F, GS, H, I, L, MT, PA, RA, S, T, TG**

LITTLE RIVER CANYON
NATIONAL PRESERVE
National Park Service
2141 Gault Ave., North
Fort Payne, AL 35967
(205) 845-9605   **BT, BW, C, CK, F, GS, H, HR, I, L, MB, PA, RC, S, T, TG**

BT	Bike Trails	**CK**	Canoeing, Kayaking	**F**	Fishing
BW	Bird-watching			**GS**	Gift Shop
C	Camping	**DS**	Downhill Skiing	**H**	Hiking

HR	Horseback Riding
I	Information Center

MOBILE–TENSAW RIVER BOTTOMLANDS
Alabama Div. of Game and Fish
PO Box 7245
Spanish Fort, AL 36577
(334) 626-5153   **BW, F, H**

NATURAL BRIDGE
PO Box 342
Natural Bridge, AL 35577
(205) 486-5330
    Admission fee   **GS, H, I, MT, PA, T**

PAYNE LAKE RECREATION AREA
Talladega National Forest
Shoal Creek Ranger District
450 Rte. 46
Heflin, AL 36264
(205) 463-2272   **BW, C, F, H, MB,**
                              MT, PA, S, T

RUSSELL CAVE NATIONAL MONUMENT
National Park Service
Rte. 1, Box 175
Bridgeport, AL 35740
(205) 495-2672   **BW, GS, H, I, MT, PA, T**

SEQUOYAH CAVERNS
Rte. 1, Box 302, Valley Head, AL 35989
(205) 635-0024; (800) 843-5098
    Admission fee; open seven days a
    week March–November; open week-
    ends December–February; handicapped
    accessible   **BT, C, F, GS, H,**
                              MT, PA, S, T, TG

TALLADEGA NATIONAL FOREST
U.S. Forest Service
2946 Chestnut St.
Montgomery, AL 36107-3010
(334) 832-4470   **BW, C, F, H,**
                              MB, MT, PA, S, T

TUSKEGEE NATIONAL FOREST
U.S. Forest Service
125 National Forest Rd. 949
Tuskegee, AL 36083
(334) 727-2652   **BW, C, F, H, HR,**
                                  MB, MT, PA

**WEEKS BAY NATIONAL ESTUARINE
RESEARCH RESERVE**
National Ocean Service
11300 Rte. 98, Fairhope, AL 366532
(334) 928-9792
    Group tours by prearrangement; handi-
    capped-accessible boardwalk trail
        BW, CK, F, GS, H, IC, MT, PA, T, TG

**WHEELER NATIONAL
WILDLIFE REFUGE**
U.S. Fish and Wildlife Service
Rte. 4, Box 250, Decatur, AL 35603
(205) 350-6630 (visitor center)
(205) 353-7243 (office)
    Complex includes Watercress Darter,
    Fern Cave, and Blowing Wind refuges
        BW, CK, F, H, HR, I, MT, PA

FLORIDA

ALEXANDER SPRINGS RECREATION AREA
Ocala National Forest
Seminole Ranger District
40929 Rte. 19, Umatilla, FL 32784
(352) 669-3522
    Includes portion of Florida National
    Scenic Trail; some day use fees; no mo-
    torized boating; canoe rentals or launch
    your own   **BT, BW, C, CK, F, H,**
                              I, MB, MT, PA, RA, S, T

ANCLOTE KEY STATE PRESERVE
Florida Div. of Recreation and Parks
c/o Gulf Islands GEOpark
1 Causeway Blvd.
Dunedin, FL 34698
(813) 469-5918 (Caladesi Island); (813)
469-5942 (Honeymoon Island/Gulf Islands)
    Primitive camping; bring water and bug
    spray   **BW, C, CK, F, H, S**

**APALACHICOLA BLUFFS
AND RAVINES PRESERVE**
The Nature Conservancy,
NW Florida Program
PO Box 393, Bristol, FL 32321
(904) 643-2756   **BW, H, MT**

APALACHICOLA NATIONAL FOREST
U.S. Forest Service
PO Box 579, Rte. 20
Bristol, FL 32321
(904) 643-2282
(Apalachicola Ranger District);
(904) 926-3561 (Wakulla Ranger District)
                    BT, BW, C, CK, F, H,
                    HR, MB, MT, PA, S, T

**ARCHIE CARR NATIONAL
WILDLIFE REFUGE**
U.S. Fish and Wildlife Service
c/o Merritt Island National Wildlife Refuge
PO Box 6504, Titusville, FL 32780
(407) 861-0667

L	Lodging	**PA**	Picnic Areas	**RC**	Rock Climbing	**TG** Tours, Guides
MB	Mountain Biking	**RA**	Ranger-led Activities	**S**	Swimming	**XC** Cross-country Skiing
MT	Marked Trails			**T**	Toilets	

BAHIA HONDA STATE PARK
Florida Div. of Recreation and Parks
36850 Overseas Hwy.
Big Pine Key, FL 33043
(305) 872-2353
 Reservations required for overnight accommodations **BW, C, CK, F, GS, L, MT,**
         PA, RA, S, T, TG

BIG CYPRESS NATIONAL PRESERVE
National Park Service
33100 Tamiami Trail East
Ochopee, FL 33943
(941) 695-4111
 Primitive camping; be prepared for hiking through wet swampy areas
    BW, C, CK, F, GS, H, I, MB, RA, T

BIG TALBOT ISLAND STATE PARK
Florida Div. of Recreation and Parks
12157 Heckscher Drive
Jacksonville, FL 32226
(904) 251-2320
 Vehicle admission fee **BT, BW, CK, F,**
         H, MB, MT, PA, S

BISCAYNE NATIONAL PARK
National Park Service
PO Box 1369
Homestead, FL 33093-1369
(305) 230-7275; (305) 230-1100
(reservations and schedules)
 Tent camping accessible by boat only;
 boat tours and snorkel trips available
 through concessionaire
     BW, C, CK, F, GS,
     I, PA, PA, RA, T, TG

BLACKWATER RIVER STATE FOREST
Florida Div. of Forestry
11650 Munson Hwy.
Milton, FL 32570
(904) 957-4201 **BT, BW, C, CK, F, H,**
    HR, I, MB, MT, PA, RA, S, T, TG

CALADESI ISLAND STATE PARK
Florida Div. of Recreation and Parks
c/o Gulf Islands GEOpark
1 Causeway Blvd.,
Dunedin, FL 34698
(813) 469-5918; (813) 469-5943
(Gulf Islands GEOpark)
 Accessible by boat only; primitive
 camping **BW, C, CK, F, GS, H, I,**
     MT, PA, RA, S, T, TG

CANAVERAL NATIONAL SEASHORE
National Park Service
308 Julia St., Titusville, FL 32796
(904) 428-3384 (information)
(407) 267-1110 (headquarters)
 South district includes Kennedy Space
 Center (closed three days prior to Space
 Shuttle launch); permit required for backcountry camping and horseback riding
    BW, C, CK, F, H, HR,
    I, MT, PA, RA, S, T, TG

**CEDAR KEY NATIONAL
WILDLIFE REFUGE**
U.S. Fish and Wildlife Service
16450 NW 31st Pl., Chiefland, FL 32626
(352) 493-0238   **BW**

**CHASSAHOWITZKA NATIONAL
WILDLIFE REFUGE**
U.S. Fish and Wildlife Service
1502 SE Kings Bay Dr.
Crystal River, FL 34429
(352) 563-2088
 Accessible by boat only **BW, CK, F, S**

CORKSCREW SWAMP SANCTUARY
National Audubon Society
375 Sanctuary Rd., Naples, FL 33964
(941) 657-3771 **BW, GS, MT, PA, T**

**CROCODILE LAKE NATIONAL
WILDLIFE REFUGE**
U.S. Fish and Wildlife Service
PO Box 430510
Big Pine Key, FL 33043-0510
(305) 872-2239
 Not open to public

**CRYSTAL RIVER NATIONAL
WILDLIFE REFUGE**
U.S. Fish and Wildlife Service
1502 SE Kings Bay Dr.
Crystal River, FL 34429
(352) 563-2088
 Accessible by boat only **BW, CK, F, S**

**DEVILS MILLHOPPER STATE
GEOLOGICAL SITE**
Florida Div. of Recreation and Parks
4732 NW 53rd Ave., Gainesville, FL 32601
(352) 955-2008
(352) 462-7905
 Admission fee; open 9 A.M. to 5 P.M.
   BW, GS, H, I, MT, PA, T, TG

BT	Bike Trails	**CK**	Canoeing, Kayaking	**F**	Fishing	**HR**	Horseback Riding
BW	Bird-watching			**GS**	Gift Shop		
C	Camping	**DS**	Downhill Skiing	**H**	Hiking	**I**	Information Center

DRY TORTUGAS NATIONAL PARK
National Park Service
40001 State Rd. 9336, Homestead, FL 33034
(305) 242-7700   **BW, C, F, GS,**
       I, PA, RA, S, T

EVERGLADES NATIONAL PARK
National Park Service
40001 State Rd. 9336
Homestead, FL 33034
(305) 242-7700
   Summer weather extremes; wilderness
     precautions   **BT, BW, C, CK, F, GS,**
       H, I, L, MT, PA, RA, T, TG

FAKAHATCHEE STRAND STATE PRESERVE
Florida Div. of Recreation and Parks
PO Box 548, Copeland, FL 33926
(941) 595-4593
   One swamp walk per month November
   to February, reservations required
       BW, CK, F, H, RA

FALLING WATERS
STATE RECREATION AREA
Florida Div. of Recreation and Parks
1130 State Park Rd.
Chipley, FL 32428
(904) 638-6130   **BW, C, F, I, MT, PA, S, T**

FLORIDA CAVERNS STATE PARK
Florida Div. of Recreation and Parks
3345 Caverns Rd.
Marianna, FL 32446
(904) 482-9598
(904) 482-1228 (camping reservations)
   Parking fee; cave tours daily 9 A.M. to
   4:30 P.M. (fee)   **BW, C, CK, F, GS, H,**
       HR, I, MT, PA, RA, S, T, TG

FLORIDA NATIONAL SCENIC TRAIL
Florida Trail Association
PO Box 13708, Gainesville, FL 32604-1708
(800) 343-1882; (904) 942-9300 (Forest
Service); (352) 378-8823 (Trail Association)
       BW, C, CK, F, H, MT, PA, S

GREAT WHITE HERON
NATIONAL WILDLIFE REFUGE
U.S. Fish and Wildlife Service
PO Box 430510, Big Pine Key, FL 33043-0510
(305) 872-2239
   Information center at National Key Deer
   Refuge; most of area accessible by water
   only   **BW, CK, F, I, S**

GULF ISLANDS NATIONAL SEASHORE
National Park Service
1801 Gulf Breeze Pkwy.
Gulf Breeze, FL 32561
(904) 934-2600; (904) 934-2621 (visitor
center)
     BT, BW, C, F, H, I, MT, PA, RA, S, T, TG

HIGHLANDS HAMMOCK STATE PARK
Florida Div. of Recreation and Parks
5931 Hammock Rd., Sebring, FL 33872
(941) 386-6094   **BT, BW, C, GS, H, HR,**
       MB, MT, PA, RA, T, TG

HOBE SOUND NATIONAL
WILDLIFE REFUGE
U.S. Fish and Wildlife Service
PO Box 645, Hobe Sound, FL 33475
(407) 546-6141   **BW, CK, F, H,**
       I, MT, RA, S, T

HONEYMOON ISLAND
STATE RECREATION AREA
Florida Div. of Recreation and Parks
c/o Gulf Islands GEOpark
1 Causeway Blvd., Dunedin, FL 34698
(813) 469-5942; (813) 469-5943
       BT, BW, CK, F, GS, H,
       HR, I, MT, PA, RA, S, T, TG

J. N. "DING" DARLING
NATIONAL WILDLIFE REFUGE
U.S. Fish and Wildlife Service
1 Wildlife Drive
Sanibel, FL 33957
(941) 472-1100
   Parking fee; some day use fees; five-
   mile wildlife drive for cars and bikes;
   ranger-led winter walks
     BT, BW, CK, F, GS, H, I, MB, MT, RA, T

JOHN PENNEKAMP
CORAL REEF STATE PARK
Florida Div. of Recreation and Parks
MM 102.5 Overseas Hwy., PO Box 487
Key Largo, FL 33037
(305) 451-1202   **BW, C, CK, F,**
       GS, I, MT, PA, RA, S, T

JONATHAN DICKINSON STATE PARK
Florida Div. of Recreation and Parks
16450 SE Federal Hwy.
Hobe Sound, FL 33455
(407) 546-277   **BT, BW, C, CK, F, GS, H,**
       HR, I, L, MB, MT, PA, RA, T, TG

L	Lodging	**PA**	Picnic Areas	**RC**	Rock Climbing	**TG**	Tours, Guides
MB	Mountain	**RA**	Ranger-led	**S**	Swimming	**XC**	Cross-country
	Biking		Activities	**T**	Toilets		Skiing
MT	Marked Trails						

267

JUNIPER SPRINGS RECREATION AREA
Ocala National Forest
Lake George Ranger District
17147 East Rte. 40
Silver Springs, FL 34488
(352) 625-3147
> Some day use fees; no motorized boating; canoe rentals or launch your own
> **BW, C, CK, F, H, I, MB, MT, PA, RA, S, T**

KEY LARGO NATIONAL MARINE SANCTUARY
National Ocean Service,
Sanctuary and Reserves Div.
PO Box 1083, Key Largo, FL 33037
(305) 451-1644
> Scuba diving **BW, F, I, S**

KEY WEST NATIONAL WILDLIFE REFUGE
U.S. Fish and Wildlife Service
PO Box 430510
Big Pine Key, FL 33043-0510
(305) 872-2239
> Accessible by boat only; information center at National Key Deer Refuge
> **BW, CK, F, I, S**

LAKE WOODRUFF NATIONAL WILDLIFE REFUGE
U.S. Fish and Wildlife Service
PO Box 488
De Leon Springs, FL 32130-0488
(904) 985-4673
> Ranger-led activities by appointment only
> **BT, BW, CK,F, H, I, RA, T**

LIGNUMVITAE KEY STATE BOTANICAL SITE
Florida Div. of
Recreation and Parks
PO Box 1052, Islamorada, FL 33036
(305) 664-4815
> Accessible by boat only; tours Thursday through Monday 10 A.M. and 2 P.M. (fee)
> **BW, CK, RA, T, TG**

LITTLE TALBOT ISLAND STATE PARK
Florida Div. of
Recreation and Parks
12157 Heckscher Drive
Jacksonville, FL 32226
(904) 251-2320
> Vehicle admission fee
> **BW, C, CK, F, H, I, MB, MT, PA, RA, S, T, TG**

LOWER SUWANNEE NATIONAL WILDLIFE REFUGE
U.S. Fish and Wildlife Service
16450 NW 31st Pl.
Chiefland, FL 32626
(352) 493-0238 **BW, F, MB**

LOXAHATCHEE NATIONAL WILDLIFE REFUGE
U.S. Fish and Wildlife Service
10216 Lee Rd.
Boynton Beach, FL 33437-4796
(407) 734-8303 **BW, CK, F, GS, H, I, MT, RA, T**

MERRITT ISLAND NATIONAL WILDLIFE REFUGE
U.S. Fish and Wildlife Service
PO Box 6504
Titusville, FL 32782
(407) 861-0667
> May be closed during shuttle launch operations **BW, CK, F, GS, H, I, MT, RA**

MYAKKA RIVER STATE PARK
Florida Div. of Recreation and Parks
13207 Rte. 72
Sarasota, FL 34241
(941) 361-6512; (941) 361-6515
> **BT, BW, C, CK, F, GS, H, HR, I, L, MT, PA, RA, T, TG**

NASSAU WILDLIFE MANAGEMENT AREA
Florida Div. of Wildlife
Rte. 7, Box 440
Lake City, FL 32055
(904) 758-0525 **BW, C**

NATIONAL KEY DEER REFUGE
U.S. Fish and Wildlife Service
PO Box 430510
Big Pine Key, FL 33043-0510
(305) 872-2239
> Ranger-led activities during winter only; information center open weekdays
> **BW, I, MT, RA**

OCALA NATIONAL FOREST
U.S. Forest Service
325 John Knox Rd.
Woodcrest Office Park, Ste. S-100
Tallahassee, FL 32303
(904) 942-9300 **BT, BW, C, CK, F, H, HR, I, MB, MT, PA, S, T**

BT	Bike Trails	**CK**	Canoeing, Kayaking	**F**	Fishing	**HR**	Horseback Riding
BW	Bird-watching			**GS**	Gift Shop		
C	Camping	**DS**	Downhill Skiing	**H**	Hiking	**I**	Information Center

OSCEOLA NATIONAL FOREST
U.S. Forest Service
PO Box 70
Olustee, FL 32072
(904) 752-2577   BW, C, F, GS, H, HR,
                         I, MB, MT, PA, S, T

PAYNES PRAIRIE STATE PRESERVE
Florida Div. of Recreation and Parks
Rte. 2, Box 41
Micanopy, FL 32667
(352) 466-3397; (352) 466-4100
                    BT, BW, C, CK, F, H,
                    HR, I, MB, MT, PA, RA, T, TG

**PELICAN ISLAND NATIONAL
WILDLIFE REFUGE**
U.S. Fish and Wildlife Service
c/o Merritt Island National
Wildlife Refuge
PO Box 6504,Titusville, FL 32780
(407) 867-4820   BW, F

RICE CREEK SANCTUARY
Georgia-Pacific Corporation
PO Box 158
East Palatka, FL 32131
(904) 328-2796
(800) 343-1882 (Florida Trail Association)
  Call before visiting
          BT, BW, H, MB, MT, PA, T

SAINT GEORGE ISLAND STATE PARK
Florida Div. of Recreation and Parks
HCR, Box 62
Saint George Island, FL 32328
(904) 927-2111
  Excellent fall and spring viewing of
  transgulf migrants, especially warblers
                    BW, C, CK,
                    F, H, MT, PA, S, T

SAINT JOSEPH PENINSULA STATE PARK
Florida Div. of Recreation and Parks
Rte. 1, Box 200
Port Saint Joe, FL 32456
(904) 227-1327   BW, C, CK, F, H, L,
                         MT, PA, RA, S, T

**SAINT MARKS NATIONAL
WILDLIFE REFUGE**
U.S. Fish and Wildlife Service
PO Box 68, Saint Marks, FL 32355
(904) 925-6121   BT, BW, CK, F, GS, H,
                         HR, I, MB, MT, PA, RA, T

**SAINT VINCENT NATIONAL
WILDLIFE REFUGE**
U.S. Fish and Wildlife Service
PO Box 447
Apalachicola, FL 32329
(904) 653-8808   BT, BW, CK, F, H, I

**SAN FELASCO HAMMOCK
STATE PRESERVE**
Florida Div. of Recreation and Parks
2720 NW 109th Lane
Gainesville, FL 32606
(352) 462-7905
  Admission fee   BW, H, I, MT, RA

TIGER CREEK PRESERVE
The Nature Conservancy,
Central Florida Office
225 E. Stuart Ave.
PO Box 1199
Lake Wales, FL 33853
(941) 678-1551   BW

**TIMUCUAN ECOLOGICAL AND
HISTORIC PRESERVE**
National Park Service
12713 Ft. Caroline Rd.
Jacksonville, FL 32225
(904) 251-3537; (904) 641-7155
          BW, CK, F, GS, H, I, RA, T

TORREYA STATE PARK
Florida Div. of Recreation and Parks
HC 2, Box 70
Bristol, FL 32321
(904) 643-2674
          BW, C, H, MT. PA, T, TG

**TURTLE MOUND
ARCHAEOLOGICAL SITE**
National Park Service
Canaveral National Seashore
308 Julia St.
Titusville, FL 32796
(904) 428-3384; (407) 267-1110
  Primitive camping   BW, C, CK, F, H,
                         HR, I, MT, PA, RA, S, T, TG

WACCASASSA BAY STATE PRESERVE
Florida Div. of Recreation and Parks
PO Box 187
Cedar Key, FL 32625
(352) 543-5567
  Primitive camping, first-come first-
  served; accessible by boat only   C

L	Lodging	**PA**	Picnic Areas	**RC**	Rock Climbing	**TG** Tours, Guides
MB	Mountain	**RA**	Ranger-led	**S**	Swimming	**XC** Cross-country
	Biking		Activities	**T**	Toilets	Skiing
MT	Marked Trails					

**WAKULLA SPRINGS
(EDWARD BALL) STATE PARK**
Florida Div. of Recreation and Parks
1 Spring Drive
Wakulla Springs, FL 32305
(904) 922-3632
(904) 224-5950 (reservations)
　Snorkeling in swimming area
　　　BW, GS, H, L, MT, PA, RA, S, T, TG

GEORGIA

**AMICALOLA FALLS STATE
PARK AND LODGE**
Georgia Parks, Recreation
and Historic Sites Div.
418 Amicalola Falls Lodge Dr.
Dawsonville, GA 30534
(706) 265-8888　　　**BT, BW, C, F, GS,
H, I, L, MB, MT, PA, RA, T, TG**

ANNA RUBY FALLS SCENIC AREA
Chattahoochee National Forest
Chattooga Ranger District
PO Box 196, Clarkesville, GA 30523
(706) 878-3574
　Parking fee　　　**BW, F, GS, H,
I, MT, PA, RA, T**

**BANKS LAKE NATIONAL
WILDLIFE REFUGE**
U.S. Fish and Wildlife Service
Rte. 2, Box 3330, Folkston, GA 31537
(912) 496-7836　　　**BW, CK, F, PA, T**

BIG HAMMOCK NATURAL AREA
Georgia Wildlife Resources Div., Game
Management Section
1773-A Bowen's Mill Hwy.
Fitzgerald, GA 31750
(912) 423-2988 ˉ　　　**BW, F, H, MT**

BROXTON ROCKS PRESERVE
The Nature Conservancy of Georgia
1401 Peachtree St. NE, Ste 236
Atlanta, GA 30309
(404) 873-6946
　Must call in advance　　　**BW, H**

CHATTAHOOCHEE NATIONAL FOREST
U.S. Forest Service
508 Oak St.
Gainesville, GA 30501
(770) 536-0541　　　**BT, BW, C, CK, F,
GS, H, HR, I, MB, MT, PA, RA, RC, S, T**

CLOUDLAND CANYON STATE PARK
Georgia Parks, Recreation
and Historic Sites Div.
Rte. 2, Box 150, Rising Fawn, GA 30738
(706) 657-4050　　　**BW, C, GS, H,
I, L, MT, PA, S, T**

COHUTTA WILDERNESS
Chattahoochee National Forest
Cohutta Ranger District
401 Old Ellijay Rd., Chatsworth, GA 30705
(706) 695-6736
　Primitive camping　　　**C, F, H, HR**

**CROCKFORD-PIGEON
WILDLIFE MANAGEMENT AREA**
Georgia Wildlife Resources Div.
2592 Floyd Springs Rd., NE
Armuchee, GA 30105
(706) 295- 6041
(706) 638-3944
(check station)
　Primitive camping　　　**BT, BW, C, F, H,
HR, I, MB, MT, RC**

CUMBERLAND ISLAND NATIONAL SEASHORE
National Park Service
PO Box 806, St. Marys, GA 31558
(912) 882-5671　　　**BW, C, F, H, I,
MT, PA, RA, S, T**

**ED JENKINS NATIONAL
RECREATION AREA**
Chattahoochee National Forest
Toccoa Ranger District
990 East Main St., Suite 1
Blue Ridge, GA 30513
(706) 632-3031　　　**BW, C, CK, F,
H, HR, MB, MT**

FRANKLIN D. ROOSEVELT STATE PARK
Georgia Parks, Recreation
and Historic Sites Div.
Box 2970, Rte. 190 E
Pine Mountain, GA 31822
(706) 663-4858　　　**BW, C, F, GS, H, HR,
I, L, MT, PA, RA, S, T**

**GRAY'S REEF NATIONAL
MARINE SANCTUARY**
National Ocean Service
10 Ocean Science Circle, Savannah, GA 31411
(912) 598-2345
　Scuba diving; public aquarium display
　on Skidaway Island, Savannah　　　**F, I**

BT	Bike Trails	**CK**	Canoeing,	**F**	Fishing	**HR**	Horseback
BW	Bird-watching		Kayaking	**GS**	Gift Shop		Riding
C	Camping	**DS**	Downhill	**H**	Hiking	**I**	Information
			Skiing				Center

HEGGIE'S ROCK PRESERVE
The Nature Conservancy of Georgia
1401 Peachtree St. NE, Ste. 236
Atlanta, GA 30309
(404) 873-6946
   Must call in advance   **BW, H**

KEOWN FALLS SCENIC AREA
Chattahoochee National Forest
Armuchee Ranger District
PO Box 465
La Fayette, GA 30728
(706) 638-1085   **BW, H, PA, T**

LAKE CONASAUGA RECREATION AREA
Chattahoochee National Forest
Cohutta Ranger District
401 Old Ellijay Rd.
Chatsworth, GA 30705
(706) 695-6736   **BT, BW, C, CK, F,**
              H, HR, MB, MT, PA, S, T

LEWIS ISLAND NATURAL AREA
Georgia Wildlife Resources Div.
Game Management Section
One Conservation Way
Brunswick, GA 31523-8604
(912) 262-3173
   Access by boat   **BW, C, CK, F**

OCONEE NATIONAL FOREST
U.S. Forest Service
508 Oak St.
Gainesville, GA 30501
(770) 536-0541
   Trail map available; primitive camping
             BT, BW, C, CK, F, H,
             HR, I, MT, PA, RA, RC, S, T, TG

**OKEFENOKEE NATIONAL
WILDLIFE REFUGE**
U.S. Fish and Wildlife Service
Rte. 2, Box 3330
Folkston, GA 31537
(912) 496-7836   **BW, C, CK, F, GS, H, I,**
              L, MT, PA, RA, T, TG

**PANOLA MOUNTAIN STATE
CONSERVATION PARK**
Georgia Parks, Recreation
and Historic Sites Div.
2600 Rte. 155 SW
Stockbridge, GA 30281
(770) 389-7801   **BW, CK, GS, H,**
              I, MT, PA, RA, T, TG

PANTHER CREEK RECREATION AREA
Chattahoochee National Forest
Chattooga Ranger District
PO Box 196,
Clarkesville, GA 30523
(706) 754-6221   **BW, C, F, H, MT, PA, T**

PIEDMONT NATIONAL WILDLIFE REFUGE
U.S. Fish and Wildlife Service
Rte. 1, Box 670
Round Oak, GA 31038
(912) 986-5441
   Tours by prearrangement; special-use
   fishing permit required; six-mile wildlife
   area   **BW, F, H, I, MT, RA, T**

**PROVIDENCE CANYON STATE
CONSERVATION PARK**
Georgia Parks, Recreation
and Historic Sites Div.
Rte. 1, Box 158
Lumpkin, GA 31815
(912) 838-6202   **C, GS, H, I, MT, PA, T**

RAVEN CLIFFS FALLS
Chattahoochee National Forest
Chattooga Ranger District
PO Box 196
Clarkesville, GA 30523
(706) 754-6221
   Self-registration before hiking
             BW, C, F, H, MT

RICH MOUNTAIN WILDERNESS
Chattahoochee National Forest
Toccoa Ranger District
990 East Main St., Ste. 1
Blue Ridge, GA 30513
(706) 632-3031   **BW, C, F, H, MB**

SAVANNAH COASTAL REFUGES
U.S. Fish and Wildlife Service
Parkway Business Center
1000 Business Center Dr.
Savannah, GA 31405
(912) 652-4415
   Pets not allowed; day-use only
             BW, F, H, MB, MT, S, T, TG

SPREWELL BLUFF STATE PARK
Georgia Parks, Recreation and Historic
Sites Div.
740 Sprewell Bluff
Thomaston, GA 30286
(706) 646-6026   **CK, F, H, PA, S**

L	Lodging	**PA**	Picnic Areas	**RC**	Rock Climbing	**TG** Tours, Guides
MB	Mountain Biking	**RA**	Ranger-led Activities	**S**	Swimming	**XC** Cross-country Skiing
MT	Marked Trails			**T**	Toilets	

STEPHEN FOSTER STATE PARK
Georgia Parks, Recreation and
Historic Sites Div.
Rte. 1, Box 131, Fargo, GA 31631
(912) 637-5274
(912) 637-5325
BW, C, CK, F, GS, H, I, L,
MT, PA, RA, T, TG

SWEETWATER CREEK STATE
CONSERVATION PARK
Georgia Parks, Recreation and
Historic Sites Div.
PO Box 816, Lithia Springs, GA 30057
(770) 732-5871
Parking fee   BW, CK, F, H,
MT, PA, RA, T, TG

TALLULAH GORGE STATE PARK
Georgia Parks, Recreation
and Historic Sites Div.
PO Box 248
Tallulah Falls, GA 30573
(706) 754-7970   BT, BW, C, CK, F, GS,
H, I, MB, MT, PA, RA, RC, S, T

UNICOI STATE PARK
Georgia Parks, Recreation
and Historic Sites Div.
PO Box 849, Helen, GA 30545
(706) 878-2201   BW, C, F, GS, H, I,
L, MB, MT, PA, RA, S, T

WASSAW NATIONAL WILDLIFE REFUGE
U.S. Fish and Wildlife Service
Parkway Business Center
1000 Business Center Dr., Ste. 10
Savannah, GA 31405
(912) 652-4415
Occassionally closed to public during
fall and winter deer hunts; group tours
by prearrangement
BW, F, H, MB, MT, S, TG

SOUTH CAROLINA

ACE BASIN NATIONAL WILDLIFE REFUGE
U.S. Fish and Wildlife Service
PO Box 848
Hollywood, SC 29449
(803) 889-3084
Be prepared for insects and the possibil-
ity of snakes spring through fall
BW, F, H

ANDREW PICKENS RANGER DISTRICT
Sumter National Forest
112 Andrew Pickens Circle
Mountain Rest, SC 29664
(864) 638-9568   BW, C, CK, F, GS, H,
HR, I, MT, PA, RA, S, T, TG

ASHMORE HERITAGE PRESERVE
South Carolina Dept. of Natural Resources
Heritage Trust
PO Box 167, Columbia, SC 29202
(803) 734-3894
Hikers be prepared to cross two streams
BW, F, H, MT, S

BEAR ISLAND
WILDLIFE MANAGEMENT AREA
South Carolina Div. of Wildlife and
Freshwater Fisheries
Rte. 1, Box 25, Green Pond, SC 29446
(803) 844-2952
BT, BW, F, H, PA

BUZZARD ROOST HERITAGE PRESERVE
South Carolina Dept. of
Natural Resources Heritage Trust
PO Box 167, Columbia, SC 29202
(803) 734-3894   BW, H, MT

CAESARS HEAD STATE PARK
South Carolina State Park System
8155 Geer Hwy., Cleveland, SC 29635
(864) 836-6115
Hiking registration required; trailside
camping   BW, C, GS, H,
I, MT, PA, RA, T

CAPE ROMAIN NATIONAL
WILDLIFE REFUGE
U.S. Fish and Wildlife Service
5801 Rte. 17 North, Awendaw, SC 29429
(803) 928-3368
Boat access only; ferry to Bull Island
from Moore's Landing
BW, CK, F, H, I, MT, PA, T

CAPERS ISLAND STATE PRESERVE
South Carolina Div. of Marine Resources
217 Fort Johnson Rd., PO Box 12559
Charleston, SC 29412
(803) 762-5043   BT, BW, C, CK, F, H, S

CAROLINA SANDHILLS WILDLIFE REFUGE
U.S. Fish and Wildlife Service
Rte. 2, Box 330, McBee, SC 29101
(803) 335-8401   BW, F, H, I, MT, PA, T

BT	Bike Trails	**CK**	Canoeing, Kayaking	**F**	Fishing	**HR**	Horseback Riding
BW	Bird-watching			**GS**	Gift Shop		
C	Camping	**DS**	Downhill Skiing	**H**	Hiking	**I**	Information Center

**CHATTOOGA NATIONAL WILD
AND SCENIC RIVER**
Sumter National Forest
4931 Broad River Rd.
Columbia, SC 29210-4021
(803) 561-4000
   Primitive camping   **C, CK, F, H, HR, S**

**CONGAREE SWAMP
NATIONAL MONUMENT**
National Park Service
200 Columbia Sims Rd.
Hopkins, SC 29061
(803) 776-4396
   Primitive backcountry camping; free
   permit required
   BW, C, CK, F, GS, H, I, MT, PA, RA, T, TG

**EASTATOE CREEK
HERITAGE PRESERVE**
South Carolina Dept. of
Natural Resources Heritage Trust
PO Box 167, Columbia, SC 29202
(803) 734-3894
   Primitive camping   **BW, C, F, H, MT**

EDISTO BEACH STATE PARK
South Carolina State Park System
8377 State Cabin Rd.
Edisto Island, SC 29438
(803) 869-2156   **BW, C, F, GS, I,
    L, MT, PA, S, T**

ELLICOTT ROCK WILDERNESS
Sumter National Forest
4931 Broad River Rd.
Columbia, SC 29210-4021
(803) 561-4000
   Primitive camping   **BW, C, F, H**

ENOREE RANGER DISTRICT
Sumter National Forest
20 Work Center, Whitmire, SC 29178
(803) 276-4810
   Includes the former Tyger Ranger District; tours by prearrangement
    **BT, BW, C, CK, F, H,
    HR, I, MB, MT, PA, S, T**

**EVA RUSSELL CHANDLER
HERITAGE PRESERVE**
South Carolina Dept. of
Natural Resources Heritage Trust
PO Box 167, Columbia, SC 29202
(803) 734-3894   **BW, H, MT**

**FLAT CREEK HERITAGE PRESERVE
AND FORTY ACRE ROCK**
South Carolina Dept. of
Natural Resources Heritage Trust
PO Box 167
Columbia, SC 29202
(803) 734-3894   **BW, F, MT**

FOOTHILLS TRAIL
Foothills Trail Conference
PO Box 3041
Greenville, SC 29602
(864) 467-9537   **BW, C, CK, F, H, I,
    L, MT, PA, RA, S, T**

FRANCIS BEIDLER FOREST
National Audubon Society
336 Sanctuary Rd., Harleyville, SC 29448
(803) 462-2150
    BW, CK, I, MT, PA, RA, T, TG

FRANCIS MARION NATIONAL FOREST
U.S. Forest Service
4931 Broad River Rd.
Columbia, SC 29210-4021
(803) 561-4000   **BT, BW, C, CK, F, GS,
    H, HR, I, MB, MT, PA, RA, T, TG**

**GLASSY MOUNTAIN
HERITAGE PRESERVE**
South Carolina Dept. of
Natural Resources Heritage Trust
PO Box 167, Columbia, SC 29202
(803) 734-3894   **BW, H, MT**

HITCHCOCK WOODS NATURAL AREA
Hitchcock Foundation
PO Box 1702, Aikin, SC 29802
(803) 642-0528
   Day use only; horse-drawn carriages; no
   motorized vehicles   **BW, H, HR, MT**

HUNTING ISLAND STATE PARK
South Carolina State Park System
2555 Sea Island Pkwy.
Hunting Island, SC 29920
(803) 838-2011   **BW, C, F, GS, H, I,
    L, MT, PA, RA, S, T**

JONES GAP STATE PARK
South Carolina State Park System
303 Jones Gap Rd., Marietta, SC 29661
(864) 836-3647
   Hiking registration required; trailside
   camping   **BW, C, F, H, I, MT, PA, RA, T**

L Lodging	**PA** Picnic Areas	**RC** Rock Climbing	**TG** Tours, Guides	

MB Mountain
    Biking
	RA Ranger-led
	    Activities
		S Swimming
		T Toilets
			XC Cross-country
			    Skiing
				273

MT Marked Trails				

LEWIS OCEAN BAY HERITAGE PRESERVE
South Carolina Dept.of
Natural Resources Heritage Trust
PO Box 167
Columbia, SC 29202
(803) 734-3894   **BW, H**

**LITTLE PEE DEE
HERITAGE PRESERVE**
South Carolina Dept. of
Natural Resources Heritage Trust
PO Box 167,
Columbia, SC 29202
(803) 734-3894   **BW, CK, F, H**

LONG CANE RANGER DISTRICT
Sumter National Forest
810 Buncombe St.
Edgefield, SC 29824
(803) 637-5396   **BT, BW, C, CK, F, H,
                          HR, I, MB, MT, PA, S, T, TG**

MOLLYS ROCK
Sumter National Forest
Enoree Ranger District
20 Work Center,
Whitmire, SC 29178
(803) 276-4810   **F, MT, PA, T**

**MOUNTAIN BRIDGE WILDERNESS AND
RECREATION AREA**
South Carolina State Park System
8155 Geer Hwy
Cleveland, SC 29635
(864) 836-6115
   Hiking registration required; pre-
   arranged tours   **BW, C, F, GS, H, HR,
                          I, MT, PA, RA, T, TG**

OCONEE STATE PARK
South Carolina State Park System
624 State Park Rd.
Mountain Rest, SC 29664
(864) 638-5353
   Cabins available; park store open spring
   weekends and all summer
                      **C, CK, F, H, L, MT,
                          PA, RA, S, T**

PEACHTREE ROCK PRESERVE
The Nature Conservancy
PO Box 5475
Columbia, SC 29250
(803) 254-9049   **BW, H, MT, TG**

**PINCKNEY ISLAND NATIONAL
WILDLIFE REFUGE**
U.S. Fish and Wildlife Service
Parkway Business Center
1000 Business Center Drive, Ste. 10
Savannah, GA 31405
(912) 652-4415
   Tours for groups only by appointment;
   motorized vehicles not allowed past park-
   ing lot   **BT, BW, CK, F, H, MT, TG**

SAND HILLS STATE FOREST
South Carolina Forestry Commission
PO Box 128, Patrick, SC 29584
(803) 498-6478   **BT, BW, C, F, HR, PA**

SANTEE COASTAL RESERVE
South Carolina Div. of Wildlife and Fresh-
water Fisheries
PO Box 167
Columbia, SC 29202
(803) 254-9049 (TNC)
                  BW, CK, F, H, MT, PA, T, TG

**SANTEE NATIONAL
WILDLIFE REFUGE**
U.S. Fish and Wildlife Service
Rte. 2, Box 370
Summerton, SC 29148
(803) 478-2217   **BW, F, H, I, MT**

**SAVANNAH NATIONAL
WILDLIFE REFUGE**
U.S. Fish and Wildlife Service
Parkway Business Center
1000 Business Center Dr., Ste. 10
Savannah, GA 31405
(912) 652-4415
   Tours for groups only by appointment
                      BT, BW, F, H, MT, T, TG

**SAVANNAH RIVER BLUFFS
HERITAGE PRESERVE**
South Carolina Dept. of
Natural Resources Heritage Trust
PO Box 167, Columbia, SC 29202
(803) 734-4037   **BW, H, MT**

**STEVENS CREEK
HERITAGE PRESERVE**
South Carolina Dept.
of Natural Resources Heritage Trust
PO Box 167
Columbia, SC 29202
(803) 734-3894   **BW, F, H, MT**

BT	Bike Trails	**CK**	Canoeing, Kayaking	**F**	Fishing	**HR**	Horseback Riding
BW	Bird-watching			**GS**	Gift Shop		
C	Camping	**DS**	Downhill Skiing	**H**	Hiking	**I**	Information Center

SUMTER NATIONAL FOREST
U.S. Forest Service
4931 Broad River Rd.
Columbia, SC 29210-4021
(803) 561-4000   **BT, BW, C, CK, F, H, HR, MB, PA, S**

TABLE ROCK STATE PARK
South Carolina State Park System
246 Table Rock State Park Rd.
Pickens, SC 29671
(864) 878-9813   **BW, C, F, H, I, L, MT, PA, RA, RC, S, T**

TOM YAWKEY WILDLIFE CENTER
South Carolina Div. of Wildlife
and Freshwater Fisheries
Rte. 2, Box 181, Georgetown, SC 29440
(803) 546-6814
Tours by reservation only; boat access
to outer beaches by public vendors in
Georgetown   **BT, BW, C, CK, F, H, TG**

WATSON HERITAGE PRESERVE
South Carolina Dept. of
Natural Resources Heritage Trust
PO Box 167
Columbia, SC 29202
(803) 734-3894   **BW, C, F, H, MT**

WILDCAT WAYSIDE
South Carolina State Park System
1205 Pendleton St.
Columbia, SC 29201
(864) 836-6115 (Caesars Head State Park);
(864) 878-9813 (Table Rock State Park)
    BW, H, PA

WOODS BAY STATE PARK
South Carolina State Park System
Rte. 1, Box 208
Olanta, SC 29114
(803) 659-4445
    BW, CK, F, MT, PA, RA, T

ABOVE: *American artist Winslow Homer visited Florida seven times from 1885 to 1904. Here he tours the Homosassa River with two guides.*

L	Lodging	**PA**	Picnic Areas	**RC**	Rock Climbing	**TG**	Tours, Guides
MB	Mountain Biking	**RA**	Ranger-led Activities	**S**	Swimming	**XC**	Cross-country Skiing
MT	Marked Trails			**T**	Toilets		

INDEX

PHOTOGRAPHY CREDITS

All photography by Tony Arruza except for the following:

16–17: Robert M. Hicklin, Jr., Inc., Spartanburg, SC

32, left: Dan Dempster/Dembinsky Photo Associates (DPA), Owosso, MI

32, top right: Arthur Morris/Birds As Art, Deltona, FL

51, top left: Anthony Mercieca/DPA

51, top right: Leonard Lee Rue III, Blairstown, NJ

78: American Philosophical Society, Philadelphia, PA

98: Georgia Museum of Art, The University of Georgia, Gift of Mrs. Will Moss, Athens, GA (Acc. #59.646)

103: Arthur Morris/Birds As Art

111: Len Rue, Jr., Blairstown, NJ

127: Adam Jones/DPA

134: Mark J. Thomas/DPA

135: Carl R. Sams II/DPA

140: New-York Historical Society, New York, NY

147, top: Arthur Morris/Birds As Art

148, top: Jim Battles/DPA

148, bottom: Skip Moody/DPA

174: New-York Historical Society

185: Spencer Museum of Art, University of Kansas, William Bridges Thayer Memorial, Lawrence, KS (Acc. #28.1796)

196, bottom: Jeff Foott, Jackson, WY

204: Gail Shumway, Bradenton, FL

206: John Gerlach/DPA

207: Marilyn Kazmers/DPA

217: Jeff Foott

219: Gail Shumway

229, left: Bill Lea/DPA

259: Library of Congress, Washington, D.C.

275: Bowdoin College Museum of Art, Brunswick, ME, Gift of the Homer Family

ACKNOWLEDGMENTS

The editors gratefully acknowledge the professional assistance of Tish Fila, Susan Kirby, and Patricia Woodruff. We wish to thank those site managers and naturalists whose time and commitment contributed to this volume. The following consultants also helped in the preparation of this volume: Stephen H. Bennett, Biologist, South Carolina Heritage Trust Program; Mark W. Glisson, Chief, Florida Bureau of Natural and Cultural Resources; Kent Hanby, State Lands Forester, State of Alabama Department of Conservation and Natural Resources; Tom Patrick, Georgia Natural Heritage Program; Butch Proulx and Robert S. Wilhelm of John Pennekamp Coral Reef State Park; Dallas Rhodes, Professor and Chair of Geology, Whittier College; and Keith P. Tomlinson, Principal Naturalist, Biogeographic, Inc.

U.S.A. $19.95
Canada $27.95

THE SMITHSONIAN GUIDES TO NATURAL AMERICA

This extraordinary series of comprehensive, practical, lavishly illustrated guides takes you to the national parks and forests and beyond, into thousands of wilderness preserves and nature sanctuaries throughout the United States, including hidden trails and lesser-known scenic spots, from canyons to waterfalls to migratory-bird refuges. Stunning color photographs and vivid narration feature wildlife, wildflowers, and landforms, while clear explanations of ecology and human impact deepen your understanding of America's natural beauty.

- More than 185 color photographs
- Original, full-color relief maps throughout
- More than 160 sites, including national, state, and local parks and private reserves
- Addresses and telephone numbers for every site

"Everything looks great. These guides make you want to travel." —*Los Angeles Times*

"Gorgeous color photographs . . . breathtaking geographic and ecological attractions."
—*Newsday*

"A beautiful and practical series . . . designed actually to be used." —*Parade*

Random House, Inc., New York, N.Y. 10022
http://www.randomhouse.com/
Printed in U.S.A. 1/97
© 1997 Smithsonian Institution

ISBN 0-679-76480-1

51995

EAN

9 780679 764809